MW00769987

Inspiration & Interpretation

Inspiration &

Interpretation

A Theological Introduction
to Sacred Scripture

Denis Farkasfalvy, O.Cist.

THE CATHOLIC UNIVERSITY OF
AMERICA PRESS • *Washington, D.C.*

Copyright © 2010
The Catholic University of America Press
All rights reserved
The paper used in this publication meets the minimum
requirements of American National Standards for Information
Science—Permanence of Paper for Printed Library Materials,
ANSI Z39.48-1984.

∞

Library of Congress Cataloging-in-Publication Data
Farkasfalvy, Denis M., 1936–
Inspiration and interpretation : a theological introduction
to Sacred Scripture / Denis Farkasfalvy.
p. cm.
Includes bibliographical references (p.   ) and index.
ISBN 978-0-8132-1746-8 (pbk. : alk. paper)
1. Bible—Inspiration.   2. Bible—Hermeneutics.
3. Catholic Church—Doctrines.   4. Bible—
Inspiration—History of doctrines.   5. Bible—
Criticism, interpretation, etc.—History.   6. Catholic
Church—Doctrines—History.   I. Title.
BS480.F32 2010
220.6088'282—dc22   2010007520

In memory of my parents
In honor of all my teachers
In gratitude to all my students

Contents

Inspiration &
Interpretation

INTRODUCTION

This book is the fruit of a lifelong fascination with the presuppositions of biblical theology, specifically with the relationship between the doctrine of inspiration and hermeneutics. I can best introduce the book, then, by giving an account of its genesis.

Beginnings: Inspiration in St. Bernard

The present volume grew out of a project I undertook as a young student in Rome: an investigation of the biblical exegesis of St. Bernard of Clairvaux. As I realized the complexity of this topic, I began to research St. Bernard's understanding of scriptural inspiration in the hope of finding a clearer approach to his exegesis as a whole. Soon this "preliminary" study took center stage and became the topic of my doctoral dissertation in theology. My professor, Jean Leclercq, O.S.B., the editor of the critical edition of St. Bernard's complete works, though he was an eminent scholar on Bernard, felt that he knew little about Bernard's doctrine of inspiration. So he showed my work to two of his friends, both first-class theologians: Henri de Lubac, S.J., and Pierre Benoit, O.P. De Lubac, with his characteristic modesty, remarked that, although "no expert on Bernard," he suspected that in Bernard's works there is more material on this topic than I had detected, and so he encouraged me to pursue my work further. On the other hand, Fr. Benoit, a recognized authority on biblical inspiration, saw little hope that the study of monastic authors would shed significant light on the modern problems of the subject.[1] A few years later, when my dissertation was published, I received a third input from a book review and a letter by Luis Alonso Schökel, who was working on the English edition of his book *La Palabra Inspirada*.[2] In his letter he commended my efforts to recover the patristic and medieval heritage about inspiration; he too thought that the doctrinal history of inspiration needed much more research.

Recent History of the Theology of Inspiration

Following these promptings, I turned to the works of Irenaeus. It was in the framework of an ecumenical faculty seminar, in which biblical and patristic scholars of various denominations cooperated for decades, that I began to study Irenaeus and other authors of the second century.[3] Returning to Rome in 1974 for biblical studies, I had a chance to meet Fr. Alonso Schökel. His assessment of the future of the study of inspiration was pessimistic. I was surprised, for I certainly had not realized that in Catholic theology the pre-conciliar excitement about this topic was rapidly fading and, in fact, would soon expire.

The title of a German publication appearing in that same year could have opened my eyes; it proclaimed quite literally "the end of the theology of inspiration" and suggested that a brand new approach be taken which postulated no supernatural origin for the biblical text.[4]

That this change in the theological climate was heralded long

1. Pierre Benoit, *Inspiration and the Bible,* trans. J. Murphy-O'Connor and M. Keverne (New York: Sheed and Ward, 1965).
2. Denis Farkasfalvy, *L'inspiration de l'Écriture Sainte dans la théologie de saint Bernard* [The Inspiration of Holy Scripture in the Theology of Saint Bernard], Studia Anselmiana 53 (Rome: Herder, 1964). Luis Alonso Schökel, *The Inspired Word,* trans. Francis Martin (London: Herder, 1967).
3. Denis Farkasfalvy, "Theology of Scripture in St. Irenaeus," *Revue bénédictine* 78 (1968): 319–33; "Prophets and Apostles: The Conjunction of the Two Terms before Irenaeus," in *Texts and Testaments,* ed. W. E. March, 109–34 (San Antonio, Tex.: Trinity University Press, 1980); William R. Farmer and Denis M. Farkasfalvy, *The Formation of the New Testament Canon* (New York: Paulist Press, 1983).
4. Oswald Loretz, *Das Ende der Inspirationstheologie. Die Chancen eines Neubeginns* [The End of the Theology of Inspiration. Chances for a New Beginning] (Stuttgart: Katholisches Bibelwerk, 1974).

in advance I learned only later. In a book published in 1991, Helmut Gabel calls attention to an intervention by Bishop Simon from India at Vatican II, in which he proposed that the Council abandon the concept of biblical inspiration altogether as both obsolete and misleading, having proven itself useless for the Church by causing confusion and providing no help.[5] Gabel's book describes how, in the second half of the twentieth century, one theological model after another succeeded in eroding the tradition regarding biblical inspiration bit by bit, eventually almost entirely washing it away. His work begins with the neo-scholastic model of inspiration as it was presented in the draft prepared by the Second Vatican Council's Preparatory Commission under the title *De fontibus revelationis*. This text was rejected in the first session of the Council, and was eventually replaced by a substantially different conceptual model, on which the Apostolic Constitution *Dei Verbum* was based. But the theological journey which Gabel's book describes began several years before Vatican II and went beyond the Council, passing through even more radical phases during the post-conciliar period. We will now briefly outline this journey.

Vatican II and *Dei Verbum*

It was during the years immediately following the Second World War that a new epoch of Catholic theology emerged in which a series of eminent personalities showed keen interest in the issues and questions of revelation, inspiration, inerrancy, and canon, all of which had been left unresolved by Vatican I. In France, Henri de Lubac and Yves Congar began to study them in the context of patristic studies.[6] In Germany Karl Rahner launched a speculative essay about biblical inspiration, in which he asked that this concept be thought

5. Helmut Gabel, *Inspirationsverständnis im Wandel* [Changing Understanding of Inspiration] (Mainz: Grünewald, 1991), 99–101.
6. Henri de Lubac, *Histoire et Esprit. L'intelligence de l'Écriture d'après Origène* (Paris: Aubier, 1950). An English translation appeared fifty-eight years later: *History and Spirit: The Understanding of Scripture according to Origen*, trans. A. E. Nash (San Francisco: Ignatius Press, 2008). Yves Congar, *La Tradition et les traditions* [The Tradition and the Traditions] (Paris: Fayard, 1960).

over from fresh beginnings.[7] Congar and Rahner were among the most prominent members of the commission appointed by Paul VI to prepare the new conciliar text about revelation, which eventually became the Apostolic Constitution *Dei Verbum*. It must have been, however, mainly the work of Congar, whose thought and style are recognizable in the text, while there is little or no trace of Rahner's thought about the collective concept of biblical inspiration. Even so, most studies published shortly after the Council paid more attention to the issues Rahner raised about inspiration than to the thoughts of Congar. Luis Alonso Schökel, John McKenzie, Dennis McCarthy, Norbert Lohfink, and Pierre Grelot are some of the most important authors who, each in a somewhat different way, tried to extend or concretize Rahner's suggestions about biblical inspiration as a divine action building up the early Church into the definitive community of salvation of the end times.[8] Rather than focusing on the "primitive church," they extended the concept of collective inspiration to both Israel and the Church following upon it as two phases of the one People of God.

Following in the footsteps of modern exegesis, all these authors show great concern for reformulating the concept of inspiration as an extended process in which groups and chains of individuals in a historical sequence contributed to the formation of the biblical books, and virtually all leave behind the traditional "single author" model of inspiration. By shifting the emphasis more or less radically from chosen individuals to a chosen collectivity as the focus of the transmission of divine revelation, they transpose the traditional concepts about charisms given to individuals (both preachers and writers) and present them as part of the broader reality of a divinely sponsored

7. Karl Rahner, *Über die Schriftinspiration* [Inspiration in the Bible], Quaestiones disputatae 1 (Freiburg in Br.: Herder, 1961). In English: *Inspiration in the Bible*, trans. C. H. Henkey (New York: Herder, 1961).
8. Alonso Schökel, *Inspired Word*. John McKenzie, "The Social Character of Inspiration," *Catholic Biblical Quarterly* 24 (1962): 115–24. Dennis McCarthy, "Personality, Society and Inspiration," *Theological Studies* 24 (1963): 253–76. Norbert Lohfink, "Über die Irrtumlosigkeit der Schrift und die Einheit der Schrift," *Stimmen der Zeit* 174 (1964): 161–91. Pierre Grelot, *La Bible: Parole de Dieu* (Paris: Tournai, 1965).

collective authorship. It was in response to such efforts that Loretz came to the conclusion that the original theological model had become outdated and was now to be abandoned. By proclaiming "the end of the theology of inspiration," he declared that for describing an anonymous process by which religious traditions are transmitted in writing by multiple redactors, the traditional concepts of inspired "hagiographers" and a joint divine-human authorship of biblical texts create more problems than they can solve. Likewise, he proposed to abandon the concept of infallibility and inerrancy because, once the texts' historically conditioned character is fully recognized, their limitations in expressing knowledge become self-explanatory.

Obviously, Catholic theology was by then obliged to remain within the parameters of *Dei Verbum*. Yet the new exegetical climate which followed the Council made most Catholic exegetes merge with their Protestant colleagues and, therefore, the traditional concept of inspiration was only poorly upheld and only narrowly applied.[9] This situation is reflected in Raymond F. Collins's article on inspiration in the *New Jerome Biblical Commentary* of 1990. As Collins states, "Conservative Protestant scholarship has produced most of the recent literature on inspiration; liberal Protestants often effectively deny inspiration by silence."[10] His own views about inspiration express a new dichotomy between the "prophetic models" used preponderantly in the past and the various "contemporary models" in which social, psychological, literary, and ecclesial considerations prevail.[11] But these distinct models have an important common characteristic: they freely allow theologi-

9. An effort to expand the traditional treatise of biblical inspiration in accord with both *Dei Verbum* and the new Catholic exegesis emerging after the Council is signaled by Bruce Vawter, *Biblical Inspiration* (Philadelphia: Westminster, 1972).

10. Raymond E. Brown, Joseph A. Fitzmyer, and Roland E. Murphy, eds., *The New Jerome Biblical Commentary* (Englewood Cliffs, N.J.: Prentice Hall, 1990), 1031.

11. A similar but ultimately much more simplistic view is expressed by Paul J. Achtemeier when he distinguishes between the "liberal" and "conservative" views of biblical inspiration and, afterwards, proposes to transcend the traditional "prophetic model." He agrees with Collins in noting the "silence" of the majority of biblical scholars: "There is, of course, a third option and it is the one that has been chosen by the vast majority of biblical scholars who are not conservative. That option is simply to say nothing about the problem." *Inspiration and Authority of the Bible* (Peabody, Mass.: Hendrickson, 1999), 84.

cal aspects to crumble away.[12] Of course, the need for rescuing theological exegesis was soon felt on all levels of church life, from basic preaching to biblical scholarship. An early call for renewing biblical studies came from Albert C. Outler, a prominent Methodist professor of church history and a Protestant observer at the Second Vatican Council. At the fall meeting of the Society of Biblical Literature in 1983, he challenged his audience to develop a "post-critical" model of exegesis, which he also termed "post-liberal" and "post-enlightenment."[13] Outler's call was eventually followed, albeit with varying delays, first by evangelicals,[14] but also by Catholics.[15]

Early Interpretation and the Canon

These developments were greatly influenced by the patristic renewal that prepared Vatican II, as increasingly more attention was paid to the early history of interpretation and the presuppositions which governed ancient Christian exegesis.[16] In many cases conservative Protestants—mostly evangelicals—began to show a newly developed interest in the patristic sources not only for exegesis, but also

12. An exception is the well-balanced but much too short essay by Robert Gnuse, *The Authority of the Bible, Theories of Inspiration, Revelation and the Canon of Scripture* (New York: Paulist Press, 1985).

13. His essay was published under the title "Toward a Postliberal Hermeneutics," *Theology Today* 42 (1985): 281–91. See also Denis Farkasfalvy, "In Search of a Post-critical Method of Biblical Interpretation for Catholic Theology," *Communio* 4 (1986): 288–307.

14. See a résumé and evaluation from an evangelical perspective by Daniel J. Treier, *Introducing Theological Interpretation of Scripture* (Grand Rapids, Mich.: Baker Academic, 2008), 11–36. Instead of "post-critical" or "post-liberal" he speaks of a "postmodern" trend in exegesis.

15. The most important works by which Treier was also inspired are Francis Martin, *Sacred Scripture, The Disclosures of the Word* (Naples, Fla.: Sapientia, 1999); Luke Timothy Johnson and William S. Kurz, *The Future of Catholic Biblical Scholarship: A Constructive Conversation* (Grand Rapids, Mich.: Eerdmans, 2002); and Matthew Levering, *Participatory Biblical Exegesis: A Theology of Biblical Interpretation* (South Bend, Ind.: University of Notre Dame Press, 2008). The latter work contains in its final pages (263–302) the richest and fullest bibliography in English on the subjects.

16. An excellent assessment of this trend is presented by Peter Casarella in his introduction to the 2000 edition of a selection of writings by Henri de Lubac under the title *Scripture in the Tradition*, originally published by Herder in New York in 1968, then re-released by Crossroad in 2000.

for the theology of revelation, inspiration, and interpretation. A new interest in the canon, especially in the canon of the New Testament, has also produced numerous valuable publications.[17] Such works went well beyond studying the canon as a "list of books" and began to explore the authority of the Bible and the theological basis for the various pre-canonical collections of the biblical books.[18] Newly discovered and edited apocryphal books usually had a double effect on historians and theologians. On the one hand, some tended to relativize the status of the books which eventually—and possibly for merely historical reasons—"made it into the canon." On the other hand, there arose an interest in investigating, with more pressing urgency, the factors which actually shaped the canon and brought about its reception and establishment as one of the most stable Christian institutions over the centuries.

"Canonical exegesis" is now a frequently used term. A growing consensus has formed about the need for a new context in which both canon and inspiration could be discussed constructively beyond the perspectives of the historical-critical method, and new foundations could be provided for theological exegesis.[19] This book came about amid such initiatives, but with special effort to continue promoting the historical-critical method in studies of both the Bible and the early Church Fathers as well as medieval and monas-

17. Cf. Brevard Childs, "The Canon in Recent Biblical Studies: Reflections on an Era," *Pro Ecclesia* 14, 1 (2005): 26–45, reprinted in C. Bartholomew et al., *Canon and Biblical Interpretation,* Scripture and Hermeneutics 7 (Grand Rapids, Mich.: Zondervan: 2006), 33–57. For the Old Testament see especially Peter Enns, *Inspiration and Incarnation* (Grand Rapids, Mich.: Baker Academic, 2005); for the New Testament, Harry Y. Gamble, *The New Testament Canon: Its Making and Meaning* (Philadelphia: Fortress Press, 1985).

18. Craig D. Alert, *A High View of Scripture? The Authority of the Bible and the Formation of the New Testament Canon* (Grand Rapids, Mich.: Baker Academic, 2007). Based mostly on evangelical Protestant exegesis and patristic scholarship, this book is a remarkable attempt to formulate an "evangelical theology of Scripture." Of special note is its "Post-Script" on page 173.

19. One must mention the impact of Brevard Childs's initiative of canonical exegesis and the steadily expanding circle of those exegetes who move in the same or in a similar direction. The very fact that in his book *Jesus of Nazareth* (Freiburg: Herder, 2007) Benedict XVI joined those who see canonical exegesis in a positive light indicates that it may represent a milestone in the history of both biblical scholarship and ecumenism.

tic authors. In fact this work is committed to keeping in evidence those many essential links that connect the history of exegesis not only with the history and the theology of the canon but also with the various understandings of biblical inspiration. My highest priority in this study is to integrate within the context of Catholic theology both information and insights which we can draw from the various theological disciplines: New Testament studies, patristics, medieval theology, and various parts of fundamental (or foundational) and systematic theology.

This variety of disciplines and a close adherence to the fullness of the Catholic Tradition under the guidance of the Magisterium set great challenges for my research, particularly because many questions treated here have not been sufficiently researched in monographic studies. This last remark applies especially to the history of the doctrine of biblical inspiration, which has not been seriously investigated for the past century. Moreover, what little research has been done in this field primarily focuses on the background of the Thomistic theory (a rather narrow "prophetic model") of inspiration, which was often mistaken for the Church's official or "traditional" doctrine.

Because of the multidisciplinary character of this study, I consider it important to preface it with a theological outline stating both its starting point and the sequence of its main topics.

The Starting Point

From its inception Christianity possessed sacred books.[20] The Christian Church, emerging initially from among the people of Israel and with a claim to the religious heritage of Israel, kept the holy books of the Jews and claimed them as its own. Yet the Christians engaged in a new interpretation of these ancient writings. The old-

20. Throughout this book, but mainly for the articulation of my own argument, I take a "synthetic" and mostly theological view of canon and canonicity, rather than entering into a detailed discussion of the many historical details, for which monographic research remains to be done. Such an approach may leave open several details and various hypothetical scenarios based upon them.

est documents of Christianity testify that the first Christians understood both Jesus and his deeds and the experiences governing their faith as events revealing the meaning of the holy writings of the Jews. The Church, however, went beyond the mere use and interpretation of the sacred writings received from Judaism. Soon after it began to preach its message by word of mouth, it was confronted with the need to put the Christian message into written documents. Already in the lifetime of the first Christian generation, and quite urgently at the time when Christ's first disciples began to face death, various communities and church leaders perceived the need to fix the first Christian preaching in written form; this led to the efforts of producing and collecting the earliest documents of Christian literature. Thus a new set of writings came about and began, in a rather short period of time, to obtain among Christians an authoritative status equal to or even higher than the one possessed in the Church by the holy books of old.

When dealing with biblical inspiration in the context of Catholic theology, one of the main tasks is to reconstruct the process by which a twofold Christian Bible was formed: how were the books of the "Old Testament," apparently "inherited" from the chosen people of Israel, to be joined to a new collection of books that testifies to the "New Covenant" or "New Testament" established by Jesus, the promised Messiah?

Christianity and Its Books

In studying this process, one must not lose sight of the fact that the Christian Church neither came about as the product of literary activities, nor saw itself imprisoned by written words. The Christians' use of the sacred books of the Jews was governed by a new understanding which developed from their faith in Christ. They expressed their faith in Christ within their communities and among outsiders not through the propagation of written documents but rather by oral preaching and personal witnessing, which meant that the new literary output created by the early Christians was secondary to their faith life. Meanwhile, as the first generation approached their death, conscious efforts were made by the early Church to fix and solidify in written documents the tradition received from the apostolic community.

Christians believed from the very beginning that God's Word and Spirit, which had formed the history and faith of Judaism, were actively present in Christ and his Church. Christians saw themselves—both their faith and their communities—as issuing from a new presence of God's Spirit. It was this Spirit who began acting in their midst with an unprecedented intensity, and who enabled them to discover a new meaning in the ancient sacred writings. This meaning was new in its actuality, yet authentic and thus "original," because it was divinely intended. Just as they saw Christ as God's Word made flesh, they also regarded him as the culmination and fullness of all the riches that the Scriptures offered. This understanding, however, did not arise merely from literary study of the ancient texts. Rather, enlightened and inspired by God, they discovered a new vision based on both old texts and new facts, that is, the new divine interventions in history, all of which were centered on Jesus' deeds and teaching.

This new interpretation of the ancient texts led in turn to the production of new literary works. The writings of the New Testament therefore have two dimensions: they express a new understanding of the Scriptures of old, and they also document the facts and experiences upon which this new understanding is based. *One could even say that, born with books in one hand, Christianity soon had to produce new books with the other.* Their own self-perception led the first Christians to cling to the books inherited from the Jews but also to produce new books of their own, books containing as God's own word the preaching of the first Christian generation, that is, Scriptures with a dignity comparable to the holy writings of the Jews. One must add that it was this self-understanding of the Church as the *locus* and instrument of the Spirit's presence and action in the world which prevented the Christian Church from becoming a "religion of books." Christians continued to proclaim and witness to their faith *viva voce* and claimed still to experience God's presence and activity within their ranks and expanding institutional structures.

The history enunciated above defines the basic questions which the Catholic theology of inspiration must treat. What does it mean for Christians to believe in the Scriptures as the word of God? In what sense and on what basis can they be convinced that, through the books taken over from Judaism, God spoke to all people and keeps on speaking today? How do we answer these same questions about the books of the New Testament? In what sense are these books distinguished, on the one hand, from the sacred books of other religions and, on the other hand, from other literary products of ancient Judaism or early Christianity, even if contemporary with the sacred Scriptures of one or the other of the two Testaments?

Furthermore, if in the books of the Scriptures Christian faith finds the word of God in a unique and special way, how does that belief translate into exegetical practice? How do we concretely honor the divine inspiration of these books? And how do we account for all their human qualities, which include strengths and limitations, culturally conditioned features, historically dated attitudes and pronouncements, and imperfections on a literary or doctrinal level? How does the investigation and interpretation of these documents clarify problems of Christian faith, promote private and common prayer life, and, according to the ultimate motivation of the religious quest, facilitate an encounter with God in a given context of a contemporary spiritual, intellectual, or emotional experience?

Inspiration, Canon, Interpretation, and Their Interconnection

In the theological tradition of the Church the problems outlined here are divided into two large categories. The first group consists of questions treating the origins of the sacred books as divinely inspired literary products (theology of inspiration) and therefore normative for the Church (canon and canonicity); the second group concerns the principles and methodology of interpreting biblical texts (biblical hermeneutics). This division is helpful and even necessary, but the two groups of questions cannot be treated separately. In fact, when we examine the beliefs and practices of the Church regarding the use of the Bible in the early Christian centuries (even just the first thirteen centuries), we can see a close interdependence between theories of inspiration and hermeneutical practices. Christian theologians and exegetes have made statements about the inspired character of sacred texts or about the inspiration of their authors most frequently for the sake of explaining their method of interpretation. In other words, principles of inspiration have been explained or supported usually in the context and for the sake of exegesis. One may even say that ancient Christianity formed and specified its belief about inspired authors and texts for the sake of developing or supporting the principles that governed the use of Scripture in theological discourse. At the same time, the role of scriptural arguments in theological debate naturally prompted reflection and research about the normative status of the sacred text, the nature of its inspired character, and the presuppositions that such beliefs imply about what induced the human authors to produce, under God's influence, divinely inspired texts.

Much of the material of our theological tradition concerning inspiration is the product of "regressive analysis": attempts to give account, in retrospect, of the necessary and sufficient conditions that govern the exegetical process. But also conversely, once the principles of inspiration and canonicity have been stated, theologians often proceeded, by deduction, to point out the implications of these principles for explaining the sacred texts.

All this, of course, should cause no surprise. In the Christian experience, beliefs in the normative role of Scripture as God's biblical Word always preceded detailed reflection about the way that the inspired books came about as products of both human and divine causes; therefore, it is natural to expect any theory of inspiration to have been preceded historically by some kind of exegetical practice. Usually, concrete methods of biblical hermeneutics (and the difficulties which they engendered) were at work in determining both the point of departure and the direction in which one had to move when investigating the Church's faith in the Bible. Yet as soon as theologians began to build doctrinal systems, they deduced rules of hermeneutics from their understanding of inspiration. Ultimately, though, exegetical practice and theoretical reflection about inspiration continue to search for mutual consistency and logical coherence.

The interconnectedness of inspiration, canonicity, and interpretation in the Catholic tradition forced me throughout this study to keep an eye on two components: history and systematics. The gradual development and enrichment of the concepts involved in the Church's reflection on the Scriptures cannot be understood by a purely historical method. I needed to sketch the various models of interpretation that demanded changes to the concept of inspiration and required, within a developing ecclesiology, an increasingly complex understanding of the canon and the interpretive roles of Tradition and Magisterium. In this way, the book eventually merges an overview of the history of interpretation with a doctrinal history of inspiration and canon, and ends with the sketch of a doctrinal synthesis serving systematic theology.

The reader is invited on a winding journey along this path still rarely trodden, which calls for much patience and caution.

I. "ACCORDING TO THE SCRIPTURES"

The Old Testament in the Apostolic Church

Faith in Christ and the Scriptures of Old

At its first emergence, the Christian faith—the faith of the primitive Church—appeared to be in close connection with "scriptures," the Holy Scriptures of Israel. The oldest extant document about the belief in the resurrection of Jesus, First Corinthians, from the years AD 54–57, explicitly states such a connection: "First of all I have given over to you what has been given over to me, that Christ died for our sins *according to the scriptures,* was buried and rose from the dead *according to the scriptures*" (1 Cor 15:3–4).[1] It is not an easy task to determine what scriptural text (or texts) the Apostle or his sources had in mind here: are these specific texts, such as Isaiah 53 or Hosea 6:2?[2] Some translations tried to minimize the importance of the reference

---

1. J. Fitzmyer dates First Corinthians to AD 57. See "Paul" in *The New Jerome Biblical Commentary,* ed. R. E. Brown, J. A. Fitzmyer, and R. E. Murphy (Englewood Cliffs, N.J.: Prentice Hall, 1990), 1336. J. Murphy-O'Connor dates it "most probably" to AD 54, "The First Letter to the Corinthians," ibid., 799. However, Paul cites in this letter the apostolic kerygma, which he delivered to the Corinthians at his first preaching. Thanks to Acts 18, with its reference to the proconsul L. Junius Gallio, Paul's first preaching in Corinth is very closely dateable. Gallio was proconsul in Corinth in 51–52 (ibid., 798). Thus Paul's previous preaching of eighteen months must have begun no later than the early part of 51. But if in 51 a Christian creedal formula is used, then that formula must have been circulating for a considerable time before that date. It may be a fair estimate to say that 1 Cor 15:3–4 represents the apostolic faith in its primitive formulation at some fifteen years after Jesus' crucifixion.

2. Hos 6:2 is a most attractive candidate because it refers to a specific chronological detail (the "third day") of the apostolic kerygma. However, in 1 Cor 15:3–4 this chronological reference is combined with other details like the "burial" and, therefore, the word "Scriptures" also alludes to Is 53:9.

to the Scriptures by rendering the Greek preposition κατὰ as "in accordance with," meaning an unspecified "agreement" with the Scriptures rather than the fulfillment of prophecies.[3] But the text's reference to the Scriptures cannot be reduced to some vague agreement. We must quote in Greek the opening phrase of the sentence: παρέδωκα γὰρ ὑμῖν ἐν πρώτοις, ὃ καὶ παρέλαβον (15:3). Paul speaks about transmitting tradition (a technical sense of παρέδωκα), a tradition which is being passed on in a chain of transmissions. The pair of verbs παρέδωκα/παρέλαβον indicates the alternating actions of giving and receiving. Since ἐν πρώτοις modifies the act of giving ("I passed on"), we must also conclude that not only the Messiah's death, burial, and resurrection, but also their scriptural attestation are "of first importance."[4] This is why we should prefer to interpret 1 Corinthians 15:3–4 as referring not only to one or just a few scriptural attestations, but to scripture in its totality.[5]

Hence Paul does not speak only of *some* scriptural "anticipation" of Jesus' life-mission. He does what in preaching and in catechesis the apostolic Church generally did: he presupposes the faith which the people of Israel have put in their sacred writings and regards these writings as the authentic word of God. In the Acts of the Apostles this same claim is made by the Christian missionaries every time they address a particular Jewish community. According to Acts, even Paul, who claimed to be a missionary to the Gentiles,[6] begins his activities in each city by preaching in the Jewish

3. The New American Bible, the Jerusalem Bible, the Revised Standard Version, and the New Revised Standard Version have "in accordance with," while the King James, New King James, and New English translations have the more literal "according to." The issue is not a matter of style but of substance for interpretation.

4. This is what most modern translations have: "as of first importance" (New American Bible, Revised Standard Version, New Revised Standard Version). The expressions "to you first of all" (King James and New King James) and "to you in the first place" (New Jerusalem Bible) are incorrect if "first of all" is understood as modifying "to you."

5. Paul clearly expresses his understanding of the role of the Scriptures in supporting the kerygma in Rom 1:1–4. These verses summarize in pre-Pauline terms the content of the apostolic preaching, centered on the death and resurrection of Christ. The expressions "offspring of David" and "spirit of sanctification" are not used by Paul anywhere else. Here Paul also says that God has "promised all this long ago through his prophets in the Holy Scriptures" (1:2).

6. Gal 1:16; 2:2 and 8. See also 1 Thes 2:16.

synagogues, from which he recruited his first followers. When approaching Jews, Paul argues for the gospel always on the basis of the Scriptures. A summary of Paul's activities in Rome at the end of Acts captures this method of evangelization well: "And he expounded the matter to them from morning till evening, testifying to the kingdom of God and trying to convince them about Jesus both from the Law of Moses and from the prophets" (Acts 28:23).[7] By examining Peter's speech at Pentecost (Acts 2:14–36) or Paul's preaching in Antioch of Pisidia (Acts 13:15–41) or Philip's dialogue with the Ethiopian courtier (Act 8:26–38), we are led to the conclusion that the argument of a Christian preaching to Jews (or, in general, to those who belong to the Mosaic Covenant) always starts off with texts from the Old Testament. It is on such a basis that Christian missionaries try to prove that Jesus is the Messiah and the Son of God.

How convincing such argumentation may appear to a modern audience—or, if there is one, to "an independent jury" of historical-critical exegetes—is not the point here. After all, in the first century AD, the cultural-religious context and the method of dealing with history were quite different. For our purpose, it should suffice to state that the first Christian missionaries presupposed the authority of the Old Testament, began with passages from the Jewish Scriptures, and based their arguments on them.

The sources, however, go much further. In the practice of the apostolic Church the Scriptures were not only regarded as tools to prove the truth of Christianity. The arguments went also in the opposite direction: believing in Christ provided the key to the Scriptures. According to St. Luke, the risen Lord explains to his Apostles that through his passion and resurrection "everything written about me in the Law of Moses and in the prophets and psalms must be fulfilled," and with this "he opened their minds to understand the

---

7. "Moses and the Prophets" is equivalent to "the Law and the Prophets," meaning the totality of Sacred Scriptures. See in Mt 5:17; 7:12; 11:13; Lk 16:16, 29; Jn 1:45; Acts 26:22; Rom 3:21. The reference to the triplet "Law—Prophets—Writings," from which the current Hebrew acronym for "Bible" (TANACH) has been derived, might have its earliest known appearance in Lk 24:44 ("Moses—Prophets—Psalms") but this alone does not prove that the expression itself antedates the Apostle Paul.

Scriptures" (Lk 24:44–45). This conviction, that one can fully understand the Scriptures only in Christ, is well visualized by a passage in the book of Revelation: the Lamb, appearing "as if it had been slain," takes up a sealed scroll, breaking its seven seals (Rev 5:1–7) and thus revealing the meaning of all history.[8] Indeed, as our earliest sources testify, the Church of the Apostles considered itself a fully entitled proprietor of the Scriptures of old, capable of understanding and announcing their meaning.[9] Thus not only is faith in Christ built upon the Scriptures, but, correspondingly, this faith introduces the believer into a full and authentic understanding of the Old Testament.

Jesus' Message and Person Linked to the Scriptures in the Gospels

The conviction by which the primitive Church considered the Scriptures of the Old Testament its own is rooted in Jesus' own thought and preaching. During his ministry he often started from scriptural passages and continually referred to biblical texts. When preaching in the synagogues, he read and explained biblical passages. For this we can find many examples in all the four gospels.

According to Luke, when Jesus preached in the synagogue of Nazareth, he commented on Isaiah: "The Spirit of the Lord is on me. He anointed me to bring good tidings to the poor" (Is 61:1). After the reading, he rolled up the Scripture text and sat down. In the synagogue all eyes were fixed on him. He began to speak: "Today

---

8. In fact, a contemporary exegesis easily appropriates such an understanding of Rev 5:1–5. The Lamb "as if slain" and animated by the Spirit (5:6–7) opens the transcendental meaning of history, which coincides with that of the totality of the Scriptures. See Ugo Vanni, *Lectura del Apocalipsis* [Reading the Apocalypse] (Pamplona: Verbo Divino, 2005), 181–83.

9. The oldest texts are found in the Pauline epistles. In Romans, after quoting Ps 69:10, Paul continues: "For whatever was written in former days was written for our instruction, so that by steadfastness and by the encouragement of the scriptures we might have hope" (15:4). In 1 Corinthians he writes about Deut 25:4: "Or does he not speak entirely for our sake? It was indeed written for our sake" (9:10). Subsequently, after quoting from Ex 15–17, he concludes: "These things happened to them to serve as an example, and they were written down to instruct us, on whom the ends of the ages have come" (10:11).

this scripture has been fulfilled in your hearing" (Lk 4:18-21). Of course, this statement by Jesus matches what Jesus says at the end of the same gospel (Lk 24:44-45) and thus creates for this book an impressive programmatic inclusion. There is no justification for supposing that Luke (or Luke's source) manufactured both scenes out of either thin air or theological creativity. On the contrary, the passage about Jesus' preaching in Nazareth carries the marks of authenticity as it reflects Jesus' self-understanding that he is the one who fulfills the Scriptures. A multiplicity of diverse yet converging testimonies points in this direction.

In Matthew 11:4-6 a chain of quotations from Isaiah also has a programmatic purpose.[10] A delegation from John the Baptist approaches Jesus and asks him to clarify his identity. Jesus' reply is based on Isaiah 61:1-2, the same text with which his preaching begins in Luke. Here again, the scriptural quote is used not only for describing in what sense Jesus claims to be the Messiah, but also as a "catalogue of messianic deeds," revealing the meaning and significance of Jesus' first ministry in Galilee as presented by Matthew 4:16-9:38.[11] Thus, on a level deeper than any synoptic source theory could explain the connections between Matthew and Luke, the beginning of Jesus' Galilean ministry, in which he presents his "credentials" to his first audiences in the various synagogues, is essentially linked to Isaiah 61:1-2 as a text which, in unison with his deeds, certifies his identity.

In a sketchier but similar way, the opening lines of Mark's gospel lead in the same direction. Here also, "the beginning of the gospel" (1:1) is connected with a reference to Isaiah (verse 2).[12] The Old Testament texts (Is 40:3, with Ex 23:20 and Mal 3:1) which Mark uses here to introduce John the Baptist were not chosen at random. They point

10. According to W. D. Davies and Dale C. Allison, *The Gospel According to Saint Matthew* (Edinburgh: T & T Clark, 1991), 242, the chain also includes 26:19; 29:18; 35:5-6; 42:7, 18; and 61:1.

11. "'The deeds of Christ' is a key phrase. . . .It refers back not only to the miracles in chapters 8-9, but also to the Sermon on the Mount, 5-7, interpreting Jesus' authoritative words and mighty deeds as messianic." Ibid., 242.

12. Robert H. Gundry, *Mark: A Commentary on His Apology for the Cross* (Grand Rapids, Mich.: Eerdmans, 1993), 31.

to the "Law" (Exodus) and to "the Prophets" (Isaiah and Malachi), basically in the same way Paul does in Romans when he states that, although apart from law, "now the righteousness of God has been disclosed, and is attested by the Law and the Prophets (3:21)," that is, by the totality of the Scriptures.

Luke, the author of the third gospel and of Acts, is one of the New Testament authors who note most carefully the connection between faith in Christ and the Scriptures of the Old Testament. But the other evangelists express very similar thoughts; they differ only in approach and emphasis. Matthew's account of the Sermon on the Mount is filled with references to the Mosaic legislation. Jesus as Legislator continues the Torah, although on a higher level and with a higher rank than Moses, as evident from the recurring phrase: "You heard it said to those of old . . . now I tell you" (Mt 5:21, 27, 33, 38, and 43). This means that Jesus legislates for no other purpose than to "bring to completion" or "to a fullness of perfection" the Law and the Prophets (5:17).[13] In John the testimony of the Scriptures is a crucial issue. Jesus' enemies argue from the Scriptures: "But some said, 'Is the Christ to come from Galilee? Has not the scripture said that the Christ is descended from David, and comes from Bethlehem, the village where David was?" (Jn 7:41–42). In reply, those who reject Jesus are said to be rejecting Moses as well, for the acceptance of the books of Moses would result in accepting Jesus: "Your accuser will be Moses in whom you have put your hope. If you believed in Moses, you might believe me, just as well, for he wrote about me." (Jn 5:45–46)

Mark's gospel appears to contain relatively few explicit state-

---

13. The sentence reads: "Do not think that I have come to abolish the law or the prophets; I have come not to abolish but to fulfill." That this refers to all the Scriptures is clear from the technical meaning "Law and Prophets." The meaning of the verb "to fulfill" is differently interpreted by the commentators, but is evidently opposed to "abolishing"; hence it means enhancement and confirmation. When followed by an infinitive or a subordinate clause of purpose (starting with ἵνα), the verb ἦλθον ("I have come") expresses typically a goal or purpose, i.e., the purpose of Jesus' mission (cf. Mt 9:13/Mk 2:17; Mt 10:34–35 [three times]; Mt 20:28/Mk 10:45; Lk 12:49; 19:10; also Jn 9:39; 10:10, 41; 12:9, 27, 47). Thus, regardless of how we determine the meaning of "fulfillment" for the Scriptures, this sentence links the purpose of Jesus' existence to the vindication and validation of the Scriptures.

ments about the value of the Scriptures, mostly because, in general, it contains more narrative than didactic passages. Yet this gospel also shows Jesus repeatedly referring to the Scriptures (cf. Mk 2:25; 4:12; 7:6–11), and habitually teaching in synagogues (1:21; 3:1; 6:2). His messianic identity is clearly indicated and outlined by means of scriptural references (12:10–11, 36–37), although—in typical Markan style—without directly asserting that Jesus fits anybody's image of an expected Messiah.

One item of the triple synoptic tradition is of particular importance. The parable about the wicked vinedressers defines in three very close parallel renderings (Mt 21:33–46; Mk 12:1–12; Lk 20:9–19) Jesus' role and mission in continuity with the Old Testament as a whole. The comparison of Israel to a vineyard originally is rooted in Isaiah (5:1–7). In Jesus' parable, however, the vineyard is only a peripheral theme referring back to the old scriptural comparison. In the center of the story stand the vineyard's owner and his servants, who are being sent one by one to the vinedressers (or tenant farmers) to pick up the fruits they owe as payment to the owner. The servants symbolize Israel's prophets being sent in unbroken succession. As they all fail to carry out their mission, the owner finally sends his own son, whom the vinedressers kill. In the parable Jesus' coming is presented as the culminating event which concludes a succession of divine missions by which the prophets of the Old Testament have been dispatched in steady but unsuccessful succession. The parable harkens back in particular to a notion emphasized in the book of Jeremiah: God's communications with his people result in an unrelenting sequence of messengers who are sent "early on and unceasingly" but are ignored.[14] Thus, in this parable, based on texts from both Isaiah and Jeremiah, Jesus stands at the end of a series of prophetic missions as the peak of the whole series.[15] While standing in

14. The expression *hashkem w^eshalo^ach* appears to be a formula repeated three times in Jeremiah: 7:25; 25:4; 35:15. The prophets are always called in these texts "the servants." Literally the expression means "early and sending," translated in contemporary Bibles as a hendiadys: "sending persistently." A variant of it appears three more times in Jeremiah (26:6; 29:19; and 34:14).

15. There is a Dominical saying curiously formulated in Lk 11:49 ("the Wisdom of

continuity with the servants, he, the Son, is of higher rank than any of the previous messengers, and so his mission also transcends that of the servants sent before him.

The Church's Bible

In theological literature we often meet the assumption, supposedly self-evident, that the Church "inherited" the Old Testament Scriptures from Judaism.[16] However, this would say both too much and too little. Too much, because at the time that the Church began to use the Holy Scriptures of Israel, the Hebrew Bible's canon had not yet been formalized and thus did not circumscribe a closed collection of books. Only after the First Jewish War, around AD 90, was a final list of holy books adopted in Judaism. One must, therefore, say that the Christian Church *took over* and *began* to use books, which, at a later time, Judaism eventually included in its canon of Scriptures. But a good number of early Christians included in this collection some additional books about which, at the time of the Christian origins, Judaism had as yet formed no consensus. Eventually the Jews decided not to include these contested books in the Hebrew Bible.[17] Consequently, the sacred writings of Israel used

God said, 'I will send them prophets and apostles, some of whom they will kill and persecute'"), which many exegetes regard as a quotation from some unidentified source, but is more probably a loose and re-interpreted rendition of the hendiadys occurring in Jeremiah about the prophets sent "early on and persistently." If we assume a semitic original, the second member of the word-pair with a different vocalization *(shaluach)* could have given rise to the formula "prophets and apostles" as we have it in Luke, for which there is a triple variant, "prophets and wise men and scribes," in Mt 23:29. See more about this in Denis Farkasfalvy, "Prophets and Apostles, The Conjunction of the Two Terms before Irenaeus," in *Texts and Testaments* ed. Eugene W. March, 109–34 (San Antonio, Tex.: Trinity University Press, 1980).

16. A renewed theological interest in inspiration and canon seems to come from this perspective. See the subtitle "Canon Issues Are about the Church" in Craig D. Allert, *A High View of Scripture?* (Grand Rapids, Mich.: Baker Academic, 2005), 75–78.

17. We will treat further below the differences between the Catholic and the Protestant canons of the Old Testament. At this point we only explain that, contrary to popular notions, Christians did not automatically take over an already existent Jewish canon, for the latter had not been finalized before the end of the first century. Thus, even with regard to the Old Testament, the faith of the Christians has novel features, albeit its interest in Scriptures was ultimately derived from Jewish views.

by early Christianity came to contain several more books than the Hebrew Bible of the late first century. Thus some products of Jewish religious literature obtained canonical status in Christian communities, while "Judaism" (the Jewish groups that survived beyond the destruction of the Second Temple) ultimately decided not to include them in their canon. Historically, therefore, the nascent Church did not take over a ready-made canon of the Old Testament but rather made its own decisions about how to select from among the sacred books of the Jews.[18]

The books not included in the Jewish canon yet regarded as Scripture by various Christian communities caused few and only minor disputes among the early Christian churches, and led to no schisms or confessional splits in the first fifteen hundred years. Called "apocrypha," they were used with more or less frequency across various Christian churches. The issue of including and using or neglecting the apocrypha depended very much on whether a local church or a group of churches used the Septuagint, a Greek translation of the Bible that included the apocrypha, or eventually prepared a new translation with more or less independence from the Septuagint. As happened in the Latin Church, and also in Syriac Christianity, translating the Old Testament from Hebrew texts resulted in assigning different canonical status to the books of the Hebrew Bible and to the apocrypha. However, the exclusion of the apocrypha became a divisive confessional issue only at the time of the Reformation.

We also said that speaking of "inheriting" the Old Testament from Judaism affirms, in some sense, too little. This is so because the faith that Christians have in the inspiration and canonicity of the Old Testament coincides only partially with what Jewish communities believe about their holy books, even about those they hold in

18. Much confusion about this issue comes from the fact that the scriptural canon of the Pharisees was reasonably well defined at the beginning of the first century, but Judaism became identical with Pharisaism only after the Second Jewish War, when all other factions disappeared. See D. Barthélemy, "L'état de la Bible juive depuis le début de notre ère jusque la deuxième révolte contre Rome" [The State of our Bible from the Beginning of Our Era until the Second Jewish War], in Le Canon de l' Ancien Testament [The Canon of the Old Testament], ed. J.-D. Kaestli and O. Wermelinger, 9–45 (Geneva: Labor et Fides, 1984).

common with Christians. There are, of course, important theological concepts and expressions that Jews and Christians share about the Bible. According to both Jews and Christians, the Scriptures contain God's word transmitted through chosen individuals (Moses, David, the patriarchs, the prophets, and others). These transmitters of God's word—including the authors of the holy books—were prompted by the Spirit of God to speak or write, and thus to put into human words, God's word addressing his people. Such concepts and expressions about "the Scriptures," which reflected the Church's Jewish origins, found their way into the apostolic teaching and thus into the New Testament.

Nevertheless the early Church formed some radically new concepts about the biblical texts as it developed its own ideas about revelation. For Christians, belief in the Scriptures became an integral part of their faith in Christ. Certainly, the members of the early Church with a Jewish background simply retained their Jewish ideas about the Bible, but, because of their faith in Christ's messianic identity and divinity, they also began to read the Hebrew Bible with a new outlook and gave it a new interpretation. Among Gentile Christians a slightly different process took place. They would first learn about Jesus, and only as a second step would they begin to regard the biblical books of the Old Testament as Jesus' "pre-history," and therefore as sacred.

All in all, the use and interpretation of Scripture by the early Christian Church is not a mere imitation of a practice pre-existent in Judaism but a new theological program based on the apostolic faith in Christ. In the practice of the nascent Christian Church, the Jewish holy books function and are interpreted as documents of a Christ-centered salvation history with its full and true meaning apparent only in the light of the Church's faith in Christ. Christians were being taught to read the Scriptures in the context of this new vision of faith. They debated and defended them, but remained convinced that their understanding of these writings penetrated the Scriptures more fully and adequately than the views of those, including most Jews, who read the Scriptures without believing in Christ. This explains what we quoted from Paul (Rom 15:4) as a comprehensive statement: "All that has been written" (he means here all the sacred writings of Israel) has been written "for us" (that is, for the Christian Church). He expresses here the claim which the first Christian generation—and even apostolic Christianity before Paul—formulated: the Scriptures belong to them, and their own Christological interpretation fulfills the Bible's ultimate purpose and enables its correct and full comprehension.

II. "I AM WRITING TO YOU"

The Origins of the New Testament

How Did the Apostolic Preaching Produce Written Documents?

As we observed before, the Christian faith was first spread not by written word but by missionaries who preached *viva voce*.[1] Narratives about the deeds and sayings of Jesus, as well as the memory of his teachings, were spread and preserved by live proclamation entrusted to oral tradition. To the extent we know, the first products of Christian literature did not deal with the life of Christ, not even with the collection of his sayings, but consisted of the exhortations and the theological, moral, or pastoral comments of missionaries.[2] As most contemporary scholars assume, none of the canonical gospels was composed before AD 60. The Gospel of Mark is frequently dated

1. To define precisely the initial point of the process which led to the formation of the New Testament canon is of great importance. I do not agree with the widespread notion that the New Testament is basically a duplication of the Jewish writings used in the Church from its beginnings. In the words of Harry Gamble, "Thus the Scriptures of Judaism and literature produced within Christianity were read together in the context of Christian worship. This did not presume or imply that Christian writings possessed the inspired or oracular character of the Jewish Scriptures, but the associated use of these different books of religious literature led over time to a scriptural estimate of Christian writings and to their grouping as a counterpart to Jewish scriptures." Harry Gamble, *The New Testament Canon: Its Making and Meaning* (Philadelphia: Fortress Press, 1985), 59.

2. How early there existed collections of "Dominical sayings" cannot be easily determined. There are scholars who would even project the existence of notes taken from Jesus' preaching during the Lord's ministry. Yet no early collection of Jesus' sayings, including the Gospel of Thomas, can be regarded in their currently available form as earlier than Paul's authentic epistles.

at the beginning of the Jewish War or, at the earliest, a few years before. Even those who claim the literary priority of Matthew's gospel would rarely date it earlier than AD 60, and often it is dated around 70 or later. An earlier date could be assigned to only a few books of the New Testament, among them the early letters of Paul. They were not motivated, however, by the intention of producing a new set of "holy books," but by pastoral reasons. To the extent we can reconstruct the dates and events of Christian origins, we can say with probability that all twenty-seven books of the New Testament were written in the last forty to fifty years of the first century, and that possibly a few of them were written even later, though not later than the two subsequent decades. The production, collection, and preservation of these writings played an important role in the process by which the first generation of Christians transmitted their faith, theological thinking, and moral teaching to the following generation.

Even if the earliest New Testament books were written in the years 50–60 (First Thessalonians, Galatians, Romans, and First and Second Corinthians are dated to this period), their collection, preservation, and dissemination (beyond the original addressees) required several decades; only thereafter could there have been a process of "canonization." This process, however, began in the last years of the first century and attained some stability in most church communities within the next century.[3] The formation of the New Testament canon was motivated by various, complex reasons. It was certainly

---

3. The earliest known canonical list of the New Testament is preserved in the *Muratorian Fragment*. It is dated at about AD 200, mostly because of its reference to *The Shepherd*, a work written "most recently" *(nuperrime)* by Hermas, "the brother of Pius, bishop in the city of Rome." Recent efforts by A. Sundberg ("Canon Muratori: A Fourth-Century List," *Harvard Theological Review* 66 [1973]: 1–41) arguing for fourth-century provenance have not obtained scholarly consensus (see E. Ferguson, "Canon Muratori: Date and Provenance," *Studia Patristica* 17, 2 [1982]: 677–83). Since Hermas and his brother Pius are firmly dated in the middle of the second century, the term *nuperrime*, referred to in the document as "our times" *(nostris temporibus)*, remains an insurmountable obstacle for Sundberg's thesis. The beginnings of a canonization process appear as early as the date of composition of 2 Peter, usually assigned to around AD 125. This document makes reference to "all the letters of Paul," an expression implying some collection of the Pauline letters. These letters all speak of God's patience with mankind, delaying the Day of Judgment (2 Pt 3:15).

quickened by the passing on of the first Christian missionaries. After their departure, the Church experienced an urgent need both to rely on written documents and to define its doctrinal legacy and social structures as inherited from the first apostolic generation.[4]

Pseudepigraphy in the Formation of the New Testament

One particular feature of this process was the production of "pseudepigraphic" works. A minority of authors deny the existence of such books in the canon as a matter of principle.[5] Some of the difficulty may come from the unfortunate connotation of the terms "pseudepigraphy" and "pseudonym." Any word linked to the term "pseudo" evokes a sense of falsehood and falsification, which are, indeed, incompatible with the inspired character of the biblical books and their authors. But the issue is not merely one of terminology.[6] There is no reason to exclude a priori the possibility of extended or secondary au-

4. A "generation" usually means about twenty-five years. However, in early Christian history the function of remembering is claimed to span over fifty years. As we will see below, this issue has special importance with regard to the identity of the Apostle John, and to his death, which is said to have occurred at an advanced age (after AD 100), as well as to the claim that St. Polycarp of Smyrna, living until the middle of the second century, remembered having seen him. Linked to these is Irenaeus's claim of having known Polycarp, so that a live chain of memory and tradition is being formed (Irenaeus—Polycarp—John—Jesus) from the time of Jesus to the end of the second century.

5. Terry L. Wilder, *Pseudonymity, the New Testament and Deception* (Lanham, Md.: University Press of America, 2004). The author's thesis is that by pseudonymity the Church deceptively extended the set of authentic apostolic writings, and falsified Christian heritage. Such an understanding makes a group of committed Christian scholars unwilling to consider the existence of pseudepigraphy in the New Testament. Representative of this view is Earl Ellis's essay "Pseudonymity and Canonicity of New Testament Documents," in *Worship, Theology and Ministry in the Early Church*, ed. M. Wilkins and T. Paige, 213–24 (Sheffield: Sheffield Academic Press, 1993). More hospitable to pseudonimity in the canon is David G. Meade, *Pseudonymity and Canon* (Tübingen: Mohr, 1987).

6. One could, in fact, search for better terms than "pseudepigraphy." For example, speaking of secondary or "attributed" authorship would not only avoid offending but would also express more correctly the shades of authorship. Particularly helpful is D. Meade's assessment: "Attribution in the pseudonymous Petrine and Pauline epistles must be regarded as an assertion of authoritative tradition, not of literary origin." *Pseudonymity and Canon*, 193.

thorship: documents might have been ascribed to leading apostolic figures although written down, even composed, by their disciples, and circulated in good conscience and with honest intentions under apostolic names. This is all the more plausible because the concepts of authorship and authority, which were used in antiquity within a wide range of analogous meanings, must not be harmonized with our modern conception of literary authorship and originality. In fact, the production of apostolic letters by an Apostle's disciples and their attribution by the author to an Apostle might have been part of a disciple's recognized role. If so, this would understandably have played an important role in the formation of the New Testament canon.

One must not hesitate to admit that it was the task of the disciples, acting as secondary authenticators and working posthumously on behalf of the original Apostles, to carry out the collection and edition of Paul's or Peter's letters.[7] The names Mark, Silvanus, Timothy, Titus, and others have been remembered in connection with such functions. By the same token, one may legitimately assume that "editing" Pauline or Petrine tradition involved not only editorial changes to an otherwise complete text, but also more creative forms of intervention in composition (writing and rewriting). In this book we will assume such secondary authenticity (a posthumous and attributed Pauline authorship) for the pastoral letters (1–2 Timothy and Titus) and for Second Peter. Many authors think similarly about Ephesians, James, and Jude, but due to lack of clarity in the arguments we see no need to make a judgment on the issue. Nor do we see any reason to speak of "false attribution" (pseudonymy), "false superscription" ("pseudepigraphy"), or "false authorship" as tools of intentional deception in the sense some critics use these terms. Such works may be considered truly apostolic books in the same sense in which tradition called the gospels of Mark and Luke *evangelia apostolica* and their authors *viri apostolici*. Although Mark and Luke have never been classified among the Apostles and must not be thought of as original eyewitnesses of Jesus, from the second cen-

7. See this put in the context of second-century Christianity by Gamble, *New Testament Canon*, 36–41.

tury both evangelists and their gospels have been regarded as "apostolic."[8]

The attachment of superscriptions to the gospels ("according to Matthew," "according to Mark," "according to Luke," and "according to John") has attracted new attention in recent decades. Some scholars may still hold on to the position that all four gospels were originally anonymous works, and only later, perhaps shortly after their composition, once *several* of the gospels were being used simultaneously, were they attributed to various authors in order to distinguish them from each other. In short, they were assigned to fictitious authors and through them to one or another prominent apostolic personality whose name was known to the local church.

Such theories are regularly linked to doubts about the correctness of these attributions. These theories, however, lack probability, breaking down on two issues. First, if they were *initially* circulated and only afterward given titles, how can one explain that each was attributed unanimously to the same author, with no trace of diversity in their traditional authorship? Second, choosing authors like "Mark" and "Luke" for these "anonymous compositions" would have been pointless, unlikely, and ineffective. Mark and Luke are only marginally known co-workers mentioned in the apostolic letters; they did not qualify as eyewitnesses to Jesus' ministry.[9] Assigning their names to a gospel would have only indirectly conferred an apostolic status on it. Just the reverse is more likely: Mark and Luke obtained notoriety and importance because of their association with their respective gospels. Moreover, "authorship" in antiquity did not mean what it

8. Both Irenaeus (*Adversus haereses* III, 1, 1) and Tertullian (*Adversus Marcionem* IV, 2) consider Mark and Luke apostolic gospels. When they identify Mark as Peter's "disciple and interpreter" and Luke as Paul's "follower," they show clear awareness that apostolicity could be verified by authorship through a disciple. Interestingly, in the second century Catholics and Marcionites agreed on the *reason* for which Marcion accepted Luke as the only authentic gospel: a tradition affirming Luke's association with Paul. Similar reasoning is present in the ancient gospel prologues and Papias's fragments reporting about Mark's association with Peter. See Hans-Joachim Schulz, *Die apostolische Herkunft der Evangelien* [The Apostolic Provenance of the Gospels] (Freiburg: Herder, 1995), 62.

9. Papias emphatically states that Mark was no eyewitness. Luke says indirectly the same thing about himself in the prologue of his gospel (Lk 1:1–4) when stating that he consulted eyewitnesses for assuring a firm basis for his work.

means today: it might have coincided with being the writer of a text, but oftentimes it pointed back to the "authority" of the person from whom the substance of the book's content originates, rather than to a sole literary author who is *the one and only* writer of the book. Just as the concept of a ghostwriter still exists today, so also in antiquity commissioning the writing of a book was common and the use of redactors was just as well known as it is today.[10]

Neither "secondary authorship" nor the identity of the authors as provided by early Church writers or early manuscripts should be judged in a global way. The question of authorship comes with many nuances and each case must be decided individually. All in all, the assumption that "Mark" and "Luke" are correctly identified as the authors of the respective gospels is by far the best explanation for the early and unanimous attribution of these gospels to them. There is also solid tradition for some kind of factual connection between the Apostle Matthew and the first gospel, although we must not necessarily grant him the same kind of authorship as the one attributed to Mark and Luke. But the linkage of the Apostle "Matthew" with the first gospel means at least this much: the tradition of oral preaching which obtained a fixed literary expression in the Gospel of Matthew goes back to the tax official Jesus converted in Capernaum, and that this person had been chosen by Jesus as one of the Twelve. In the case of the fourth gospel, the issue is again somewhat different. Although a number of disputed questions about the identity of the author or authors of the Johannine writings have not been resolved, one cannot discard the tradition about the Apostle John (son of Zebedee) having played a substantial role in founding the tradition from which the fourth gospel took its origin. In this sense of the word, we can, therefore, affirm that tradition's claim for an "apostolic origin" of each canonical gospel is rooted in facts.

A more diverse concept of apostolic authorship is manifest in the rest of the New Testament, and one cannot make for each book the

10. It is not only legitimate but highly probable that the Silvanus mentioned in 1 Pt 5:12 was the literary redactor of 1 Peter, since one rightly assumes that Peter was, if not outright illiterate, less than sufficiently trained for composing such a text.

same historical claims. On one end we see authentically apostolic letters (for example Romans or Galatians) penned or dictated by the Apostle Paul. Further along we must regard the canonical gospels as oral teaching formed into solid literary compositions by writers who belonged to the personal entourage of the first Apostles. Finally, on the other end of the spectrum, we find books of attributed or secondary authorship like the pastorals and Second Peter. The Letter to the Hebrews constitutes a special case: its author was a matter of guesswork even in antiquity. Yet these uncertainties did not prevent it from obtaining canonical authority and being eventually recognized as canonical by all Christian denominations.[11]

In the history of the New Testament canon there appear both a remarkable restraint in accepting dubious literary products and a conscious effort to extend apostolicity to *some* early "post-apostolic" (or "sub-apostolic") works, that is, recognizing in *some* cases the production of new works under old names as legitimate. A good example of such a case is Second Peter, especially when compared to First Peter. The authenticity of First Peter has been quite firmly and widely accepted, from as early as Papias and onward even to several modern critics. With a high degree of probability one can say that it contains a so-called "circular letter" to the churches of Asia Minor issued under the authority of Peter. Again, there is no simpler explanation for its early and universal acceptance than the assumption that it was produced under Peter's supervision even if with the assistance of a "secondary author," a certain Silvanus (1 Pt 5:12), who is also mentioned a few times in Pauline letters (1 Thes 1:1; 2 Thes 1:1; and Col 1:19) as well as, under the variant name of "Silas," in Acts (twelve times in Acts 15–18). But Second Peter is quite probably of a later origin and must be considered posthumous. Yet its being "a second letter by Peter" is essential to its composition, since it constitutes a conscious follow-up to First Peter: "This is now, beloved, *the second letter I am writing to you*" (2 Pt 3:1). On the other hand, the text curiously mentions at its very beginning Peter's imminent "departure," or "exodus," propheti-

11. The insertion of Hebrews among the Pauline letters was neither universally recognized nor an absolutely necessary condition for its canonical status.

cally foreknown to him and motivating him to compose this second letter: "I think it right, *as long as I am in this body*, to refresh your memory, since I know that my death will come soon, as indeed our Lord Jesus Christ has made clear to me" (2 Pt 1:13–14). These features indicate that the writer not only regarded First Peter as authentic, but felt entitled to attach to it a second letter—after all, the first itself was written "through Silvanus" and not by the Apostle alone. But by referring to the Apostle's imminent death, the author of the second epistle effectively shows that, in his understanding, no further addition to Peter's letters may be constructed.[12]

In the case of Second Peter, then, we have the model for attaching a pseudonymous work to an earlier authentic work for the sake of completing it, even while blocking efforts to create (further) pseudonymous letters. Perhaps this is the way to understand how a kind of appendix was attached to the Gospel of John (chapter 21), not only to complete some unfinished theological agenda, but also to report the death of the "Beloved Disciple," and thus render impossible the production of any further extension of the fourth gospel. The last verse even goes so far as to make any further proliferation of similar work futile and, therefore, it has become a tool to help protect not only John's gospel but the whole collection of the four canonical gospels from further accretion (see Jn 21:25).

Something similar may be observed regarding the Pauline pastorals. Modern exegesis likes to emphasize that the three documents' pseudepigraphic character is rooted in an effort to mask the increasing institutionalization of the Church in the late first century. Yet, more important, it should be noted that the pastorals ultimately provide for an effective closure of the Pauline corpus. For after Second Timothy, a written monument to the Apostle's *martyrdom*, one cannot conceive of further posthumous works written in his name. By observing that the pastorals are presented as the last Pauline letters,

12. In other genres (gospel and apocalypse) there have been significant efforts made to extend the Petrine corpus: the *Apocalypse of Peter* shows up in the *Muratorian Canon* (dated to around AD 200). But the addition of the *Gospel of Peter* created problems for bishop Serapion in the early third century, as reported by Eusebius, *Historia ecclesiastica* VI, 12, 3.

we again come to the conclusion that the production of secondary apostolic letters was an essential part of a process which brought closure to the body of normative documents rather than encouraged a proliferation of such works.

Apostolic Preaching and the New Testament Scriptures

Canonical Gospels

Each of the four gospels demonstrably carries in its title and content a conscious, intentional attachment to the apostolic preaching. Each links up to a name that, in the context of the canon, is connected with a major apostolic figure of the first proclamation of the faith.

The closing of the Gospel of Matthew explains such a linkage most explicitly. In the final scene, as Jesus appears to the Eleven and declares the beginning of his messianic reign ("all power has been given to me in heaven and earth"), he entrusts to their care his whole teaching mission and all the precepts he has given. Their task is to "make disciples of all nations" and to promulgate the divine commands, a new legislation, which Jesus has provided them (Mt 28:16–20). This scene really conveys to the reader that the content of the book has become, by the will of the risen Christ, the material of continued preaching destined for all peoples of all times. Of course, the preaching entrusted here to the care of the Eleven preceded the composition of the book itself. But it was supposed to be continued by preaching what is contained in the book, which is the intended use of the book itself.

Although the book's immediate importance may appear secondary to that of the preaching, the book actually obtains its significance and authority from the very empowerment to preach that Christ gave to the Eleven as he sent them into the whole wide world. The last sentence of the book is, therefore, of extraordinary importance: "Behold I am with you until the consummation of the world." The reigning Christ, when commissioning the Eleven, guarantees his abiding presence for and with them until their task is completed. Here again the book points beyond itself: it declares the ongoing presence of the enthroned Messiah with his messengers, assuring in this way authenticity, normative authority, and never-ending trustworthiness for the preaching that they begin under his command.

The self-understanding of Matthew's gospel, then, is clearly part of a larger reality: the self-understanding of the Church. For the Church uses this book while retaining not only the historical memory of Jesus' deeds and teaching, but also Jesus' actual and effective presence as the ultimate guarantee of the truth and authority for the Church's teaching. The authenticity of the teaching is not a matter of checking the material exactness of its contents against other human records. The author is fully aware that the guarantee of truth resides not in human accuracy, but in the risen Christ's actual presence in the Church. The reader of Matthew's book realizes at this point why the narration of more encounters between the disciples and the risen Christ would be of no consequence for the Matthean author. Thus the book aptly concludes by declaring that the ongoing presence of Christ with his disciples is the ultimate basis for all ecclesial activities, including the very creation in the Church of authentic records of Jesus' deeds and teaching (Mt 28:16–20). Thus the conclusion of the Gospel of Matthew is an appendix of "self-authentication." Not only does it identify the content of the book as a whole with what has been entrusted to the Eleven to proclaim, but it also includes Jesus' promise of remaining with them as a guarantee that the gospel book "according to Matthew" authentically teaches what Jesus taught to his chosen disciples.[13]

Mark's gospel expresses a different facet of the Church's self-understanding. Consider the title of the work: "The beginning of the gospel of Jesus Christ, the Son of God" (1:1). The Greek word

13. There is no way of deciding the exact time when the title Εὐαγγέλιον κατὰ Μαθθαῖον became part of the transmitted document. However, the presbyter whom Papias quotes (not just Papias, but a source that chronologically preceded him at the end of the first century) attributes this gospel to the Apostle Matthew. To this we add that, by cross-referencing Mt 9:9 and 10:3, the Gospel of Matthew alone identifies the Apostle Matthew as a witness to Jesus' ministry from its beginnings in Capernaum. This argument focuses not as much on the authorship of Matthew by one of the Twelve as on the claim of the gospel's credibility as it presents itself as closely connected with the witness of the Twelve, who were charged with their ministry by Jesus and received the promise of his ongoing assistance.

εὐαγγέλιον belongs to the earliest layer of the ancient Christian vocabulary used for designating the Christian message. From the opening of Paul's letter to the Romans (1:1–4), a document dated without much dispute to around AD 57, we know that this word was closely associated with the self-understanding of the first Christian missionaries. Paul declares that he has been "segregated for the εὐαγγέλιον," that is, his whole life has been put into its service by divine election and call (see also Rom 1:16; Gal 1:11–12; 1 Cor 9:16–18). Such close rapport between apostleship and "the gospel" is not a particularly Pauline notion, nor is it simply derived from some idiosyncratic Pauline concept. The link of the essential content of Romans 1:1-4, which describes the εὐαγγέλιον, to pre-Pauline formulas is widely recognized. Both the style and the vocabulary of the passage reveal that Paul was drawing from previous tradition. This is, of course, quite understandable, for he is addressing a Christian community that he had had no chance to meet before. Since Romans is the only Pauline letter addressing a non-Pauline community, it is natural to expect that he should begin his letter by using phrases broadly employed by Christian missionaries, including those who converted the Christians of Rome.

In his other writings, Paul makes it quite clear that, when he describes himself as an Apostle of Christ, he compares himself to those who were eyewitnesses of Jesus' earthly life (1 Cor 9:1–5), and also to those whom elsewhere he called "the pillars" of the Church (Gal 2:9). These texts express a paradoxical notion of his apostleship: while recognizing that he was not one of the original Apostles, he formulates his claim to a direct divine call, accompanied by a personal vision of the risen Christ (Gal 1:1, 15–16). He patterns the understanding of his call and the authority he received from God both according to and against the authority which he recognizes in the Twelve.[14] According to time and rank, he distinguishes *his* own call to be an Apostle from *their* personal call by the earthly Jesus and

14. How Paul related and ranked James, the brother of the Lord, to rest of the "pillars" mentioned in Gal 2:9 or to the Twelve is of lesser significance, and must not detain us here.

their firsthand experience of the resurrection (see 1 Cor 15:5–9), even while he compares his call to theirs.

When Mark begins his composition with the term εὐαγγέλιον, he inserts his work into a Pauline setting, and ties it more broadly to both the apostolic preaching and the Apostles themselves, who, endowed with special qualifications and authority, began to spread the Christian message. As the book's title or first sentence, Mark 1:1 also links the book specifically to the witnesses of the resurrection.[15] From this point of view, the possible absence of resurrection appearances from the original ending of Mark is of little importance. By the time the Roman community received Mark's written gospel, it had possessed at least for a decade a Pauline epistle with clear statements about Jesus' bodily resurrection as constitutive of their faith. In all probability they also possessed a copy of First Corinthians with a traditional list of appearances of the risen Lord (1 Cor 15:1–8; esp. verse 3). In general, at the time the gospel message was put in written form, the experience of the risen Christ was recognized as the essential basis of Christian faith and preaching.

This may of course lead some to assert that narratives about the risen Christ typically belonged to the conclusion of a gospel according to the patterns of the "genre" (as documents describing the Lord's words and deeds); therefore, such scholars might suggest that to assume that Mark's gospel ended with 16:8 raises many questions and solves none.[16] It is quite interesting to note that Mark's concep-

15. Whether or not Mk 1:1 can, indeed, be called in a technical sense the "title" of the book remains debatable. Yet, directly or indirectly, Mk 1:1 designates the book as a rendition of the Christian εὐαγγέλιον. By this I mean that, if the verse refers to the preaching of John the Baptist, it describes John's preaching as an initial phase or "beginning" of the εὐαγγέλιον, and thus, at least in an implicit sense, the rest of the book, dealing with the deeds and words of Jesus, would be regarded as εὐαγγέλιον. However, verse 1:1 may constitute an "incipit" (a heading) for the composition and may be translated as "Here begins the εὐαγγέλιον of Jesus Christ, Son of God." In that case the word εὐαγγέλιον designates more directly and explicitly the subject matter of the book.

16. The last verse of Mark is the subject of unending debate. For a summary of its present state see Kelly R. Iverson, "A Further Word on Final *Gar*," *Catholic Biblical Quarterly* 68 (2006): 79–94. Independently of the final γάρ in Mk 16:8, the assumption that verse 14:28 ("But after I am raised up, I will go before you to Galilee") was left hanging in suspense with no fulfillment or explanation would imply that the author had unclear notions about how to close a literary composition.

tion of the apostolic preaching is characterized primarily by an effort to anchor it in the actual participation of the Twelve in Jesus' own preaching of the gospel. Repeatedly (cf. 3:14–15; 6:7–13, 30–32) he describes how, already in Jesus' lifetime, the Twelve were sent to act in Jesus' name and with his power, and to do what he was doing.[17] If we look at all these elements of Mark's gospel, there is certainly enough evidence for concluding that the book is not merely about the mission and ministry of "the Twelve" but stays in continuity with that same ministry—indeed, is the product and the extension of it. According to its author's intention, this gospel cannot be understood apart from its claim that there is a connection between the activities of Jesus and the ongoing work of his chosen disciples.

An even more acute awareness of this connection between a written gospel and the apostolic preaching appears in Luke's gospel. The main difference arises from Luke's unique project: he alone composed a two-volume work in which the narration of "what Jesus did and taught" (Acts 1:1) is followed by the story of Christian origins in the form of a history of the apostolic preaching, particularly the missionary activities of Peter and Paul. The preface of the first volume (Lk 1:1–4) carefully and concisely formulates the thesis that Luke's work is essentially linked to the testimony of "eyewitnesses and ministers of the word," who first spread the Christian message. He speaks of the role of tradition, the task of collecting information from eyewitness sources, returning to the origins, aiming at a certain completeness of information, and providing an ordered narrative with accuracy.

Here for the first time a certain historical and literary consciousness joins with the self-understanding of a believer and servant of

17. In this regard the compact sentence introducing the selection of the Twelve is quite remarkable: "He chose Twelve so that they might be with him, and that he might send them to preach and that they might have the power of expelling demons." This statement levels off considerably the role of the Twelve before and after the Resurrection. Mk 6:7–13 is surprisingly close to what we found in Matthew's last verses: preaching, power, and "being with Jesus" constitute in Matthew and Mark practically the same concept of apostleship. The difference is that in Mark all these functions are rooted in original election of the Twelve and not in an empowerment that follows the Resurrection.

the Church community. He aims at providing "solidity to the words" of the Church's preaching by using the procedures of ancient historiography. Handling his task as a qualified "professional," Luke is the first to realize that he can achieve his objectives only if his work encompasses both the history of Jesus and the history of the early Church as two consecutive phases of one single divine intervention in human history. What appears at the end of Matthew only as a barely sketched projection—the sending off of the disciples into the totality of space and time—takes concrete shape in Luke's work. By applying a geographic outline, his book's structure exhibits in spatial terms the expansion of the Christian movement: its beginnings in Galilee lead to the peak events of crucifixion and resurrection in Jerusalem; then the beginnings of the Jerusalem church meander through numerous developments until they lead to a final transfer of the gospel to the Gentiles, symbolized by Paul's arrival in Rome. There, although Paul is a prisoner destined for martyrdom (his farewell in Acts 20:32–38 leaves no doubt),[18] he announces the message and teaching "about the Lord Jesus Christ with full confidence and unhindered" (Act 28:31).

The author's awareness of purpose and motivation are also manifest in John's gospel, specifically regarding the work's relationship to the preaching and teaching functions of the Church. There is a close relationship between the gospel's prologue and John's first letter, especially its first chapter. Both texts' central topic is the Eternal Word, who appears in the realm of flesh and thus becomes the object of sense experience: "What we have seen and heard and touched by hand." The "we" of both texts (1 Jn 1:1–3 and Jn 1:14) is an "apostolic we," which refers to a special group of privileged eyewitnesses endowed with the task and mission of witnessing.[19] By their testi-

18. The speech of Miletos makes no sense unless both writer and reader know that Paul in fact never had a chance to see the Christians of Asia Minor again.

19. See Raymond Brown's comment: "'We have seen' seems to be a reference to apostolic witness, like the Prologue to First John." *The Gospel of John I–XII,* The Anchor Bible 29 (Garden City, N.Y.: Doubleday, 1966), 34. The "we" in both texts cannot be simply identified with the "Johannine community," as Brown's later works and other commentators suggest.

mony, these witnesses extend their communion (κοινωνία) with the Word of God to all men who are willing to receive their preaching with faith. The Johannine writings, and especially the gospel, have the task of extending this communion of life with God, achieved through the Incarnate Son: "What we have seen and heard we proclaim now to you, so that you too may have fellowship (κοινωνία) with us; for our fellowship is with the Father and with his Son, Jesus Christ" (1 Jn 1:3).[20]

It is no coincidence that among all the books of the New Testament, it is in the Johannine writings that the Greek verb γράφειν occurs most frequently. In a remarkable way the second chapter of First John points out the role and importance of "apostolic writing" in the Church.[21] It is obviously an extension of the apostolic preaching, but it is also a function coordinated to the role of an "abiding" teaching by the Spirit working "from within" the believer:

> My little children, I am *writing* these things to you so that you may not sin. . . .
>
> He who says "I know him" but disobeys his commandments is a liar, and the truth is not in him; but whoever keeps his word, in him truly love for God is perfected. By this we may be sure that we are in him: he who says he abides in him ought to walk in the same way in which he walked.
>
> Beloved, I am *writing* you no new commandment, but an old commandment that you have had from the beginning; the old commandment is the word that *you have heard*. Yet I am *writing* you a new commandment that is true in him and in you, because the darkness is passing away and the true light is already shining. . . .
>
> I am *writing* to you, little children, because your sins are forgiven on account of his name. I am *writing* to you, fathers, because you know him who is from the beginning. I am *writing* to you, young peo-

20. It is this distinction of "we" and "you" (the latter in plural) in 1 Jn 1:3, which excludes the possibility that the "we" of verse 1 would mean the Johannine community.

21. The linkage between the "apostolic writing" and "the apostolic preaching" is by no means an exaggeration except for the fact that the use of the term "apostle" is absent from both John's gospel and the Johannine letters. However, what the author of 1 John is "writing" about can be well referenced to the Farewell Discourses, addressed to the Twelve so that they might transmit their message "to those who will believe after them" (Jn 17:20).

ple, because you have conquered the evil one. I *write* to you, children, because you know the Father. I *write* to you, fathers, because you know him who is from the beginning. I *write* to you, young people, because you are strong and the word of God abides in you, and you have overcome the evil one. . . .

I *write* to you, not because you do not know the truth, but because you know it, and you know that no lie comes from the truth. . . .

Let what you heard from the beginning abide in you. If what you heard from the beginning abides in you, then you will abide in the Son and in the Father. And this is what he has promised us, eternal life.

I *write* these things to you concerning those who would deceive you. As for you, the anointing that you received from him *abides* in you, and so you do not need anyone to teach you.[22]

In the above passage running through 1 John 2:1–26, the expression "I write" is repeated eleven times. "Writing" corresponds here, on the part of the recipient, not to "reading" but to "hearing": a hearing of "what was announced and heard from the beginning" and "abides" in the believer. The repeated act of "writing," therefore, serves to extend and solidify what was originally heard; by being enshrined in written records, the content of faith remains accessible for ages to come.[23]

The books of the New Testament connected in the tradition with the name of the Apostle John attribute also elsewhere a special importance to writing for helping to extend the Church community. The first conclusion of John's gospel clearly states that writing serves the purpose of eliciting and confirming faith: "Now Jesus did many other signs in the presence of (his) disciples that are not *written* in this book. But these are *written* that you may (come to) believe that

22. Each occurrence of "I write" or "I am writing" is followed by a reference to major topical issues of the fourth gospel. A short list can be given for the following: for "walking in the same way" see Jn 15:10; for giving a new commandment see Jn 13:34; for "sins forgiven on account of my name" see Jn 15:3; for "the word of God abiding in you" see Jn 15:4; for "you abiding in the Son and in the Father" see Jn 15:5–8; for the "promise of eternal life" see Jn 17:2; and for the anointing that abides and takes care of further teaching see Jn 14:26 and 16:13.

23. This argument ties in with Richard Bauckham's observation that, in the context of the apostolic preaching, "tradition" (παράδοσις) is not a matter of oral preaching but includes both vocal *(viva voce)* and written transmission. Richard Bauckham, *Jesus and the Eyewitnesses* (Grand Rapids, Mich.: Eerdmans, 2006), 264–71.

Jesus is the Messiah, the Son of God, and that through this belief you may have life in his name" (20:30–31). Furthermore, the concluding passage of John's gospel has some striking resemblance to the opening verse of Mark about the beginning of the gospel "of the Messiah, the Son of God." One may remark that, in view of the literary genre of a gospel, it should not be surprising to see "writing" and the function of confirming the faith in Jesus as "Messiah and Son of God" linked in both Mark and John. Yet what John says about his work's lack of completeness must appear rather surprising. While Mark may be seen as sketchy and incomplete by default and to a fault, John's work purposefully claims to be only a selective "anthology" of the Jesus tradition: "Jesus has performed many more signs in the sight of his disciples which are not written in this book" (Jn 20:30).[24] Thus, although the written work originated in preaching, the book makes no claim to be coextensive with what was transmitted by oral ministry. This point is, apparently, so important for the fourth gospel that its so-called second conclusion, the last verse of chapter 21, repeats the idea, by stating a priori that a complete written presentation of Jesus' words and deeds is not even possible: "There are also many other things that Jesus did, but if these were to be described individually, I do not think the whole world would contain the books that would be written" (Jn 21:25).

This might be the end of a development: a recognition of the vital importance of the written record of the apostolic preaching combined with the refusal to reduce all surviving tradition about Jesus to written records. This conviction is later reflected by Papias's testimony: "For I did not suppose that the things from the books would aid me so much as the things from the living and abiding voice."[25]

---

24. The Gospels of Matthew and Luke give the impression that, at least in principle, they tried to achieve a kind of completeness in their presentation of the early tradition about Jesus. This is quite clear in Luke's prologue: ἔδοξε κἀμοὶ παρηκολουθηκότι ἄνωθεν πᾶσιν ἀκριβῶς καθεξῆς σοι γράψαι (1:3). Matthew's last verses indicate that the content of his book became from that time on the subject of oral preaching which Jesus intends to accompany with his lasting presence until the end of the world. This is, indeed, not very distant from what Papias says about the "living and abiding voice."

25. Eusebius preserved this in his *Historia ecclesiastica* III, 39, 3. The "living and abiding voice" reflects both an ancient *topos* (*viva vox* is to be preferred to written

The Apostolic Letters

Dependence on apostolic preaching is also of capital importance for the rest of the books in the New Testament. The letters that, on account of their factual Pauline origin, form the core of the Pauline corpus frequently indicate that they were regarded, by both writer and recipients, as substitutes for Paul's actual presence.[26] By assuming that at least Ephesians and possibly also Colossians are pseudepigraphic, we may better define their relationship to Paul's preaching, rather than weakening it. Because of their doctrinal character, stated in less personal but more concise terms, they appear to be depositories of Pauline teaching. Yet it is not necessary to assume that they are posthumous. It does not take too much imagination about (and experience of) persecution to accept that letters sent from prison were probably not dictated or penned by the prisoner, but were composed by delegated emissaries, regardless of whether the texts were actually distributed posthumously or earlier.[27]

The strong Pauline tradition in Asia Minor, which survived beyond the lifetime of the Apostle and was integrated into the Pau-

---

sources) and a Johannine usage (see Jn 6:27; 1 Jn 2:14, 17; 3:15; 2 Jn 1:2). A detailed analysis of this double root of the phrase is found in Richard Bauckham, *Jesus and the Eyewitnesses* (Grand Rapids, Mich.: Eerdmans, 2006), 21–30.

26. In the concluding chapters of many of the epistles there are passages containing phrases like "I come (to you)," in order to express that Paul wants to *continue* his discourse with the recipients *viva voce*. Rom 15:23, 29, 32; 1 Cor 16:2; 14:6; 2 Cor 12:14, 20, 21; 13:2, 10; Phil 1:26–27; 2:24. The pastorals contain only one such statement, but with quite a contrast: "I hope to come to you soon, but I am writing these instructions to you so that, if I am delayed, you may know how one ought to behave in the household of God" (1 Tm 3:14). 2 Timothy, however, repeatedly speaks of Timothy's coming to Paul: "you come" (2 Tm 3:1; 4:9, 13).

27. The overlapping lists of individuals to be greeted at the end of Colossians (4:9–17), Philemon (10, 23–24) and 2 Timothy (4:10–21) may be a good indicator that Paul's message was extended through letters coming from his imprisonment with notes appended about the identity of the people in charge of his spiritual legacy. Since one of these letters (Philemon) is doubtlessly authentic, but 2 Timothy is, according to a wide majority of scholars, pseudepigraphic, these letters may give the best evidence for a "school" of Pauline disciples which collected, organized, and fixed Paul's apostolic heritage. 2 Timothy might have had the same function which 2 Peter had. Its place at the end of the collection makes it clear that the apostle, now deceased, could not have issued further letters. One easily concludes that such letters could not have come about without being known to his disciples who were with him at his last imprisonment.

line churches' blossoming life, is attested in many independent ways. Acts (18:9–10) records Paul's continued teaching for nearly three years in Ephesus, the capital of the province of Asia Minor, and there is no basis for questioning the reliability of this information.[28] A letter by Clement of Rome to the Corinthians, written on behalf of the Roman community around the year 96, contains several specific references to Paul and his letters.[29] The letters of Ignatius of Antioch, written around the year 115 to several of the churches of Asia Minor and the church of Rome, also show a keen awareness about the impact of Paul's letters,[30] as do the extant texts of Polycarp, bishop of Smyrna, the leading ecclesiastical figure of the region, writing shortly thereafter to the Philippians.[31] Consequently, the collection of the Pauline letters must have taken place in Asia Minor at a rather early point, so that Second Peter's reference to "all of Paul's letters" (3:15) can be interpreted concretely as "all pieces" of a known collection.[32]

A most unusual corroboration of the process by which the Pauline corpus was formed is the letter to Philemon, the only authentic letter that addresses an individual and thus has some characteristics of a private letter addressed to an individual on account of an individual affair. Since we can rightfully assume that Paul wrote many such letters, the question must be raised: why did this one and only this one survive? The simplest explanation is that the person or persons in possession of this letter—Philemon himself or, more probably, Onesimus, the runaway slave who carried it—played an important role in creating the collection of Paul's letters addressed to the churches.[33]

The second epistle of Peter is usually dated around or earlier than

28. The detail about the location of his preaching (that Paul rented the lecture hall of Tyrannus) confirms this impression.

29. 5:6; 47:1.

30. Eph 12:2; Rom 4:3. Ignatius might, in fact, be imitating Paul's letter writing.

31. Phil 3:2; 4:1; 9:1.

32. See Peter Trummer, "Corpus Paulinum—Corpus Pastorale," in *Paulus in den neutestamentlichen Spatschrifte,* ed. Karl Kertelge, 122–45 (Freiburg in Br.: Herder, 1981).

33. Cf. Phlm 10; Col 4:9. The precarious juridical status of a runaway slave is the best explanation for the survival of the letter. Onesimus could have preserved it for his own security in order to use it as a proof that he was no longer a slave on the run.

AD 125. Thus by that time at the latest a Pauline collection of letters was in existence. In 2 Peter 3:15–16, within the reference to Paul's letters lies a doctrinal issue concerning the time of the *parousia*. Second Peter refers to "the patience of our Lord," a topic on which "our beloved brother Paul wrote to you according to the wisdom given him"; he is "speaking of this as he does *in all his letters*."[34] Thus, it seems that the controversies about the *parousia* are linked to controversies about the interpretation of Paul's letters: "There are some things in them hard to understand, which the ignorant and unstable twist to their own destruction, as they do *the other scriptures*." By classifying the Pauline letters as "scriptures," Second Peter sufficiently explains why Paul's letters have been carefully preserved and shows that their interpretation matters; by the year 125, Paul's apostolic preaching is regarded as matching "the scriptures" in dignity and importance. At the same time, it is clear from 2 Peter 3:15–16 that the two Petrine epistles were regarded as being on equal, if not stronger, footing with "all the epistles" of Paul, since according to this text the Petrine letters are said to give guidelines and approval for the interpretation of Paul's letters.[35]

The "hermeneutical confrontation" between Peter and Paul reflected in 2 Peter 3:15–16 might shed some additional light on the need that motivated Paul's disciples to continue and complete the process of codifying the Apostle's heritage and to use for this purpose the

34. The expression ἐν πάσῃ ἐπιστολῇ in Ignatius's *Letter to the Ephesians* 2:12 makes the existence of a Pauline collection of letters at the beginning of the second century virtually certain.

35. 2 Peter contains several more or less explicit references to 1 Peter. The clearest of them is 2 Pt 3:1–2: "This is now, beloved, *the second letter* I am writing to you; in them I am trying to arouse your sincere intention by reminding you that you should remember the words spoken in the past by *the holy prophets,* and the *commandment of the Lord* and Savior spoken through your *Apostles*." This sentence needs to be recognized as testifying to an "embryonic" but only virtually complete canon of Scripture in the sub-apostolic Church. Its reference to "prophets," the "commandment of the Lord," and "the apostles" forms the triptych, later recognized as "Prophets—Gospels—Apostles." The continuation of this passage, including 2 Pt 3:15–16, makes it clear that what 2 Peter understands as the teaching of the Apostles is not only some oral tradition but a collection of Pauline letters and two letters of Peter. A reference to Peter's approaching martyrdom ("since I know that my death will come soon, as indeed our Lord Jesus Christ has made clear to me," 2 Pt 1:14) manifests that the letter does not envisage more than two Petrine letters ever to be included in the canon.

same literary genre that Paul had invented and used for multiplying his presence in the churches: the apostolic letter. To be more specific: why were the "pastorals," three posthumous letters addressed to Timothy and Titus, composed? Their purpose was to leave behind written documents about Pauline church order and to link the fundamental principles of church tradition with the memory of Paul's life and death and with the written documents of his teaching.

The pastoral letters had an immense impact on the shape of the Pauline tradition. Although, already in Romans, Paul called himself "the apostle to the Gentiles" (11:3), it was under the influence of the pastorals that Paul's figure was put on a separate apostolic "pedestal." He appears in the pastorals as an apostle on a "solo" mission: an apostle and teacher set apart for the Gentiles (see 1 Tm 1:1, 2:7; 2 Tm 1:1, 11). The pastorals set the pattern of referring to Paul as "the Apostle" without further qualification. This usage might have been re-enforced and rapidly disseminated under the influence of Marcion, for whom Paul was Jesus' only legitimate "Apostle."[36] In any case, soon both Marcionites and anti-Marcionites began to call Paul "the Apostle," a title retained even in our day.

One may assume that the rest of the books of the New Testament have been attached to the canon in analogous ways, even if in many cases the exact process of canonization and the precise reasons for promoting it are less well known. Second Peter certainly uses and completes First Peter and at the same time coordinates the theological and literary legacy of the two Apostles. This is achieved in a balanced manner and would have seemed satisfactory to the Pauline communities. For, due to the image cast of Peter in First and Second Peter, as well as of Paul in Galatians and in Second Corinthians,

36. Marcion's canon of scriptures consisted of two parts, τὸ εὐαγγέλιον and ὁ ἀπόστολος, the first was based on the Gospel of Luke, the second was a collection of apostolic letters but only by the Apostle Paul. Several authors rightly insist that Marcion's central thesis was not so much about recognizing only the Pauline letters, but about recognizing only one Apostle: Paul. See also Harry Gamble, *Books and Readers in the Early Church: A History of Early Christian Texts* (New Haven, Conn.: Yale University Press, 1995). While vigorously rejecting Marcion's position, the anti-Gnostic fathers of the second and third centuries reinforced the usage appearing in the pastorals and promoted by Marcion (Irenaeus, Tertullian) as they began referring to Paul as "the Apostle."

both Peter and Paul are portrayed as recipients of supernatural, even ecstatic, revelations. They are preachers and authors of letters, originators of doctrinal traditions, and finally, due to Second Peter and John 21 on the one hand, and Second Timothy on the other,, holy martyrs of blessed memory. From such a perspective the two letters of Peter, tightly linked with the Pauline corpus, form the core and bulk of the apostolic letters of the New Testament.[37]

Clearly, as was mentioned above, the letter of James aims at solving problems of interpreting Pauline theology for those steeped in the theological tradition of the Matthean gospel and aware of the legitimacy of Jewish–Christian tradition in the Church. James, the "brother of the Lord," was not one of the Twelve, yet already in Paul's lifetime he was placed alongside the original Apostles (Gal 2:9; 1 Cor 9:1–2, 15:9), so that a letter attributed to him was legitimately seen by the early Church as an "apostolic writing." The letter of Jude is a special case. It seems that it was used as an authoritative source for the composition of Second Peter. Its apostolic status was a result of both its attribution to "Jude, the brother of James," an original disciple, and its relationship to Second Peter as a major source.

The Johannine letters attained their canonical status by their connection to the fourth gospel as well as by the identification of the "presbyter" (3 Jn 1:1), the author of both the second and the third letter, with the Apostle John. This identification has been debated for a long time in one form or another, usually in connection with "the Johannine question," that is, the question posed about the authorship of the fourth gospel and the Book of Revelation. Yet the Church settled for the authority of the three Johannine letters (whose pertinence to the tradition of the fourth gospel remains unchallenged) without ever forcing on the faithful a dogmatic decision linking the identity of their author to John, the son of Zebedee.

In a similar way, the authority and status of the Book of Revelation derive from a number of factors. Its apocalyptic style, its claim

---

37. Another process of linkage between Peter and Paul comes to completion in Acts. The title itself, Acts of the Apostles, refers not so much to "apostles" in general as to the two Apostles, Peter and Paul, whose ministries are the central topic of the book.

to have been revealed by heavenly angels to a visionary who called himself John, and its demand to be considered as an inspired book (Rev 1:3, 19; 22:18) made an early impression on the sub-apostolic Church. Ultimately it was accepted into the canon as a book pertaining to the apostolic heritage of the Church. The identification of the seer with the Apostle John goes back to Justin Martyr and even to Papias.[38] Revelation's belonging to "the Johannine writings" is not necessarily a critically far-fetched proposition, even if its difference in genre and style from the fourth gospel requires that we attribute to it a literary redactor other than the one responsible for the fourth gospel or the Johannine letters. The statements of the Church which demand the admission of these books into the New Testament canon are theological in nature, not literary or historical. The apostolicity of the books requires authenticity only in the sense that they contain original and foundational teaching for the Church; the term certainly does not prejudice the exact historical process by which these books developed their literary form and shape. In the case of the Book of Revelation, the Church has allowed the survival of one

38. Justin Martyr, *Dialogus cum Tryphone* 81. Papias's witness is extant only in fragmentary quotations and references. Andrew of Caesarea in his Commentary to the Apocalypse quotes Papias as witness to the Johannine provenance of the book. Cf. J. Kürzinger, *Papias von Hierapolis und die Evangelien des Neuen Testaments* [Papias of Hierapolis and the Gospels of the New Testament] (Regensburg: Pustet, 1983), 110–11. Scholarship treats Papias's witness with remarkable confusion. The majority of leading authorities quote with approval the position of Eusebius of Caesarea, who claims that Papias confused a certain "John the Elder" with John the son of Zebedee. They usually also remark that Eusebius makes this distinction between the "two Johns" only for discrediting Papias's contention that Revelation was written by the Apostle John (the son of Zebedee). They all observe that Eusebius's agenda was to undermine the chiliasm of Revelation and to downgrade the authority of Papias, who was, in fact, an ardent millenarist. Yet most authors fail to add that Eusebius himself championed the authorship of the fourth gospel by the Apostle John and ascribed only the authorship of Revelation to John the Elder. From the nineteenth century onward Eusebius's distinction is used for quite a different agenda. These modern authors (including most recently Martin Hengel and Richard Bauckham) accept Papias's testimony in order to identify "John the Elder" with the author of the fourth gospel, not of Revelation. They do not even mention that at this point they fail to agree with Eusebius, who never disputed the apostolic origin of the fourth gospel. But the testimony of Papias is shortchanged also in another way. Our present-day textbooks continue to state that the earliest testimony about the apostolic authorship of Revelation comes from Justin Martyr, not from Papias. Incidentally, Justin Martyr admittedly depends on Papias, but virtually nobody cares to explain how he managed to misunderstand Papias and not perceive the distinction between the "two Johns."

single volume of New Testament prophecy containing apocalyptic thought. The controversies about the canonicity of the Book of Revelation in antiquity were attached to problems of interpretation: objections were made against its apostolic authority by some authorities of the early Church mostly in response to its interpretation as millenaristic, but not from historical or critical concerns about its Johannine authorship. By asserting its apostolicity, the Church promotes its interpretation in the wider context of an apostolic canon. In this way the Church counteracted its chiliastic and Montanist interpretation and affirmed its derivation from and conformity with the original presentation of the Christian message.[39]

The apostolicity of the New Testament canon is a *"theologoumenon,"* that is, a theological construct with a conceptual kernel that is theological but is, at the same time, superimposed upon the rudimentary facts of historical tradition. The theological concept in itself is not justified without reference to *some* factual historical foundation. Yet the *exact way* in which the historical basis of an apostolic origin may be verified for one book or another is not defined with authority. Nor is it required that in each case the apostolic character of a book be defined in a univocally identical way. The Magisterium of the Church, up to and including *Dei Verbum* at Vatican II, has always found it sufficient to affirm the apostolicity of the canonical books of the New Testament in some *analogous sense* of the word and without closer specification of the exact way in which the apostolic origin of a particular document is actually verified.

The Formation of the New Testament in the Second Century

In a full and technical sense, in the course of the second century, "the scriptures of the New Testament" had not yet fully devel-

39. The doubts about the scriptural character of Revelation are clearly linked to the Church's rejection of millenarism, although forms of early millenarism—like that of Papias and of Irenaeus—were not condemned officially by the Church. The Montanists assumed the apostolic authorship of both the fourth gospel and Revelation. Their teachings about "the new prophecy" were based preponderantly on John's gospel.

oped. Before Irenaeus (whose death is conventionally dated around the first couple of years of the third century) there is no evidence that Christian doctrine would be routinely and methodically demonstrated by reference to a set of authoritative books. Some of the books themselves might not have been finished and edited before the year AD 125. Moreover, the propagation of these books—even of those written in the last decades of the first century—demanded significantly more time than it would in our day. But one may say, in general, that the whole historical process which brought about the New Testament as an identifiable collection of authoritative books possessed by the Church at large did not come to its conclusion before the end of the second century. This process can be described as a sequence with several phases.

At first, oral tradition played an important part, and its importance did not fade for at least another generation, even if concurrently there was an increasing reliance on written sources. The quotations of Jesus' sayings in Clement of Rome, Ignatius, Polycarp, and Justin Martyr are made more often than not from memory. In fact, due to reliance on memory and oral sources, variant forms of the sayings can be observed within the tradition throughout the second century.

At the same time, the trend toward writing down the content of the apostolic tradition continued to produce further written documents which Church leaders and bishops regarded with growing mistrust. Apocryphal gospels, acts of different apostolic figures, apocalyptic writings, and apocryphal letters attributed to a variety of known figures of the apostolic Church were being published with claims of authenticity. It is important to remark that the forms of this apocryphal literature were based on earlier models. Yet whenever Gnostic content found expression in the apocrypha, the literary genre also underwent mutation. The Gnostic gospels, for example, show no resemblance to ancient biographies or *Vitae:* these gospels' function of reporting on the deeds of Jesus is greatly diminished or wholly lacking, as is the case with the (mostly) Gnostic logia-collection of the Gospel of Thomas. Some apocryphal gospels read very much like the Johannine revelatory discourses, or are composed in the form of dialogues between Jesus and his intimate circles. Other apocryphal gospels expand on the canonical gospels by inserting Gnostic or other theologically motivated material into the infancy narratives or the passion stories.[40]

The motivations for producing such new works were many and ever-increasing: devotion, satisfaction of curiosity, support for doctrinal needs, innovations, new trends, the influence of various ecclesial groups, some remaining in communion with mainstream Christianity, and some seceding into isolation, or appearing isolated in the eyes of the rest. Doctrinal disputes, splitting communities, and aberrant practices demanded the production of further and further "sacred writings." Most important are those writings which try to build bridges between the fundamental tenets of the Christian tradition and different streams of philosophical or religious movements in late Hellenistic society.

While this activity was growing and bearing fruit with ever-increasing fecundity, the problem of authenticity became more and more acute: what criteria can be used to sift out authentic from spurious apostolic writings? There were all sorts of efforts, rooted more or less in good faith, by various groups to enshrine their own tradition in literary documents endowed with apostolic authority by using a catchy title or a fictitious setting. From the *Didache,* or "Teaching of the Twelve Apostles," to the *Epistula Apostolorum* we see a vast number of documents that attempt to solidify liturgical and ecclesial legislation or customs in fixed literary forms. By the end of the second century this question pervaded all parts of the Church: which documents truly contain the teaching inherited from the first Christian generation and ultimately through the Apostles from Christ himself?

It was with the third or fourth Christian generation that canonicity—the authentic and normative character of allegedly apostolic

40. See a rich documentation in Raymond E. Brown, Joseph A. Fitzmyer, and Roland E. Murphy, eds. *The New Jerome Biblical Commentary* (Englewood Cliffs, N.J.: Prentice Hall, 1990), 1065–68.

writings—became a problem in the Church at large. On all fronts the Church had to engage in a battle in defense of its concept of itself; to do so, the Church had to define the authentically Christian, as opposed to the distorted, transformed, and falsified. The main engagements in this battle took place largely over decisions about literary documents: certain writings were collected and approved for public reading in the churches and, eventually, the core of this collection was declared to be authentically "apostolic" in the sense explained above.

We can observe two organically connected and somewhat overlapping phases. In both, the Church looked at its past and at itself. In the first phase, it tried to determine what it had received as original and normative from the preaching and teaching of Christ's first missionaries. In the following phase, it tried to identify those literary works in which this original and normative material was expressed and fixed in such a way that the writings, as bearers of the divine word, became basic elements in the Church's foundation: they became "Holy Scripture," and as such were indispensable for the Church because they contained guaranteed divine truth. Upon them the faith life of the community could be built, questions could be decided, regulations could be based, and certainty about authentic tradition could be assured.

III. THEOLOGY OF INSPIRATION IN THE NEW TESTAMENT

The Nascent Church's Beliefs about the Scriptures

When at its inception the early Christian Church began to use the Scriptures of Judaism, it adopted a certain way of looking at them as well as a certain way of speaking of them. Both these ways had their origin in the Old Testament. In other words, one might say that the Church's faith in the Christian Bible continued and further developed the faith that the Jews had in their Scriptures. The earliest Christian texts contain the same formulas of quotation and reference—"For it is written," "As Scripture says"—which are found in contemporary Jewish documents. These formulas not only mean that the subsequent texts are part of the Scriptures, but that what is being quoted exhibits a conclusive proof sealed by divine authority and which, consequently, is to be accepted with faith and reverence.

Such an attitude is manifest on almost every page of the New Testament, which proves that the early Church without hesitation or ambiguity taught the divine authority of the Old Testament. Scripture is the word of God and as such "cannot lose its validity" (Jn 10:35). This scriptural sense surrounds not only the Mosaic books, but also texts in which a prophet speaks as God's "mouthpiece" (cf. Acts 4:25). Even narrative texts of the Old Testament are quoted as "God's word." So, for example, in Matthew 19:4–5 a narrative passage is quoted from Genesis (2:24) with this opening: "He [the Creator] said." Here the biblical text is directly attributed to the Creator in spite of the fact that, formally, it is not a divine saying, but a statement of the human narrator speaking in his own name.

Quoting Scripture as words or statements uttered "by the Holy Spirit" was also traditional for the Old Testament, and this practice is taken up in the New Testament books. In Acts 4:25 the Apostle Peter quotes Psalm 2 by saying: "You [God] have spoken in this way by the Holy Spirit through the mouth of David." Elsewhere in Acts, Paul introduces a text of Isaiah with the introduction: "Rightly did the Holy Spirit speak when saying the following through Isaiah to our fathers" (Acts 28:25). Furthermore, the Epistle to the Hebrews repeatedly quotes Scripture as text spoken by the Spirit (3:7; 10:15). According to the Gospels of Matthew and Mark, Jesus refers to the Psalms as what "the Holy Spirit said through David" (Mt 22:43; Mk 12:36).

Two Passages about Inspiration

Two passages, 2 Timothy 3:16 and 2 Peter 1:21, are of special importance. These do not refer to specific scriptural quotations but to "the Scriptures" in general.

In 2 Timothy 3:16, Timothy is encouraged to remain faithful to the true teaching he has received and to follow the Scriptures, which he has known since childhood. The text expresses the conviction that knowledge and understanding of the Scriptures (the Old Testament) lead to faith in Christ and a correct interpretation of that faith. It is in this context that the statement is made in verse 16: "All scripture is divinely inspired, and useful for teaching." In Greek the expression "divinely inspired" is the composite term θεόπνευστος, made up of the noun θεός (God) and the verb πνεῖν ("to blow" or "to breathe"). Grammatically it would be possible to attribute to it an active meaning: "Every scripture is breathing God." However, such words made up of the noun θεός and a participle derived from a noun usually convey passive meaning: every scripture "breathed by" or "inspired by God." Thus the term θεόπνευστος means the divine activity of "breathing" (that is, God transmitting his spirit) and the noun πνεῦμα means here not "some" spirit but the Holy Spirit of God. According to the text, because *every* scripture is the product of such activity by the divine Spirit, therefore, *every* scripture is "useful" for teaching, which means that it can be successfully used for providing catechesis, for providing instruction in the Christian faith.

It is worth noting that 2 Timothy 3:16 makes no reference to the human authors of the Scriptures, nor does it contain any hint about how God "inspired" them. It speaks of the scriptural *texts* as products of divine inspiration. We may call this "objective inspiration," that is, the inspiration that results in the sacred character of a biblical text.[1] The context of 2 Peter 1:21 speaks, in general terms, about the prophetic texts of the Old Testament: "First of all you must understand this, that no prophecy of scripture is a matter of one's own interpretation, because no prophecy ever came by the impulse of man, but men moved by the Holy Spirit spoke from God." Scholars dispute what the exact referent of this "scriptural prophecy" may be in this passage. Does it refer to all Scriptures or only to texts which contain "prophecy" in a narrower sense, like the second part of the tripartite Hebrew Bible (Law–Prophets–Writings), or possibly even just some parts of these books, namely the passages which begin with the formula "Thus says the Lord"? The most likely answer is that the expression refers to the whole of the Old Testament, and regards all of it as "prophecy," that is, as texts to be interpreted in reference to Christ. This would better conform to the Christocentric interpretation of the Scriptures, a characteristic of Second Peter (and also First Peter, to which this writing is linked in many ways).[2] In any case, this verse does not speak so much of the scriptural *texts* as of their *authors,* and, in general, of the "holy men" of old, the transmitters of divine revelation. These men were "moved by the Holy

1. In view of the dilemma between an "author-focused" and a "text-focused" doctrine of inspiration, as in S. Chapman, "Reclaiming Inspiration for the Bible," in *Canon and Biblical Interpretation,* ed. C. Bartholomew, Scripture and Hermeneutics 7 (Grand Rapids, Mich.: Zondervan, 2006), 167–206, I keep the distinction of "subjective" vs. "objective" inspiration as two sides of one salvific action.

2. Another argument may be taken from 2 Pt 3:16, in which the expression "other scriptures" indicates the presence of a generalized and extended concept of the "prophetic" and "apostolic" writings, both groups being "scriptures."

Spirit," that is, they acted under his influence when expressing themselves in the Scriptures.

Thus this second passage, while referring to written biblical texts, portrays the model of the biblical (Old Testament) author as a prophetic person who "speaks" through the text. It is certainly no coincidence that the image of holy men transmitting God's word by speech merges in this passage with that of authors composing "holy writings." For centuries beforehand, Jewish tradition attributed all scriptural books to the great teachers and leaders of the past, some patent anachronisms notwithstanding: the five books of the Law were attributed to Moses (including Deuteronomy, in which Moses's death is described!), the Psalms in their totality to King David, several wisdom books to Solomon, to name but three prominent examples. Yet the designation of these "authors" is not to be judged as mere historical fiction, error, or pious exaggeration. Rather, it expresses a concept of revelation according to which God's (biblical) word comes to his people first by live teaching, combined with divine leadership and marvelous deeds, from which verbal communication and spiritual enlightenment emanate and prompt these or other individuals to engage in literary activity, and maybe even to receive divine dictation.

It was in this conceptual framework that Israel developed its traditional teaching about the Pentateuch's foundational authority, and about Moses as the author of all its passages.[3] Moreover, when the Israelites quoted the Psalms as sayings of David, or attributed the wisdom books to the celebrated wisdom of King Solomon, they were making an important connection between text and history. To our modern sense of history this "conceptual framework" might seem much too broad and sketchy, and factually inaccurate, or even "ahistorical," yet one must not forget that it was developed and consciously left intact in old times precisely in order to support a concept of revelation as history. Obviously, this way of thinking and talking had little or no concern for transmitting the names of the literary

3. Jesus speaks of Moses as "author of the Pentateuch" in accordance with this scheme: Mt 8:4; 19:8; Mk 1:44; 7:10; 10:3; 12:26; Lk 5:14; 20:28; 24:27; Jn 5:45–46; 7:19, 22–23.

authors and redactors of the texts in any modern sense of historical accuracy. It did not concern itself with distinctions between oral communication of tradition and its transmission by writing, nor did it pay any special attention to the mode in which divine assistance was provided for the writers working under the influence of the Spirit. The biblical perspective regards "the divine word" in a global sense, as if it had been directly distilled from divine action exercised in the course of human history, a history in which chosen men served as intermediaries between God and his people. In the terms of 2 Peter 1:21, God's word is "prophetic" in its messianic fulfillment, as well as in its mediation through "prophets"—divinely chosen and inspired human beings.

The faith of the early Church, therefore, took hold of the Old Testament with two basic convictions, one in the realm of *objective,* the other in the realm of *subjective* inspiration. On the one hand, the scriptural texts anticipate the arrival of Christ "in many and various ways" (see Heb 1:1); on the other hand, the people who formed and composed them were "the holy men" of salvation history acting under the special influence of the Holy Spirit.

We must realize that such an approach to Scripture in the early Church determined for most of Christian history the way in which the Bible would be treated. Twelve centuries after the time in which the New Testament books were written, the *Summa Theologiae* of Thomas Aquinas deals with scriptural inspiration under the heading of "prophecy."[4] In fact, until most recent times, "prophetic" and "biblical" inspiration remained so intertwined that all efforts to make clean-cut conceptual distinctions between them remained unclear and elusive, or at least rather imperfect.

4. In his *Summa* (II-II, 176, 2) Thomas speaks of the division of prophecy into the subcategories of "imaginary" and "intellectual" prophecy and refers to St. Jerome, who, in his commentary on the Book of Kings, made a distinction between "hagiographers" and "prophets" (PL 28, 552–554). Hans Urs von Balthasar, in his commentary on Thomas's doctrine of the charisms, points out how rich and complicated a development links St. Thomas to his patristic sources. See H. Urs von Balthasar, *Thomas von Aquin: Besondere Gnadengaben und die zwei Wege des menschlichen Lebens: Kommentar zur Summa Theologica II-II, 171–182* [Thomas Aquinas: Special Charisms and the Two Ways of Human Life: Commentary on the Summa Theologica II-II, 171–182], vol. 23 of *Die Deutsche Thomas-Ausgabe,* ed. by H. M. Christmann (Vienna: Pustet, 1958), 351–63.

There is one more important feature characterizing 2 Peter 1:21. The text reveals a line of reasoning that can be reconstructed in the following terms: Since Scripture is prophetic (because divinely inspired), it must not be interpreted by personal interpretation, but rather by apostolic teaching based on the revelation of Christ. This is so because prophecy is not the result of human efforts, but rather the fruit of the Holy Spirit's inspiration. *In other words, just as the text was produced under divine influence, so also it is to be understood according to the enlightenment by the same Spirit.* This principle was commonly held, although in general terms and without further specification, by all Church Fathers and all medieval theologians. Thus it rightly became part of the Second Vatican Council's Apostolic Constitution *Dei Verbum* (no. 12). Nonetheless, while speaking about "inspired" interpretation of various scriptural texts, one must not forget that ancient authors use the concept of inspiration in a broader (and analogous) sense. Consequently, until well into the Middle Ages, the word "inspiration" hardly ever meant specific divine acts "producing scripture," but was the generic term for any divine influence by which a person was inwardly moved to act, especially to posit signs of self-expression by speech or written work.[5]

The New Testament Doctrine of Biblical Inspiration

What has been discussed so far shows that the first Christian generation was familiar with the basic issues of biblical inspiration. These may be summarized in the following three points. First, Holy Scripture is of divine origin and of divine authority; it is God's word and it is the work of the Holy Spirit. Second, the human beings who are held to be the authors of the Bible worked under divine inspiration. They are ultimately linked to the great personalities of salvation history, through whom God communicated his thought and will

5. For this reason the use of an undifferentiated concept of inspiration can easily lead in any discussion of *biblical inspiration* to disconcerting results. See, for example, the statement, "When it comes to the issue of inspiration, the biblical data are surprisingly vague on a theory of inspiration." Craig D. Allert, *A High View of Scripture?* (Grand Rapids, Mich.: Baker Academic, 2005), 171.

to his people.[6] Third, the central topic of the Bible is the revelation of Christ; Scripture has been produced within the framework of an economy of salvation of which Christ is the center and the peak.[7]

The issues summarized here stood in focus for the ancient Church, while the written word as such drew attention only secondarily. So, for example, no matter which part of the Pentateuch they might quote, expressions like "as it is written by Moses," or "Moses said," were interchangeable. Similarly, whatever comes from a prophetic book—or one may say, in view of 2 Peter 1:21, from any part of the Old Testament—can be introduced by such formulas as "God said by the mouth of his prophet." Ancient Christian authors paid little attention to the process by which some teaching, first delivered orally, became afterwards oral tradition, and then was expressed in writing, until the written work, after adjustments and changes, obtained a final and solidified form by the hand of its latest redactors. Of course, such a process took place in the public arena of the Church. Texts were composed and then chiseled by authors, redactors, and editors. Certain elements of a primitive text could have merged with additional material or disappeared, while new elements might have been inserted or emphasized. Usually only after a period of fluctuation did a text obtain its final form and become also in the eyes of its readers a "sacred text," which had to be preserved in a stable form by the Church and transmitted with no further change. But, of course, even in a text recognized as normative textual chang-

6. Robert Gnuse, sketching the various "models" of inspiration, lists "salvation history" as a "new model." He then refers to a list of Protestant authors of a conservative bent: "George Ernest Wright, Reginald Fuller, Oscar Cullmann, John Bright, Paul Minear and many others," and adds "most importantly" C. H. Dodd. Robert Gnuse, *The Authority of the Bible: Theories of Inspiration, Revelation, and the Canon of Scripture* (New York: Paulist Press, 1985), 66–67. The theological concept of *"historia sacra,"* which unified the Church Fathers and medieval theologians from Irenaeus to early scholasticism, is quite different from *"Heilgeschichte,"* because it is neither confined to "past revelation" (ibid.,73) nor "rooted in the text" (74).

7. This is not the "Christocentric model" which Gnuse derives from Luther and detects in Karl Barth, Harnack, Käsemann, Dodd, and many contemporary authors who, however, disagree among themselves about both Christology and the historical Jesus. See in ibid., 87–94. The early Church's Christological model neither opposes nor separates Christ and Scripture, or the subjective and objective aspects of faith and experience.

es still happened, not only by accident or by mistake during copying or dictation, but also through the attempts of the textual critics, ancient and modern, to improve on it in their search for its original form.[8]

It is interesting to observe that the age which witnessed the consolidation of oral traditions into written documents paid little attention to explaining why and in what sense we may, indeed, say that "Isaiah said" or "David declared" words quoted from a fixed written text. We must not think that in ancient times people were unaware of the essential differences between oral and written sources. Yet they remained more interested in a theological scheme by which they were able to identify a sacred text with its original proclamation (and by its actual oral use in the liturgy) than they were in the process by which the words first proclaimed *viva voce* became fixed and stabilized in writing.

It is worth noting in this connection that the two most important New Testament passages about inspiration discussed above belong to posthumous ("pseudepigraphic") apostolic letters, each functioning as a concluding piece to the canonical collection of the Pauline and Petrine epistles, respectively: Second Timothy and Second Peter. In each case, the writer was acting in the name of a leading Apostle, for decades enshrined in honor as a transmitter of divine revelation, and now glorified by a martyr's death—Apostles who had deposited the apostolic traditions in written documents. As we have seen, these posthumous writings were not created for the sake of promoting new teachings insufficiently documented in the known letters of the Apostles; such an effort would have been based on the presupposition of a canon already in existence and functioning in the place of the oral tradition. Rather, they were written chiefly in order to bring

---

8. Modern textual criticism has only recently begun to realize that, as early as the first decades of the second century, Church leaders and theologians tried to correct scriptural texts by comparing manuscripts or various canonical texts, all written under the inspiration of the "same Spirit." The Gnostic and anti-Gnostic variants of the gospels and of the Pauline epistles were a major topic of debate, addressed frequently by Irenaeus, Tertullian, and others, but "corrections" were often undertaken without guile merely for the sake of improving on the text.

the canon of apostolic writings to a close or, perhaps more correctly, to manifest the canon's factual closure. The pastoral letters regard the Pauline tradition as a deposit entrusted to Paul's disciples, and Second Timothy specifically depicts the Apostle facing imminent martyrdom: "The time of my death (*analysis,* or "dissolving") is at hand" (2 Tm 4:6). Similarly, in Second Peter the Apostle states that he is writing a reminder while "in this body," but, "as the Lord Jesus Christ has revealed it" to him, he must soon "put off his body" and face his "departure" (2 Pt 1:13–15). Moreover, Second Peter, speaking of the difficulties of understanding "all letters" written by "our beloved brother Paul according to the wisdom given to him" (2 Pt 3:15), indicates the closure of a process in which *composition was followed by collection and also by the beginning of interpretation.* These passages testify to a remarkably conscious agenda: the intent to seal the apostolic deposit of teaching in vessels which posterity would be able to recognize for what they were in order to abstain from tampering with them.

Some Conclusions

We must revise the habitual ways in which we currently speak about the formation of the Christian Bible. The Church did not simply "take over" the Jewish Scriptures and add to them another set of writings. Rather, when being formed, the Church looked back at the process of sacred history from which it had taken its origins. While doing so, it began to complete and organize its remembrance of the past which had shaped its life, and to identify the way its memory was functioning in discerning the constitutive elements of Christian beliefs and standards of life. While focusing always on the Lord, his life, and his teaching, the Church quickly realized that it could keep his remembrance only by relying on the memory of the apostolic teaching and the records of the prophetic past of the Old Testament; with the passing of the first Christian generation and the sudden increase in doctrinal controversies, it had to rely on the written records. Derived from originally oral sources, the written record revealed a threefold structure: the Jesus tradition (the gospels), the preaching of the Apostles (the apostolic writings), and the word of God given to Israel (already "scripture" in pre-apostolic times and recognized in a twofold structure as "the Law and the Prophets" or "Moses and the prophets"). God's word in human texts began to coalesce in what we may call biblical inspiration in the "objective" sense: inspired texts.

The inspiration of Scripture subjectively meant the influence of the Holy Spirit upon "prophets and Apostles" as authors of the sacred books. As we saw above, this expression soon became a quasi-technical one. Rooted in history, it refers to concrete historical personalities. Nonetheless, it came to denote also a somewhat abstract, loose theological concept by which the early Church referred to various groups of people of the past. "Prophets" meant all those who mediated the word of God in the Old Testament and thus "anticipated" the coming of Christ by word or deed. "Apostles" meant those who, by their mission received from Christ, had the role of extending his historically unique life and preaching. Yet, in a special sense, by the fact that in each Testament the proclaimed word became Scripture, "prophets and Apostles" became a formula for referring to authors of all the holy books. Thus, speaking of "prophets and Apostles," churchmen, preachers, and theologians alike used a kind of Christian "jargon" referring to both human figures who, with divine election and charisma, announced the word of God, and, secondarily, to persons who by divine prompting and providence gave written form to the original preaching, thereby enshrining it in written documents. In ancient texts, the "human authors" meant first and foremost these prophetic and apostolic figures preaching God's word; quite often, however, this reference also included the fact that, by themselves or through their disciples, the "human authors" provided for written texts documenting the prophetic or apostolic preaching. Only at a relatively late period—certainly not before the advent of scholasticism—did "biblical inspiration" begin to mean the specific divine intervention by which the word proclaimed by "the prophets and the Apostles" was enshrined in the Scriptures, a process resulting in sacred texts guaranteed by God and recognized as such by the Church.

The subjective and objective sides of inspiration are interrelated; in tradition they usually appear together. God inspires the "prophets and Apostles" to preach and to write in such a way that the written records become a permanent source of God's word in the world. While the inspired character of Scripture is equally affirmed for all books of the two Testaments, it is verified analogously in individual texts according to the various ways the charisms of particular prophets and Apostles were linked to the coming of Christ, who alone is, in an ultimate sense, the Word of God, his incarnate Logos. All other expressions of the Divine Word receive their value and authenticity from him.

IV. THE EUCHARISTIC PROVENANCE
OF THE CHRISTIAN BIBLE

The literary heritage of the apostolic Church represented by the books of the New Testament is so closely and organically related to the Eucharist that one is entitled to state that all New Testament Scripture has a Eucharistic provenance.[1] This statement must not be regarded as intending to prove anything extraordinary or unexpected. Historians and Scripture scholars have, in fact, often recognized or at least tacitly presupposed that the texts that make up part of the New Testament originate in the historical, social, or cultic background of the early Church's celebration of the Eucharist.

The Apostolic Letters as Eucharistic Documents

The earliest Pauline letters were written a mere twenty to twenty-five years after Jesus' death and resurrection. They are considerably diverse in purpose and occasion. The liturgical formulas which we find in them—greetings, prayers, blessings, fragments of hymns— are unmistakable signs that they were meant to be presented to communities gathered at assemblies connected with the celebration of the Eucharist.[2]

---

1. With the gracious permission of Paulist Press, this chapter reproduces with only minor changes an article previously published: Denis Farkasfalvy, "The Eucharistic Provenance of the New Testament Texts," in *Rediscovering the Eucharist: Ecumenical Conversations*, ed. Roch A. Kereszty, 27–51 (New York: Paulist Press, 2004).

2. Oscar Cullmann, *Early Christian Worship* (London: SCM Press, 1953), 20–25, lists "psalms and hymns," formulas of benediction, doxologies, and responses, like Amen, to substantiate this claim.

One of the clearest cases for such early Christian celebrations is described in Acts 20. Here Luke narrates an assembly ending with the celebration of the Eucharist. What he describes as happening in Troas in the presence of Paul leaves little doubt: such lengthy Sunday Vigils of the Christian assembly gave ample time for reading texts even as long as any Pauline letter, like Galatians or even First Corinthians, in its entirety.[3] Of course, the Pauline letters were read, partially or in their entirety, as substitutes for the actual presence of the Apostle. After examining many liturgical greetings, doxologies, prayers, and other formulas, Oscar Cullmann comes to the following conclusion:

> The presence of so much that is liturgical here in the Pauline Epistles connects almost certainly with the fact that *the Apostle, while writing his letters, had in mind the community assembled for worship.*[4]

Thus one is fully entitled to read Paul's letters in the context of a Eucharistic celebration because Paul himself envisaged such a context.[5] Similar conclusions are valid also for letters as liturgically charged as First Peter, Ephesians, or Colossians, texts that are generally considered by exegetes to be circular letters extending or substituting for apostolic presence amidst various congregations, even if their apostolic authorship might be secondary and posthumous. The Eucharistic context of letters like Second Peter or James or Jude might be more remote, especially because these letters might only imitate the literary form of an apostolic letter without actually being addressed to concrete communities. But even if they are not meant to address a particular congregation, the most convenient way of publicizing them was in the context of the Eucharist. So, for example, in James 2:2 the term "your assembly" (συναγωγή) must be

---

3. "On the first day of the week as we were gathered to break bread, Paul was instructing them, being ready to depart on the next day. He went on and on with his message until midnight" (Acts 20:7).

4. *Early Christian Worship*, 24. Emphasis added.

5. Relying on Lietzman's research, Cullmann writes, "The closing formulae of the Pauline epistles correspond to the liturgical phrases which we find at the beginning of the old liturgy of the Lord's Supper (see especially 1 Cor 16:21–23). The reason for that is that the Lord's Supper will follow immediately after the reading of his letter" (ibid.).

thought of as a gathering of Christians in which the Eucharist was at the center.[6] The "word of truth" mentioned in 1:18 refers to such assemblies (1:22), formed from people of various social classes (2:5–9). Regardless of this letter's preponderantly exhortative and moralizing tone, its references to the "Parousia of the Lord" (5:7–8) or to prayer of healing in the Lord's name (5:13–18) may be best understood in the context of the Eucharistic services of the community addressed.

The Eucharistic Context of the Gospel Narratives

Passion and Resurrection Narratives

More intricate is the relationship connecting the structure and content of the canonical gospels with the Eucharistic celebrations of the early Church. First of all, one must notice that the narratives of the Institution of the Eucharist in Matthew, Mark, and Luke not only are chronologically linked to each passion narrative but also serve as their theological overture. From First Corinthians, in which the narration of the Institution begins with a precise chronological indicator—"On the night he was handed over" (11:23)—we see that the theological link between the Institution and the passion story goes back to Paul's first preaching in Corinth in AD 50.[7] But, of course, Paul is only quoting what he himself "received" from those who were Apostles before him.[8] Thus, we are dealing here with tradition that was handed down to him in his instruction about Jesus, that is, less than about two decades after Jesus' death and resurrection. In any case, the reference to the Institution as an overture to the passion far antedates the composition of the gospels.

Two important details should be mentioned here. First, the verb παραδίδομαι used in 1 Corinthians 11:23b (in the form παρεδίδετο), often translated as "betrayed," actually has a more technical mean-

---

6. About "the synagogue," meaning here the Christian congregation, see Bo Reicke, *The Epistles of James Peter and Jude,* The Anchor Bible 37 (New York: Doubleday, 1964), 27–28.

7. Joseph Fitzmyer, "Paul," in *The New Jerome Biblical Commentary,* ed. R. E. Brown, J. A. Fitzmyer, and R. E. Murphy (Englewood Cliffs, N.J.: Prentice Hall, 1990), 1335.

8. Notice the force of the expression τοὺς πρὸ ἐμοῦ ἀποστόλους in Gal 1:17.

ing. In fact, in early Christian Greek this verb became a specialized term charged with reference to violent death, accepted and suffered voluntarily in martyrdom.[9] At the beginning of the Institution it signifies not only Jesus' betrayal by Judas, but also his being delivered "into the hands of sinners" (see Mt 26:45; Mk 14:41) for execution (see Mt 27:26; Mk 1:15).[10] Second, from the Gospels of Luke and John, which contain several resurrection appearances, we notice that the episodes narrated about the risen Lord emphasize that, after the resurrection, Jesus and his disciples resumed their table fellowship, which had been suspended after the Institution of the Eucharist at the Last Supper. To this we will return later.

Broader Eucharistic Connections

But now the main question: do the rest of the narratives in the gospels manifest a Eucharistic link in a way comparable to that which the passion narratives show? An explicitly affirmative answer arises from a glance at the gospels.

In a number of important episodes in Jesus' ministry narrated in the gospels, there appears an intentional linkage to the Eucharist. The most obvious examples are the stories of the feeding of the multitude in the desert. Regardless of which position one follows about the so-called "doublets" (single events narrated twice), a phenomenon which, in many scholars' opinion, is the necessary result of oral transmission in the history of the synoptic tradition, the fact remains that the multiplication of loaves is, in the canonical gospels, the event narrated with the highest frequency—twice each by Matthew and Mark, once each by Luke and John. There must be a reason that this story is reproduced with such unparalleled repeti-

9. This meaning is reflected in its use in passages like Mt 10:17; Mk 13:9, 11; Lk 21:12 about persecuted Christians. The relationship of this expression with Is 53:6 is clear in First Clement 16:17 and also in Rom 8:32.

10. The fourth gospel, which does not contain the narrative of the Institution of the Eucharist, also introduces the passion story with a series of Eucharistic texts included in the Farewell Discourses, like the Parable of the Vine. For its intended Eucharistic meaning, see André Feuillet, "Le discours sur le pain de vie," in *Études johanniques* (Paris: Desclée de Brower, 1962), 83–88.

tion. No answer is convincing unless it shows that the story has been perceived in close relation to Christological and ecclesiological realities that constitute the core of the Christian faith. Of course, such a connection is verified if the story is read in a Eucharistic context. It describes the community that Jesus formed around himself to re-enact and bring to fullness the experience of Israel in the desert with thousands of people miraculously fed. Each of the six versions of the story has well-known Eucharistic overtones: the remarks about Jesus looking up to heaven, giving thanks, breaking the bread, and giving it to the disciples (Mt 14:19; 15:36; Mk 6:41; 8:6; Lk 9:16; Jn 6:11) cannot be explained otherwise. In John, the discourse of Capernaum makes these allusions explicit by providing a Eucharistic commentary about Jesus' sign in the desert. One must add that, in all four gospels, these narratives are also connected with Jesus' healings: the feeding of the multitude is intimately linked to the dispensation of divine mercy not only by teaching but by affecting physical existence by restoring the sick to health.[11]

Once we acknowledge the Eucharistic significance of these six narratives, we can easily develop a perspective in which to see the Eucharistic relevance of every narrative that mentions Jesus at common meals with his disciples or the theme of the messianic banquet, as well as of those passages in which the Kingdom of God is compared to a meal or a feast.[12]

The Narrative Pericopes of the Gospels

The canonical gospels, however, have even deeper features showing their Eucharistic provenance. These belong to the very narrative structures of the gospels. It is commonplace to speak about the familiar image of Jesus' ministry which portrays him as an itinerant teacher, a popular notion taken for granted as an actual biographi-

---

11. Cf. Mt 14:14; 15:29–31; 6:34; 7:37; 8:2; Lk 9:11; Jn 6:2. These texts belong to the immediate context of the various accounts of multiplication of loaves.

12. On Jesus' common meals with disciples, see Mt 9:10–12/Mk 2:15–17/Lk 5:27–32; Lk 7:36–50; Jn 2:2–11. On the theme of the messianic banquet, see Mt 22:2–14; Lk 17:18; 14:15-24; 15:32; 22:17–18.

cal fact. However, critical scholarship has taken issue with this image and called attention to the complexity of the factual background. This itinerant quality, strictly speaking, belongs to the literary genre of the gospels, which describe Jesus' deeds in a chain of more or less loosely linked episodes and, between episodes, assume him to be a person traveling, a human being on the road. Especially in the synoptic gospels, the larger framework into which an episode is inserted is a voyage, specifically a missionary journey, so that Jesus is always presented as *coming* from somewhere and then *departing* and moving on to some new geographic location. Although in both Matthew and Luke we find a few parallel passages stating the homelessness of the Son of Man (two in Mt 8:18–22 and three in Lk 9:57–62), there are also clear indications that in Capernaum Jesus had a permanent home to which he regularly returned. Matthew 4:13 is quite explicit about this: the three verbs of the sentence say that (1) Jesus moved away (καταλιπών) from Nazareth, (2) moved over to (ἐλθών) the city of Capernaum, and (3) there took up residence (κατώκησεν). In agreement with this interpretation, the phrase ἐν οἴκῳ in Mark 2:1 is widely understood as meaning "at home."[13] A similar interpretation would follow from Mark 9:33, which reads, "And they came to Capernaum. And as they were in the house he asked them. . ." (Καὶ ἦλθον εἰς Καφαρναούμ. Καὶ ἐν τῇ οἰκίᾳ γενόμενος ἐπηρώτα αὐτούς). Even if this were Peter's house, and even if one wanted to make the point that the emphasis is on their being "indoors," still the narrative reflects the supposition that Jesus had a permanent domicile in Capernaum.[14]

Commentators on Matthew's gospel usually point out that in its structure there appears to be a geographic outline that is important for the evangelist. But they quickly add that this peripatetic image of Jesus—he travels nonstop from place to place in a sequence of missionary episodes—is both redactional in origin and theological in

13. In Vincent Taylor, *The Gospel According to Saint Mark* (New York: Macmillan, 1966), 193, it is considered Peter's house. C. S. Mann translates it as "at home," while admitting the possibility that it was Peter's house: *Mark*, The Anchor Bible 27 (Garden City, N.Y.: Doubleday, 1986), 223.

14. Could the passage in Mt 17:24, referring to the fact that in Capernaum Jesus is reproached for not paying tax, have any other meaning?

motivation; therefore, such commentators would say, it is not based on historically identifiable journeys.

The form critics of more than eighty years ago insisted on the conclusion that the trips outlined in the synoptic gospels must not be regarded as actual travel reports but rather as products of a superficial linkage established externally among the narrative episodes of oral tradition, combining and sequencing them in a theologically comprehensible whole. This point is central to the famous contribution of K. L. Schmidt about the "framework of the story of Jesus." He insisted that the original narrators of the stories about Jesus paid little or no attention to chronological or topographical links between the individual episodes; rather, they "concentrated on the picture-like separation *(bildhafte Vereinzelung)* of the pericopes as required for a liturgical celebration."[15] Pursuing this thought, K. L. Schmidt, along with Martin Dibelius and Rudolf Bultmann, initiated the approach that reduced the importance of the links between the episodes to secondary status, without historical relevance. Consequently, synoptic research became overly fragmented, and a biographic approach to the gospels became methodologically impossible.

The next trend, redaction criticism, went even further in the same direction by suggesting that the links connecting the synoptic episodes were mere theological constructs, which most often reflect what the redactor of each gospel made of the oral tradition's complexities, as well as of his sources' sequencing of episodes. Thus, since the beginning of form criticism, it has become conventional wisdom that the formation of the gospels was intimately linked to the early Christian cult, which was the *Sitz im Leben* of most synoptic narratives. But it remained largely unspecified how this cultic/ liturgical "life situation" was to be imagined and, further, how it affected the way in which the narratives were linked together. Most important, under form criticism there was yet no explanation for

15. *Der Rahmen der Geschichte Jesu* [The Framework of the History of Jesus] was originally published in 1919 (Berlin: Trowitch und Sohn). I use a selection from a modern publication by Ferdinand Hahn, *Zur Formgeschichte der Evangelien* [About the Form Criticism of the Gospels] (Darmstadt: Wissenschaftliche Buchgesellschaft, 1985), 118–26.

why the narrative units of the gospels are linked to features of ongoing travel, that is, why the repetitious arrivals and departures form a loosely yet consistently connected chain of "comings and goings," which then appear as a constant and apparently artificial missionary meandering.

While the last eighty to one hundred years have seen many attempts to decipher the structure and sequence of the synoptic pericopes, consensus has been reached on only a few points. The view, or at least supposition, that the narratives about Jesus' ministry are inserted into a framework of traveling is one of these few commonly accepted issues. This framework both connects and separates the individual pericopes, and it depicts Jesus (and his disciples) in a chain of arrivals and departures, moving into and out of different localities in Galilee, crossing back and forth over the same lake and, in the course of these movements, encountering all sorts of people and human situations.[16]

After these considerations, we should pay special attention to the all too frequent use of the Greek verb ἔρχεσθαι and its derivates at the beginning of many gospel episodes in Matthew and Mark, as well as the use of the verb πορεύεσθαι and its derivates in Luke. In the various gospels the particular verb describing the beginnings or ends of the episodes is not always the same, but within any single gospel the redactor uniformly chiseled them into similar and even identical formulas about "coming" and "going." So, for example, the verb preferred by Matthew is προσέρχεσθαι, "to approach." At least twenty-five times in his gospel, an episode begins by using προσέρχεσθαι to describe an individual or a group of people (men or women in some physical or spiritual need) approaching Jesus.[17]

16. The fact that the evangelist Luke framed his "proper" material mostly by a lengthy and expanded travel narrative from Galilee to Jerusalem (chaps. 9–18) is the strongest indication that he had found in the sources he used this pattern of the "comings and goings" as a customary way of assembling and sequencing the narrative tradition about Jesus.

17. The various forms of verb προσέρχεσθαι are quite important for Matthew as it is an expression typical of the Matthean redactor. The verb appears altogether as often as forty-eight times in Matthew, while only four times in Mark and nine times in Luke. Yet the similarities and discrepancies between Matthew and Mark are com-

In Mark, an episode usually starts with ἔρχεσθαι , describing Jesus "coming" or quite frequently Jesus' coming with his disciples either to a specific location or simply just "coming" with no identification of place; then Jesus is either petitioned or approached or asked a question.[18] Similarly, a number of episodes begin by reporting that people congregated around Jesus; it is either his disciples, whom he has convoked, or crowds hearing about him, or some sort of a group with a need or an intention—on some occasions even his enemies, the Pharisees or the Sadducees. The assembled group then gathers around him and gives him the opportunity to address them, or to reply to them, by providing some teaching.[19]

Behind all these common characteristics of the synoptic gospels there stands a basic feature of the genre which needs to be explained. The gospels are collections of episodic narratives with Jesus as their one and only protagonist. Do these narratives, woven together by a fragile thread of ongoing physical movements, serve a common purpose, and if so, what is it? The answer lies in a fact which critics have frequently emphasized for the last one hundred years, but have failed to connect with questions of genre and composition: the Gospels are based on a tradition formed and formulated in the cultic assemblies of the early Church. So, for example, Bultmann readily states:

> One may designate the final motive by which the Gospels were produced as a cultic one (that is, the needs of common worship), if one considers that the one high point in Christian life was the gathering of the community for worship, where the figure of Jesus, his teaching

plicated and cannot be reduced to Matthew as a redactor transforming Mark's ready-made text. Of Mark's four uses of προσέρχεσθαι only three (Mk 6:35; 12:28; 14:45) have parallels in Matthew; of these only two are followed by the typically Matthean dative case αὐτῷ (6:35 and 14:45). For the use of the verb in Mk 1:31 there is no (exact) parallel in Matthew. On the other hand, for Matthew's προσέρχεσθαι + dative, we usually find in Mark ἔρχεσθαι πρός + accusative in four places (1:40; 7:1; 11:27; 12:18), and ἔρχεσθαι with no preposition in five places (2:18; 5:27; 6:29; 10:2; 14:66). At other instances, we find few further similar constructions that use synonyms like πρόσδραμον (10:17) or προσεπορεύονται (10:35) or εἰσῆλθεν (15: 43).

18. Jesus "coming": Mk 1:14, 31, 35, 39; 2:1, 13; 3:1, 13, 20, 31; 6:1, 6, 45; 7:17, 31; 8:10, 13, 27; 9:28; 10:1, 17 (twenty-one occurrences); Jesus and the disciples "coming": 1:21, 29, 38; 3:7; 5:1, 38; 6:29, 35; 8:22; 9:14, 30; 10:48 (twelve occurrences).

19. Mk 3:22; 4:1; 6:7, 30; 7:1; 8:1, 34; 10:13, 42.

as well as his life, was set before the eyes of the faithful and when, accordingly, the Gospels served for public reading.[20]

But contrary to what Bultmann and Dibelius habitually presuppose, the liturgical roots of the narratives do not imply that they were created (and manipulated) according to the changing needs of the worshipping community.[21] Rather, the insight of the form critics should help us realize that the first Eucharistic assemblies came about when Jesus' original disciples began to gather after experiencing the first evidences of his resurrection, and that, in the course of these early gatherings, there developed an organic process of recalling and retelling the memories of Jesus' ministry. It was therefore in a Eucharistic cradle provided by early Christian worship that the narrative tradition which stands behind the synoptics was formed and shaped in live exchange with an audience assembled for hearing about Jesus. These assemblies re-established the table fellowship which had been at the heart of their "being gathered" by and around Jesus. Precisely because they wanted to meet Jesus by means of these assemblies and to see their previous encounters re-enacted, renewed,

20. Rudolph Bultmann, "The Study of the Synoptic Gospels," trans. Karl Kundsinn, in *Form Criticism: Two Essays on New Testament Research,* ed. C. F. Grant, 64 (New York: Harper, 1962). The same insistence is expressed by K. L. Schmidt: "If the origin of Christianity is identified with the coming about of a religious cult—and in the last decades this understanding has been asserted with increasing force—then it is clear that the formation of early Christian literature must take place on the basis of ancient Christian cult. In my opinion for understanding the formation of the Gospels one cannot overrate the importance of the early Church's liturgical practice. The oldest form of the Jesus tradition is liturgically determined *('kultisch bestimmt')* and therefore it is filled with images and transcends history *('bildhaft und übergeschichtlich').*" *Der Rahmen der Geschichte Jesu,* 119.

21. In a brief footnote to one of his essays, K. L. Schmidt compares his position with those of Dibelius and Bultmann and remarks that Bultmann went too far by reducing *"Christuskult"* and *"Christusmythos"* to the creative activities of Hellenistic Christianity. He thinks that, in order to understand the oral tradition which antedates the written gospels *("die Vorstufen der Evangelien")* one must posit a closer connection between "cult" and "community." See K. L. Schmidt, "Die Stellung der Evangelien in der allgemeinen Literaturgeschichte" [The Place of the Gospels in the General History of Literature], in *Eucharistion, Festschrift für Hermann Gunkel,* originally written 1923, and newly edited. Now, almost eighty years later, it is fascinating to notice that the consensus of the "founding fathers" of *Formgeschichte* about a cultic *Sitz im Leben* of the gospel episodes has vanished during the subsequent reign of *Redaktionsgeschichte,* as the focus of research moved back (again) to literary analysis.

and relived, they recalled and retold their past experiences with Jesus while consuming the only "cultic meal" that the early Church had: the celebration of the Eucharist. Consequently, the narratives were formed for audiences which identified themselves with those described in the narratives, those who were being led to Christ firsthand or met him as they approached him for healing or teaching or some other benefit. In such presentations of a large selection of episodic material, Jesus is necessarily featured not merely as a figure of an objective past, defined and isolated in a frozen and distant temporal framework, but as the one who, at the beginning of an episode, "arrives" and becomes approachable once again, as the one who encounters the human needs and religious problems of living individuals, and, in these so-called "limit situations," brings again the experience of salvation, that is, a manifestation of divine mercy, a solution unavailable from merely human resources. Therefore, the framework of Jesus' life as narrated by the synoptic gospels is not a chronological segment of time or a geographically arranged missionary project, but a sequence of ongoing encounters. In them two features regularly complement each other: first, Jesus is portrayed as "the one coming," and second, as he moves from place, a variety of people approach him and reveal to him their needs.

Thus we come to the thesis that Jesus' mission and ministry as presented by the synoptics is best understood in the Eucharistic context of early Christian worship. In this context not only were the individual episodic pieces formulated, rehearsed, and fixed, but the literary genre of the compositions later called gospels also took their origin; this is how the blueprint of the model to assemble, link, and organize the units passed down by tradition took the shape of ongoing missionary journeys.

I do not claim that the episodes about Jesus, due to their use at Eucharistic celebrations, have been staged by the first Christian preachers in such a way that they would open with a fictitious "arrival" or "coming" of Jesus. Quite often the "coming" depicted at the beginning of a synoptic episode stands in a redactional passage or sentence, and contains clear marks of the evangelist as a literary redactor, and, therefore, belongs to the written form rather than to the preceding oral phase. I do claim, however, that the presentation of Jesus' ministry as peripatetic—episode after episode, he continues to arrive and be approached as he passes from place to place—is the telltale mark of the Eucharistic framework in which the Jesus tradition was chiseled first into oral patterns and afterwards into the literary compositions of our canonical gospels.

That the gospels represent a chain of discrete episodes is well accepted in both older and more recent research. I would only add that this is neither mere coincidence nor the consequence of biographic data factually remembered, although, indeed, historically speaking, Jesus spent his ministry in an ongoing process of traveling. The consistent portrayal of Jesus as the one *coming and being encountered* originates in the way memories about him were recalled, told, and retold in the presence of cultic (Eucharistic) congregations, gatherings held for the purpose of reliving the past encounters. This understanding of Jesus is not only a common feature, but an essential and constitutive one for both the gospel episodes and the early Christian celebration of the Eucharist. This consistent feature perfectly fits the gospel narratives for liturgical use, and reveals the Eucharistic mold in which the gospel tradition was cast in its primitive oral phase.

We know from Justin Martyr that, by the middle of the second century, some eighty years after the first canonical gospels were composed, they were called "the memoirs of the Apostles" and were regularly and routinely used for pericopal readings at the Eucharistic assembly. Such a use of the gospels at the Eucharist, which Justin claims was a generally accepted practice (*First Apology* no. 67), is best explained if we assume that even when still being handed on orally, they fulfilled the same function at the Eucharistic assembly, recalling the past that was to be made present again in the liturgy.[22]

22. For our position we obtain support from otherwise almost diametrically opposed authors, Oscar Cullmann and Karl Ludwig Schmidt. Cullmann states that "in the service described by Justin . . . we are not dealing with a later development," except, he adds, for a decrease of the role of the prophets and the omission of the *agape* (*Early Christian Worship,* 30). K. L. Schmidt, while reproaching Justin for having distorted the literary genre of the gospels by calling them "memoirs of the apostles," recognizes

The claim we make about the "Eucharistic cradle" of the synoptic tradition *per se* need not be applied in a rigid way to every single passage. Yet, looking for passages that could not have been formed and used in a Eucharistic context leads to surprising results. In the synoptics there are only a handful of episodic passages which would fit only poorly at an early Christian Eucharistic assembly. Such a passage is, possibly, the narrative about the death of John the Baptist in Matthew and Mark, or the inserted story about Judas' suicide in Matthew's passion narrative. These are passages in which Jesus is either not a central figure or not mentioned. Yet, these episodes appear to be detours from the narrative path of the gospels: they do not contribute to the main structure, or make only an incidental addition to the main force of the compositional framework. And, indeed, they do not begin with references to Jesus' coming, or someone's approaching him, nor do they result in a salvific encounter with him.[23]

---

that both Justin and his disciple Tatian (with his gospel harmony) stand in the line of a continuous tradition that antedated the composition of the gospels, and so "already the steps that lead to the formation of the Gospels must be explained from the liturgical practice of pericopal readings" (*schon die Vorstufen der Evangelen müssen von der Perikopenpraxis aus beleuchtet werden),* K. L. Schmidt, *Der Rahmen der Geschichte Jesu,* 206. After saying this, Schmidt quotes with approval the "very remarkable" statements of one of his great opponents, Theodore Zahn, who asserted that "all works of early Christian literature of which we know had some relationship—for a shorter or a longer period of time, in wider or narrower circles—with Christian 'anagnosis,' i.e., with some use of them in the community's liturgy" (ibid., 207, n. 164). Then Schmidt adds: "He is, indeed, justified to state that the argument about a liturgical 'Sitz im Leben' for the gospel tradition is not an issue about right and left wing, conservatives and liberals, the orthodox and the critics, but about a correct or incorrect practice of philology and theology" (ibid., 218).

23. I have no intention of claiming that all apostolic preaching took place with a Eucharistic context as its *Sitz im Leben.* This is most clear about missionary preaching such as that mentioned in Acts 5:21 in the Temple, or the various speeches given by Paul in public places (e.g., the Areopagus in 17:26–34, or in the school of Tyrannos). For the gospels, however, form-critical studies reveal not only a pre-existent oral phase but also the presence of a cultic audience which cannot be legitimately separated from the Eucharist. So, for example, when in 1 Corinthians Paul designates "the upbuilding of the church" (using the noun four times: 14:3, 5, 12, 26; plus the verb twice in 14:4) as the purpose of "speaking in the assemblies," he speaks in the same breath of "the body of Christ" for whose benefit the gifts of the Spirit are to be exercised and of the ecclesial body, which one cannot legitimately separate from the Eucharistic body of Christ. In his presentation (1 Cor 12–14), the various gifts of speech, prophecy, exhortation, and teaching, as well as the functions of the diverse members of the body, run parallel. All of them are inseparably linked to the celebration of the Eucharist (1 Cor 11).

Jesus as "the One Who Comes" in the Gospels

Does the Christology of the gospels recognize the Eucharistic feature of these compositions? More specifically, do the gospels announce explicitly who Jesus is as he keeps on coming, arriving, and being approachable? I find a positive answer to this question in the way the term ὁ ἐρχόμενος, or "the one coming," is applied to Jesus in the gospels.

A few decades ago, when it was customary to study the Christology of the New Testament by examining Christological titles,[24] scholars debated the question of whether or not this expression was in fact one such title, and if so, whether it was used by Jesus' contemporaries to designate the Messiah. Although the debate has never been settled, one can say that this term is essential for both the Christology and the eschatology of the canonical gospels.

A study of the term ἐρχόμενος in Matthew makes its meaning fully apparent. John the Baptist initiates its use when he points to the one coming after him (3:18). The term is taken up again in Matthew 11:2 by the disciples of John, who come to Jesus and ask him if he is identical with ὁ ἐρχόμενος, "the One to Come." Jesus' complete answer, presented in Matthew, is best interpreted as a catalogue of healings listed in the framework of Isaian texts (mostly Is 61:1): "Go and tell what you see, for the blind see, the lame walk, the deaf hear and to the poor the kingdom is being proclaimed." But this is not just a reference to miraculous healings of bodily ailments; Matthew makes it clear that Jesus fulfills Isaiah's prophecies also when preaching the Kingdom of Heaven to the poor (see 5:2) and when providing forgiveness as he takes upon himself our sins (8:17, quoting Is 53:4).[25] Thus the two occurrences of ἐρχόμενος, in 3:18 and 11:2, encompass the first part of Matthew's gospel and summarize Jesus' Galilean ministry.

---

24. Oscar Cullmann, *Die Christologie des Neuen Testamentes* [The Christology of the New Testament] (Tübingen: Mohr, 1957).

25. One must read in this context 9:11–13, in which the equivalence of forgiveness and healing is made explicit.

The rest of the gospel quite consistently follows the same path, for it demonstrates how Jesus continues to manifest himself as the one who is coming. This happens first in peak scenes revealing his power, as he walks on the sea (14:25) and as he reveals his glory in the Transfiguration (17:7). Both scenes emphasize his coming to the disciples.[26] Moreover, throughout the second part of the gospel every major eschatological statement and parable uses the verb ἔρχεσθαι in reference to the Parousia as the coming of the Son of Man.[27] Finally, fullness of meaning for this term is achieved in Jesus' statement before the Sanhedrin: "From now on you will see the Son of Man seated on the right hand of the Power and *coming* [ἐρχόμενον] in the clouds of the sky" (26:64). Some commentators focus on the words "from now on," while others insist that the Son of Man is not (or not exactly) a self-designation by Jesus. Yet the term ἐρχόμενον cannot be divested of its semantic link to its previous crucial occurrences in the gospel, in 3:18 and 11:2, nor is it legitimate to curtail its syntactic value as a present participle. Appearing several more times throughout Matthew's composition, it signifies essentially the unfolding character of Jesus' mission. The chain of events comprising Jesus' ministry in the gospels is nothing more than the continual coming to the people he encounters, with his final and manifest coming in divine power that unfolds with his condemnation, death, and resurrection.

In the Gospel of John, Jesus is also designated ὁ ἐρχόμενος, the one who comes after John the Baptist (see 1:15, 27). Yet here his true importance, the cosmic significance of his coming, is shown. His

26. In the episode of Jesus' walking on the sea, it is first stated that he was "coming" to them (14:25), then the same verb is used three times to describe Peter's "coming" to him (vv. 28–29), until he finally exclaims "save me" (the meaning of Jesus' name, according to Mt 1:21), and is rescued by being touched (v. 31). The episode finally ends with Jesus entering the boat and the disciples worshipping him as they make a profession of faith. One can hardly find an episode any more "cultic" and thus "Eucharistic" in both form and content. However, the Transfiguration matches it closely: it presents Jesus first "bringing" the disciples to the "high mountain" (17:1), then "coming" (προσῆλθεν) to them, touching them (v. 8), and making a statement about the resurrection of the Son of Man from the dead (v. 9).

27. Mt 16:27; 21:9, 40; 24:42–44; 25:11, 19.

coming is the central issue already in the prologue of John, in which the Logos is depicted as the true light "coming into the world" (1:9) to become flesh (1:14).[28] Several times, the physical action of coming takes on symbolic meaning (see Jesus' coming to John, as John sees him coming from a distance, in 1:29). The transcendental meaning of his coming is at times explicitly stated: he is said to be "coming from above" and "coming from heaven," (3:31–32) or he is called as "the prophet coming into the world" (6:14) and "the Son of God coming into the world" (11:27). Thus his coming is in a transcendental sense a descent, so that in the explicitly Eucharistic text about the bread of life this coming is said to be "coming down from heaven" and is associated semantically with the previous uses of the term ἐρχόμενος. The statements believers make about "the coming of the Messiah" (ἔρχεται ὁ λεγόμενος Χριστός) are expressions not only of traditional Jewish messianism, but also of Johannine theology, which describes Jesus as the subject of a process the conclusion of which is his arrival into the world, reaching its fullness in the gospel narratives (4:23–25; 7:41–42).

Seen in the light of this usage, the expressions "he came" or "he is coming," as they appear in the context of the Johannine resurrection narratives, take on an explicitly Eucharistic meaning with eschatological reference. Twice Jesus comes through closed doors (ἦλθεν in 20:19, and ἔρχεται in 20:26), and both meetings end in physical contact with his body as the disciples touch the marks of his wounds. In the third appearance "Jesus comes and takes the bread and gives it to them" (21:13). This theologically deepened Johannine usage integrates Christology, Eucharist, and a sacramentally "realized" eschatology into a unified vision of Christ's coming as an unfolding process that penetrates cosmos and history. Is such usage an esoteric, Johannine specialty, or are its roots (also) found in the synoptic tradition? The reference to the "one who is coming after me"

28. It is rightly pointed out that the theme of Jesus' coming organically expands on the synoptic sayings about the purpose of Jesus' "coming," the term he uses when explaining his mission. See Mt 5:17; 7:25, 27; 9:13; 10:34–35; Mk 1:38; 2:17; Lk 12:49; Jn 1:31; 8:14; 9:39; 10:10; 12:27, 47.

on the lips of the Baptist belongs to the oldest elements common to all the gospels. One must say the same about the phrase "blessed is the One coming in the name of the Lord" quoted from Psalm 118:26 and applied to Jesus six times in the gospels, once in each of the four descriptions of the triumphal entry to Jerusalem (Mt 23:39; Mk 11:9; Lk 19:38; Jn 12:5) and once more in a saying common to Matthew and Luke (Mt 23:39 and Lk 13:35).

Exegetically the following can be said about Jesus portrayed as "the One Coming" in the gospels. First, it translates the Hebrew expression 'asher haba', a relative clause formed with the present participle of the verb "to come" *(ba')* carrying a definite article. It appears in the quotations of Psalm 118:26 and Malachi 3:1 with the meaning of an actual but ongoing and, therefore, also future coming. Second, it offers an important complement to the notion of the "coming of the Kingdom" by referring to Jesus as the King who comes. Third, it connotes the dynamic character of Jesus' mission as a chain of comings. The term depicts his entry into the world, his encountering all sorts of people through the various episodes of teaching and healing, his travel to Jerusalem, his facing death, his return to the Father, and his institution of a new way of being present to the disciples. Finally, it puts the eschatological dimension (a future coming) of Jesus' mission and message in seamless continuity with his earthly ministry.

The Eucharistic Character of the Book of Revelation

A summary look at the Apocalypse, the only prophetic book of the New Testament canon, can greatly enhance and complete the above considerations.

The opening vision and general organization of this book insert it into the general liturgical framework of composition. André Feuillet's comments made in the 1960s are still valid:

> We should be on guard against the danger of misunderstandings with regard to the Apocalypse's liturgical character. True enough, it [this book] is not a specifically and professedly liturgical document, but

rather a prophecy and an account of visions. Still we must not lose sight of its liturgical aspects, which have been emphasized, and placed very much in relief, although not always very discretely, by modern exegetes. Most of the great visions of the Apocalypse have some sort of a liturgical flavor to them, which is basically due to their essentially eschatological orientation, characteristic of the Christian liturgy, especially of the Eucharist.[29]

The book begins with an apparition of the risen Lord on a Sunday, the Lord's day. This reference is not a casual piece of chronology about the day the vision took place, but contributes to establishing an overall liturgical backdrop for the book.[30] That the visionary sees the risen Lord on a Sunday (1:9) must be taken in continuity with the resurrection appearances in the fourth gospel, the only passages of the New Testament that emphasize Jesus' appearance on Sundays (Easter Sunday in 20:19 and a week later in 20:26). The risen Jesus appears clothed in a long white tunic with a golden sash, standing amidst seven lamps (1:13–14)—that is, he appears clothed as a high priest.[31]

The appearance of the risen Lord must be understood as his coming to the Church, which is addressed collectively by the book. As was observed already in ancient times, the seven churches to which the seven letters are addressed are intentionally numbered in order to express the entirety of the Church.[32] The idea of Jesus' coming is

29. André Feuillet, *The Apocalypse* (New York: Alba House, 1965), 85.

30. "It is not without significance that the Seer mentions that he saw his visions on 'a Lord's day' (1:10), at a time, therefore, when the Christian community was gathered together. Thus he sees the whole drama of the last days in the context of the early Christian service of worship, which, so to speak, has its counterpart and at the same time its fulfillment in the coming aeon, so that all that takes place in the gatherings of the early Christian community, seen from this side, appears as anticipation of that which in the last day takes place from God's side. Hence, the whole Book of Revelation from the greeting of grace and peace in 1:14 to the closing prayer: Come Lord Jesus in 22:20, and the benediction in the last verse, is full of allusions with the liturgical usages of the early community." Cullmann, *Early Christian Worship*, 7.

31. Cf. Otto Karrer, *Die geheime Offenbarung* [The Secret Revelation] (Einsiedeln: Benziger, 1948), 38.

32. The *Muratorian Canon,* most often dated to around AD 200, states this explicitly: *Joannes enim in Apocalypsi, licet septem ecclesiis scribat, tamen omnibus dicit.* D. J. Theron, *Evidence of Tradition* (Grand Rapids, Mich.: Baker Bookhouse, 1958), 110.

emphasized right at the beginning in the first revelatory statement of the book, introducing the description of the risen Lord with the following words: "Behold he comes [ἔρχεται] in the clouds and every eye will see him, including those who pierced him through" (1:7). This reference to the Johannine scene of the crucifixion must not be missed: the fourth gospel alone quotes Zechariah's prophecy stating that "they have seen him as he was pierced" (Zec 12:10 in Jn 19:37). The reference is quite important for the Johannine passion story, for it attests to the truly physical suffering and death of Jesus, witnessed by the Beloved Disciple (19:35–37). Its use in the Apocalypse aims unmistakably at establishing a bond between Jesus' glorious return and his violent death, between the ignominy of the past and the glory of the future. The verb "he comes," or ἔρχεται, belongs to an eschatological language, but the use of the present tense reveals as well a sense of actuality.[33]

Also quite significant is the connection with Jesus' two apparitions in John 20, where the appearance of the risen Lord likewise happens on a Sunday. On both occasions he is described not as appearing, but as coming: ἔρχεται. In addition, he is said to be appearing as the one whom they have pierced, for he invites them to view and touch his wounds, specifically the wound in his chest (20:26–27).[34] Therefore, the quotation from Zechariah provides an important bridge between a future coming "in the clouds" and the event that took place on the cross. At the eschatological coming all eyes will see on his body what the eyes of the Beloved Disciple perceived when it occurred as Jesus was pierced on the cross. This is what all the eleven disciples saw when Jesus appeared to them on the two Sundays that followed the crucifixion.

It is also important to note that the Apocalypse calls Jesus "the One who is to Come" or "the One who is coming" in a triple phrase which sounds like a liturgical formula: "The one who was, who is,

33. One of the ways this extended concept of "coming" is given emphasis is its double appearance in the prologue (1:7) and the epilogue (22:13).
34. For both appearances to the Eleven the fourth gospel uses the expression "Jesus came and stood," ἦλθεν in 20:19 and ἔρχεται in 20:26.

and who is coming" (ὁ ἦν καὶ ὁ ὢν καὶ ὁ ἐρχόμενος).[35] The Hebrew/ Aramaic origin of the formula is hardly in doubt; accordingly, the word ὁ ἐρχόμενος is a Hebraism.[36] In Hebrew one must use the present participle of the verb "to come" *(haba')* to express future existence: the one who will be. But even so, it would be incorrect to separate the word ἐρχόμενος from its etymological root, deny its basic grammatical meaning, and fail to realize that it refers to an actual coming, that is, a present-time active process of coming near and becoming present.[37]

In spite of the attempts that have been made to deconstruct the Book of Revelation into originally independent parts, the unity of the composition keeps asserting itself and again and again finds recognition.[38] It is in the unified composition that the Eucharistic links become visible. We will comment now on two issues that will complement what has been said about the gospels and the apostolic letters in this connection.

First, the seven churches are the addressees of the seven letters collectively, and it is collectively that they constitute the recipients of the book John is told to write (1:11). Therefore, one must see in

35. The shorter form, ὁ ἦν καὶ ὁ ὢν, occurs two more times (11:17; 16:5).

36. Authors point out its grammatical irregularities. A. Vögtle considers it a grammatically impossible formulation *("eine grammatisch unmögliche Formulierung")* and connects it with Hellenistic formulas of the day *(Das Buch mit sieben Siegeln* [The Book with Seven Seals] [Vienna: Herder, 1981], 20). According to J. Massyngberde Ford it functions like an expansion on the divine name, YHWH, meaning "the one who is." *Revelation,* The Anchor Bible 38 (Garden City, N.Y.: Doubleday, 1975), 376. Most satisfactory is the explanation offered by R. H. Charles: "As for ὁ ἐρχόμενος, where our author returns to the participial construction, it is clear that he uses ἐρχόμενος, instead of ἐσόμενος, with a definite reference to the contents of the Book and especially to the coming of Christ, i.7, ii. 5, 16, iii. 11, xxii. 7, 12, etc., in whose coming God Himself comes also." *The Revelation of St. John,* vol. 1 (Edinburgh: T & T Clark, 1920), 10.

37. Very helpful are the remarks by Richard Bauckham: "John has taken advantage of this usage to depict the future of God not as his mere future existence, but as his coming into the world in salvation and judgment. He has in mind no doubt those many Old Testament prophetic passages which announce that God will 'come' to save and judge (e.g., Ps 96:13; 98:9; Is 40:10; 66:15; Zec 14:5) and which early Christians understood to refer to his eschatological coming to fulfill the final purpose for the whole world, a coming he identified with the parousia of Jesus Christ." *The Theology of the Book of Revelation* (Cambridge: Cambridge University Press, 1993), 29.

38. See Richard Bauckham's remarks about "the First and the Last," as a basic literary pattern, ibid., 54–58.

the appearance of the risen Lord to the prophetic messenger a visitation intended for all the churches for which John is exercising his prophetic role. In this way the opening vision determines the framework of the whole book, as we read in 1:19: "Write down both what there is and what will come about later." In this way the prophet is told to compose a book of two parts, the first the evaluation of the present-day status of the churches (chapters 2 and 3), and the second of their future destiny (chapters 4 through 19). But both parts are addressed to all, and are a revelation about the Son of Man's coming, a revelation inspired by one and the same Spirit.

Consequently, the vision of the heavenly liturgy in chapters 4 and 5, which follow the seven letters, is a continuation of the same revelatory experience taking place on "the Lord's Day" (1:10). However, now, in verse 4:2, the prophet ascends into heaven, that is, he falls into ecstasy and obtains divine knowledge that penetrates the future.[39] As the first revelation took place in accordance with a coming of the risen Lord on a Sunday, now the second stage of revelation makes him present at the heavenly worship. This cosmic liturgy is described in concentric circles around the throne of God (4:3, 5–6): the liturgy is celebrated by twenty-four elders (4:4) and four living creatures (4:7–8) performing their homage in the first round (5:6–10), then by myriads of angels in the second round (5:11–12), and finally by a redeemed and sanctified universe (5:13–14). This scene is best understood as the fullness of the reality that takes place in the earthly, ecclesial celebration of the liturgy, a heavenly reality present in a hidden way in Christian worship.

The first action that takes place in chapter 5 is the opening of the seven seals of a book by the Lamb who had been slain, signifying the full manifestation of God's salvific will, and making possible the prophetic visions which follow. The inclusion with the liturgical scene in chapter 19, where the same assembly sings and worships, constitutes the framework of revelations about the future. Most significantly for

39. "Ascend to here and I will show you what is supposed to happen after these. Immediately I fell into ecstasy" (ἐγενόμην ἐν πνεύματι: 4:1–2).

our topic, after the seven letters in the first part and the opening of the seven seals, which is followed by an elaborate chain of apocalyptic signs in the second part, this worshipping heavenly assembly reappears, ready to celebrate the wedding feast of the Lamb. The prophet receives another order to write: "Write, happy are those invited to the wedding banquet of the Lamb" (19:9).[40] This wedding banquet is called here δεῖπνον, the noun used by Paul in First Corinthians and also by John's gospel to designate the last meal of Jesus with his disciples.[41] As soon as the seer receives the command, he falls prostrate before the messenger who has given the order, but the messenger tells him that he is just a fellow servant of the visionary prophet and must not be adored.[42]

At this point there seems to be a serious discontinuity in the book, for no description of the banquet follows. Instead, a sequence of other visions abruptly begins, most of them about the heavenly Jerusalem. Then in 22:8-9 the same scene is repeated with the messenger reappearing. The seer again falls prostrate before the messenger and is told in identical words to worship God alone. We need not discuss the various redactional theories that have been made about

40. The present-day Roman liturgy combines this verse with John's "Behold the Lamb of God" in the fourth gospel (1:29) as the form of invitation for the faithful to the Eucharistic meal at communion.

41. κυριακὸν δεῖπνον 1 Cor 11:20; Jn 13:2, 4; 21:20.

42. One must note, however, that it is not at all clear in front of whom he falls down. Charles's commentary enumerates five weighty reasons for considering 19:9b-10 as an interpolation, one of them being the dative after προσκυνῆσαι instead of accusative. But, indeed, one may rather speak of the hand of a redactor who overlooks the fact that the invitation to the Lamb's Supper was made by a voice, not by a messenger, in 19:9a. Throughout the whole vision that begins in 19:9a, no angel is mentioned whom the Seer would be adoring. Quite a curious way of combating angel worship, as the explanation of modern commentaries (Ford, Karrer, Harrington) view this passage, since no angel is mentioned throughout the vision! More probably, the original function of 19:10 was to indicate the end of the visionary experience which began with the vision of 1:10-16 and was followed with his first "fainting" as he fell to the feet of the Lord "as if dead" (1:17). Now it seems that, after the invitation to the Lamb's Supper, the same fearful experience repeats, but it signals the end of the whole chain of visions. As John is lifted from the ground, he realizes that no "divine presence" is left, for the one who awakens him identifies himself as only a "fellow-servant" and a "fellow-martyr." Such an explanation would regard the whole section 19:11-22:7 as an inserted epilogue to the book and 22:8 as a reprise of 19:9b leading to the concluding passage of the book.

this feature of the book. In any case, 19:9 must not be overlooked or marginalized. It seems to represent the final act of reconnecting to the Eucharistic framework of the book, which started with the coming of Jesus on the day of the Lord, resulted first in letters to the churches, then was followed by the ecstatic participation in the heavenly liturgy of praise, and next was led to the opening of the book with seven seals. The banquet of the marriage feast to which the seer must invite all the believers[43] is a final point of arrival—the Omega Point of sacred history at which the books' timeline ends.[44]

With or without accepting a specific redactional hypothesis about the end of the Book of Revelation, one can easily come to the conclusion that 19:11–22:8 is to be put into parentheses, so that the conclusion of John's vision continues with the command not to seal the book (22:10–11) and is followed by the repetition of the title "Alpha and Omega" first announced in the prologue (22:12), and then by three final Eucharistic references. The first of these recalls the "tree of life" (22:13), the second excludes those in grave sin from communion.[45] Finally, after repeated calls by the Bride for the Spirit's coming and by the faithful for the Bridegroom's (22:27–18), the concluding Eucharistic exclamation is pronounced: *maranatha*. This exclamation, which closes First Corinthians (16:22), a Pauline letter filled with explicit Eucharistic doctrine, is also known from the Didache (10:6) as the concluding line of a Eucharistic (or Eucharist-related *agape*) celebration. Even if one opts for an interpretation of *maranatha* based on its Syriac perfect-tense form as the original understanding of the

43. The invitation to the marriage banquet is preceded by a command connected with a macarism: "Write it down: Happy are. . ." (γράψον μακάριοι). While the command "write" runs through the whole book (in the prologue: 1:11, 19; once for each of the seven letters: 2:1, 8, 12, 18; 3:1, 7, 14), in the rest of the book it comes back only three more times, and only once again with a macarism speaking of those who have died before the Parousia, in 14:3. From such a formal point of view the command "write" in 21:5 seems to belong to an inserted appendix and not to the main outline of the whole composition.

44. Or, is it also because of a *disciplina arcani* that the liturgical pattern does not continue?

45. "Excluded are undomesticated dogs, sorcerers, the sexually immoral, murderers, idolaters, and everyone who values and practices lying" (Rv 22:15).

term, in the Book of Revelation the Greek equivalent is given as ἔρχου κύριε (22:23), an imperative of ἔρχεσθαι, which was probably the sense in which the Aramaic phrase received its Eucharistic and cultic use.

We can conclude that the *maranatha* at the end of the Book of Revelation is not a stray reference to early Christian liturgy; rather, it forms an inclusion with the opening lines of the book. The survival of its Aramaic form in both First Corinthians and the Didache testifies that, in regard to the Eucharist, Gentile churches were expected to adhere quite carefully to the tradition of the first disciples. It mattered little that by doing so they risked becoming esoteric, since an Aramaic phrase quoted aloud must have been incomprehensible. Nonetheless, one may say that the whole of the Book of Revelation is an explanation of *maranatha:* the coming of God in the coming of Jesus, both complete and to be completed.

Conclusions

In this chapter I have attempted to make a case for the thesis that the entire New Testament is of Eucharistic provenance. Doubtless the whole of the New Testament canon was written under three literary genres: the gospel, the apostolic letter, and prophetic writing (the Apocalypse). While the apostolic letters were intended to be presented to communities assembled in liturgical worship, the Book of Revelation was patterned according to an outline of the Sunday assembly as it was customarily celebrated in the late first century in Asia Minor. But even more important, I intended to show that the way our canonical gospels were composed presupposes the spread of the Jesus tradition to communities gathered in cultic assemblies to witness, experience, and respond to the coming of the Lord. The apostolic memory of the Jesus tradition was exercised in the early Church not for the sake of the biographical reconstruction of a great man's memory, but in order to present episode by episode, as well as to extend to new generations, those salvific encounters his original disciples had with him during his life and ministry.

The importance of the Eucharist as the cradle of the New Testament cannot be sufficiently emphasized. Here I add only one more thought, a logical conclusion that directly follows from this chapter and links it to the previous chapters: all scriptural texts of the New Testament arose with an eye on the Eucharistic assembly, and that assembly was the locus and framework for their ecclesial and sacramental exegesis; hence, they are all bound up with studying and preaching in service of building up (erecting, constituting, and edifying) the Church—*ad aedificationem Ecclesiae.*

V. INTERPRETATION AND CANON IN THE SECOND CENTURY

The Beginnings of Patristic Exegesis

Historical and Religious Developments Leading to Patristic Thought

The term "the patristic era" refers to a rather large time period of six to seven centuries that encompasses a wide diversity of theological schools and movements, and an immense amount of early Christian literature. Concerning too the use and interpretation of Scripture and views about the Bible, we find among the Fathers rich variety, which cannot be easily summarized without distortions or simplification. Nevertheless, with no pretense of completeness, we will attempt to sketch the process by which Christian thought gave its own account of the nature of Scripture and formed a certain method of interpretation. This method remained in use—with further modifications and enrichment but basically unchanged presuppositions—until the end of the Middle Ages. Yet, before we can speak of "patristic and medieval exegesis," we must take a closer look at the Church's development in the second century, the period in which the Christian Bible, Christian exegesis, and patristic theology were born.

By the middle of the second century Christianity had made its appearance in every important city of the Roman Empire and had extended its membership to a rapidly growing number of Gentile converts. The great debate of the first Christian generation about the Mosaic Law and its validity for Christians began to fade into the past. The position of the so-called Apostolic Council outlined in Acts 15:23–29 became the majority position. At some point around the turn of the century the separation of Christianity from Judaism became final. The two Jewish wars (AD 69–70 and 132–135) ended in the destruction of Jerusalem and the dispersion of the Jewish nation, and therefore irreversibly closed that process by which Christianity received a distinct religious and social identity. Thus, by the middle of the second century very few people considered the Christians a Jewish sect.[1] Even the authorities were clear about their distinct status. Due to the persecution of the Christians within the Roman Empire, attested to by original documents from the reigns of Trajan and Hadrian, Jews had every interest in formally declaring to all people that they had excluded from their ranks all those who had embraced the Christian faith.[2]

In this situation the Church encountered new theological challenges. It had to clarify its rapport with the philosophical and religious trends of the general pagan culture of the Empire, secure the guarantees of its institutional unity, and define the criteria of true Christian doctrine. All this could not take place without shake-ups and controversies. Most importantly, from the beginning of the second century onward for a period of about one hundred fifty years, the Church was engaged in a battle against a large and expanding group of more or less parallel religious currents commonly (and retrospectively) called Gnosticism.

The word denotes collectively a large number of philosophical and religious trends which, in the second century, shared the tendency to unify in one spiritual and intellectual synthesis a wide variety of the Greco–Roman world's religious and philosophical teachings. The basic tenets of Gnosticism came from Judaism or other religions, including Christianity, while others came from various philosophical

1. Justin Martyr's *Dialogue with Trypho* well documents the conclusion of this process of separation.

2. An exchange between the Emperor Trajan and Pliny the Younger is extant and dated AD 111. Cf. Daniel J. Theron, *Evidence of Tradition* (Ann Arbor, Mich.: Baker Bookhouse, 1980), 12–17. A letter by the Emperor to Minucius Fundatus, dated around AD 125, was preserved by Justin Martyr, *Apologia* 68, 6. Ibid., 18–19.

schools. In its attempt to be all-inclusive, religious thought in this era was decidedly syncretistic. Working with a high degree of optimism, people from various religious movements sought to bring unity to all this diversity of teaching by reorganizing it on a higher level in often very abstract and artificially systematized ways. Their aim was to create both a wider cognitive community and a stronger validation by exhibiting how different schools of religious thought could culturally and spiritually complement each other. The Gnostic movements were particularly skillful in extracting and amalgamating with their own substance the elements of diverse religious systems, including Christianity. Proceeding with a great deal of freedom and in accordance with their own presuppositions, they redefined and reformulated many Christian ideas by addition, omission, or transformation. In a very short time, Gnostic thought spread over the major cities of the Empire and infiltrated Christianity in a variety of ways.

Though there must have been many people happily embracing these new syncretistic doctrines, the Church soon mustered a vigorous self-defense on several levels. As the latest layers of the New Testament writings make clear, the Church was neither unprepared nor defenseless. Although not yet in possession of a closed canon of Scripture or a well-developed method of exegesis, it had inherited from apostolic times not only the custom of quoting Scripture and apostolic tradition but also a set of identified apostolic writings.[3] It had also adopted a "canonical principle" with the help of which it was able to make decisions about issues raised by the Gnostics' reinterpretation of the Christian faith. Since in the eyes of the first Christians the acceptance of the Christian faith was inseparable from "believing in the Scriptures," this canonical principle was also

3. Contrary to the assumption of some scholars, the earliest gospels could not have been disseminated as anonymous writings. Martin Hengel's study of the titles of the gospels in ancient manuscripts resulted in the conclusion that by about the year 120 they were uniformly named as "according to Matthew, Mark, Luke, and John." Martin Hengel, *The Four Gospels and the One Gospel of Jesus Christ* (London: SCM Press, 2000). The collection of the Pauline letters is generally accepted as having happened before AD 100 and, by definition, could not have taken place on an anonymous basis. See Harry Y. Gamble, *Books and Readers in the Early Church: A History of Early Christian Texts* (New Haven, Conn.: Yale University Press, 1995).

closely linked to the use of the apostolic tradition as the key to the interpretation of the Scriptures. This implied a canonical principle applicable to the discernment of teachings and writings representative of the apostolic faith.

The "Canonical Principle"

In sub-apostolic times—the last decades of the first century and the first decade of the second century—it became increasingly important to emphasize the idea that we have already seen in original Pauline texts, namely, that all Christians, regardless of Jewish or Gentile background, must treat the Scriptures as their own heritage: "For *whatever was written in former days was written for our instruction*" (Rom 15:3). We find similar passages also in First Corinthians, an epistle which was certainly addressed to Gentiles: "Does he not speak entirely for our sake? It was written for our sake" (1 Cor 9:10). The following passage also sounds a similar theme: "Now these things happened to them as a warning, but *they were written down for our instruction,* upon whom the end of the ages has come" (1 Cor 10:11).

The Christian canon of Scripture, including both the Jewish Scriptures and the apostolic writings, came about in an act of growing self-understanding by the Church: it recognized as constitutive of its beliefs both the apostolic traditions and the Scriptures coming from Judaism, which were regarded as holy and normative by Jesus and his disciples. In coming to this self-understanding, the Church realized that the Spirit who inspired the Jewish Scriptures was identical with the Spirit of Christ, who gave the Apostles their post-resurrectional faith and the courage (παρρησία) to understand and proclaim Christ as the one central event giving ultimate meaning to the whole divine plan of salvation.[4] This same Spirit animated the apostolic preaching: it both initiated the oral message of the Apostles and guided its ex-

4. The noun παρρησία is a term of early Christian vocabulary, characterizing a bold and public proclamation on the part of both Jesus (Mk 8:32; Jn 18:20) and the Apostles (Paul about himself: Phil 1:20; 1 John about the apostolic ministry: 1 Jn 5:14; Acts about the various missionaries of the apostolic Church: Acts 2:29; 4:29, 31; 28:29).

pression in the written records of the gospels and the apostolic letters as the truth proclaimed and preserved by the Church "built upon the Apostles and the prophets" (Eph 2:20).[5]

This "canonical principle," which led to the formation of the canon as a list of inspired books, was derived from an awareness that, to be truly Christian, beliefs must be based on the double pillar of the prophets and the Apostles. This principle is found explicitly in both the writings of the New Testament and the earliest period of the patristic era. The main scriptural passages referring to "prophets and apostles" are the following: Lk 11:49; Eph 2:20; 3:5; 4:11; and 2 Pt 3:2. Earlier formulations on which these texts depend are found in Rom 1:1–2; 1 Pt 1:10–12; and Jude 17.[6]

Using philological tools, I collected and evaluated the occurrence of such formulas in Ignatius of Antioch, Polycarp of Smyrna, the Letter of Barnabas, and Justin Martyr.[7] Beginning with Irenaeus, this "canonical principle" is abundantly documented, especially in Origen and Tertullian, and after them its use is commonplace throughout the entire patristic and medieval period. The understanding that the economy of salvation hinges on the oneness of Christ and the sameness of the Spirit is also part of the same "canonical principle." It did not come about after the canon, as if by

---

5. Most exegetes see in this sentence, as well as in Eph 3:5 and 4:11, the linkage of Christian (New Testament) prophets and Apostles. These passages are often interpreted in the same way as 1 Cor 12:28–29 to show with certainty (even if Ephesians was not written by Paul himself) that the conjunction of "prophets and Apostles" comes from Paul. Because of the expression "I have sent you prophets and Apostles" in Lk 11:49 (with a close parallel in Mt 23:34), in all these passages "prophets" may mean the prophets of old. Certainly, in the second century "prophets and Apostles" (or in reversed order: "Apostles and prophets") refers to the two Testaments, as we can see in several passages of Justin, Irenaeus, and the *Muratorian Fragment* (lines 77–78). Striking is the way in which Tertullian makes the terms "prophets" and "Apostles" functionally equivalent when he writes: *"Tam enim apostolus Moyses quam apostoli prophetae, aequanda erit auctoritas utriisque officii ab uno eodem domino apostolorum et prophetarum"* (For so is Moses an apostle as the apostles are prophets; the provenance of both offices being from the one and the same Lord of apostles and prophets). *Adversus Marcionem* IV, 24, 8–9 (*Corpus Christianorum* I, 609).

6. The verse Jude 17 mentions only the Apostles, but it appears to be the shorter and incomplete formula on which 2 Pt 2:3 depends.

7. Cf. Denis Farkasfalvy, "Prophets and Apostles: The Conjunction of the Two Terms before Irenaeus," in *Texts and Testaments,* ed. E. W. March, 109–34 (San Antonio, Tex.: Trinity University Press, 1980).

hindsight, but was posited as an a priori principle to facilitate the formation of the New Testament canon. Thus the formation of the canon is preceded by the stipulation that the ultimate norm for the content of the Christian faith is its agreement with the teaching of "the Prophets of old and of the Apostles of Christ."

The claim that God used chosen spokesmen as tools for mediating his revealed word, and that such persons left behind, directly or indirectly, written records of the revealed truth, is expressed in a variety of ways. The formulas in which we find this theme expressed in the New Testament and in the sub-apostolic texts are the following: first, the twofold formula, "the Prophets and the Apostles"; second, a threefold formula, "Law and Prophets / the Lord Jesus / his Apostles," with a variant threefold formula of "the Prophets, the Gospel, and the Apostles"; and finally, formulaic reference to the two Testaments.[8]

Thus, before there is an explicit canon as a list of books or a definite and closed collection of writings, there is in the Church an adopted routine for arguing about the faith by referring to "the Prophets and the Apostles." These references imply not only that their witness is binding for the Church, but also that the teachings which come from these sources must be assumed to be harmonious and consistent.

Since Gnosticism always aimed at developing a doctrinal system, it was very important for the Church also to think through its teaching in a more systematic manner, and to formulate it in logically coherent and consistent doctrinal statements. Therefore, it was from an anti-Gnostic perspective that the Church's first theological systems were constructed by people like St. Irenaeus and later Tertullian and Origen. Since one of their main concerns was to identify the authentic sources and criteria of the faith, it became a high priority for the Church in the second century to develop the theological notion of apostolicity.

8. Of course, the concept of the unity of the two Testaments stems from the "oneness" (sameness) of the Spirit. In reference to this point the most significant passage in the New Testament is 1 Pt 1:10–12.

The Gnostics rejected de facto important basic elements of the apostolic tradition but, at the same time, claimed to be in possession of secret traditions which, according to them, had been revealed privately to some privileged persons of the early Church, most commonly first-generation disciples. This position resulted in the circulation and promotion of many newly composed apocryphal writings appearing under the names either of the Apostles or of others of Jesus' entourage (Mary Magdalene, Nicodemus, various members of Jesus' family, etc.). Gnostic gospels with high claims of authenticity began to appear and were passed on from church to church. Consequently, the Church felt the urgent need both to define and to close the list of apostolic writings as those which contained all and only those Scriptures which could be trusted. It was in such a context that the definition of the canon of the New Testament became an issue of high priority. Most pressing was the problem of identifying which gospels were authentic—a process that began as early as the first years of the second century.

The Formation of the Four-Gospel Canon

In the development from "canonical principle" to canon, the most important step was evidently the formation of the four-gospel canon or τετραμόρφους εὐαγγέλιον, a term probably coined by Irenaeus.[9]

We do not know under what circumstance and at what exact date the four-gospel canon was formulated and in exactly what form or by what process it was received by the Church. A valid *terminus a quo* is obviously the composition and dissemination of the fourth gospel, but a *terminus ad quem* is established only with difficulty.[10]

---

9. *Adversus Haereses* III, 2, 11; II, 47–48. See D. Jeffrey Bingham, *Irenaeus' Use of Matthew's Gospel in Adversus Haereses* (Louvain: Peeters, 1998), 80–81.

10. That John was the latest canonical gospel is a rare point on which unanimity reigns among scholars. As far as tradition is concerned, the *Anti-Marcionite Prologue*, the *Muratorian Canon*, Irenaeus, Tertullian, Clement of Alexandria, and Origen explicitly assert this. Martin Hengel mentions a tradition reflected in liturgical calendars and some additional hints suggesting that John, son of Zebedee, died a martyr just as his brother did (Mk 10:35–39), which Hengel thinks must be taken more seriously than most scholars do. Martin Hengel, *The Johannine Question*, trans. J. Bowden (London:

Yet the four-gospel canon must have preceded Irenaeus's *Adversus Haereses* (written around 185), which clearly declares and upholds it. One may also be reasonably confident that the canonicity of four and only four gospels had been established before the *Diatessaron* was composed by Tatian (sometime around 160–170).[11] A similar date is suggested by a remark made by Celsus, quoted in Origen's *Contra Celsum*. Celsus accused the Christians of having corrupted the gospel from its original form to a threefold, even fourfold, and many-fold degree.[12] This would mean that around 160–170, when Celsus, one of the most widely known opponents and critics of Christianity, wrote his anti-Christian pamphlet, he had the notion that, on the one hand, a certain written document referred to as "εὐαγγέλιον" was considered by Christians to contain the whole basis of the Christian message, while, on the other hand, it existed in three or four variant (and divergent) literary forms.[13]

It seems, however, that we can take one further step back a couple of decades in dating the four-gospel canon. It was around AD 130–140 that Marcion went public,[14] first in Asia Minor then in Rome,

SCM Press, 1989), 21 and 158–59. But if, as Hengel admits, Gal 2:9 mentions around the year AD 50 that John is still a "pillar" of the Church, he could not have died together with his brother James (Acts 12:1) during the reign of Herod Agrippa (AD 40–44). Therefore, in no case does Mk 11:35–39 imply the two brothers' joint martyrdom.

11. Tatian's effort to replace the use of Matthew, Mark, Luke, and John by his *Diatessaron* presupposed that those four gospels had obtained a privileged status as the only ones with apostolic origin. The simultaneous use of the four canonical gospels could have obviously caused consternation or even scandal on account of their divergence, especially in the way they present Jesus' origins. Since many of the Gnostics omitted the infancy narratives (so the Marcionites skipped Lk 1–2 and the Ebionites omitted Mt 1–2), Tatian's effort to consolidate the four gospels into one unified narrative is readily explained.

12. "After this he says that certain of the Christian believers, like persons who in a fit of drunkenness lay violent hands upon themselves, have corrupted the Gospel from its original integrity, to a threefold, and fourfold, and many-fold degree, and have re-modeled it, so that they might be able to answer objections." Origen, *Contra Celsum* 27.

13. Celsus's report corresponds well to a linguistic anomaly that he, as an outsider to Christianity, could not have understood, let alone appreciated. For in Christian usage, the word εὐαγγέλιον meant both a message and a literary genre. By the second century, books containing Jesus' words and deeds were called εὐαγγέλια (in the plural), but in Christian usage εὐαγγέλιον meant their common content; yet when specified by the preposition "according to" (κατά) it indicated again a book in four versions with the preposition designating the author.

14. The dating of Marcion's activities is controversial. Those who make Marcion a

with his program for a single canonical gospel book, that of Luke, for which Marcion himself provided an interpolated edition.[15] H. von Campenhausen conjectured that the four-gospel canon came about in reaction to Marcion and was created by those church leaders who rejected him and eventually obtained his expulsion from the church of Rome.[16] The story seems to be more complicated, and Marcion's role in the formation of a gospel canon needs a reassessment. It is well attested that Marcion gave his followers a "canon" consisting of two books: a single-book gospel (his εὐαγγέλιον) and his "ἀποστόλικον," a collection of ten Pauline letters.[17]

Though its elimination of any conflicting stories made it quite practical, Marcion's "one single gospel" was for him and his oppo-

---

contemporary of St. Polycarp tend to date the beginnings of his career as early as that of Polycarp: between 110 and 120. Some consider the heresies mentioned by Ignatius of Antioch to include Marcionism and thus tend to move back the beginning of Marcion's preaching to the last years of the first century. Unfortunately, such studies are biased. For those who claim Marcion's originality want to date him as early as possible in order to exclude his dependency on other heretics like Cerdo and Cerinthus. The question also involves Irenaeus's historical credibility, for he seems to date Marcion's arrival in Rome around 140–150, the time of Pope Anicet, whom St. Polycarp visited in 151. Cf. R. Joseph Hoffmann, *Marcion: On the Restitution of Christianity* (Chico, Calif.: Scholars Press, 1984), 49–56. In any case, the evidence for Marcionism appearing any earlier than 125 is weak, for before Justin Martyr's *First Apology* (I, 26) no heresy is explicitly connected with Marcion's name.

15. Scholars defending Marcion prefer to see in the gospel he propagated an earlier version of Luke ("Proto-Luke"), but Tertullian offers rather strong evidence that the Marcionites possessed a text of the Lucan Gospel with well identifiable omissions and transformations, all identifiable as secondary. Since Marcion's *Apostolikon,* a collection of Pauline letters, is also at variance with the canonical text, there is enough evidence to show that he tampered with the text in order to make it conform to his interpretation. Therefore, there is no reason to assume that the Marcionite version of Luke was some form of a more original "Ur-Lukas" (Proto-Luke), more authentic than the text which orthodox Christianity possessed. This is recognized by Joseph Hoffman, who tries to defend Marcion's attitude toward the text of his gospel as consistent with his general view on Paul and the other apostles. For his "reduced or proto-type version of Luke. . .was not to be equated with the Gospel of Christ (cf. Gal 1:7; Rom 15:20) which Paul proclaimed (Rom 16:25). . . . Marcion considered his own text of the gospel as imperfect" (ibid., 110). Therefore, even those who sympathize with his attempt to "rescue Christianity" from the distortion it underwent in the first century must recognize that, in Marcion's view, the text of his own version of the gospel (of Luke) was not "unchangeable"—it had no canonical status.

16. *The Formation of the Christian Bible* (Philadelphia: Fortress Press, 1972), 198–99.

17. Galatians, 1 and 2 Corinthians, 1 and 2 Thessalonians, Ephesians, Colossians, Philippians, Romans, and Philemon; the order of the books in Marcion's collection is not quite clear.

nents not the main issue at hand. His one-gospel program directly follows from his exclusive Paulinism: only Paul's message authentically represented Christ's thought, for all other Apostles betrayed Jesus by becoming "Judaizers," that is, wanting the Church to adhere to the Mosaic Law. It is probably correct that for Marcion the choice of one apostle (Paul) at the exclusion of all others (Peter and the Twelve) was primary, and the choice of one gospel only secondary. But if so, we must add the following observation: Marcion's specific choice of Luke as his only gospel must have been a reflection of this "Paulinism." By choosing Luke, Marcion testifies, perhaps unwittingly, to a church tradition of his time, according to which Luke was a follower of Paul and his gospel possessed a "Pauline pedigree." In fact, Marcion's "canonical principle" was his exclusive Paulinism. According to early church writers Marcion thought that the expression "τὸ εὐαγγέλιόν μου" in Romans (16:25) was a straightforward reference to a literary work: that is to say, Paul refers here to Luke's gospel. Beginning with Harnack, scholars have pointed out that for Marcion's purpose, the Gospel of Mark would have been better suited. But he rejected both Matthew and Mark because of their "Petrine pedigree," and according to Marcion, Peter and the Twelve compromised the purity of the Gospel of Jesus Christ by clinging to the Torah.

Marcion's choices (both negatively, by rejecting Matthew and Mark, and positively by accepting Luke) testify to the antiquity of the titles of the gospels.[18] In these, the gospel κατὰ Μαθθαῖον was attributed directly to one of the Twelve, the gospel κατὰ Μάρκον to a writer who, according to an ancient presbyter quoted by Papias, functioned as Peter's interpreter.[19] And, of course, the gospel κατὰ

18. Martin Hengel, "The Titles of the Gospels and the Gospel of Mark," in *Studies in the Gospel of Mark* (London: SCM Press, 1985), 64–84.

19. Dating Marcion as a contemporary of Papias is consistent with these facts. But it is important to realize that Papias's fragments quote a "presbyter" of the previous generation. Cf. Denis Farkasfalvy, "The Papias Fragment on Mark and Matthew and Their Relationship to Luke's Prologue: An Essay on the Pre-History of the Synoptic Problem," in *The Early Church in Its Context: Essays in Honor of Everett Ferguson,* ed. Abraham J. Malherbe, Frederick W. Norris, and James W. Thompson, 92–106 (Leiden: Brill, 1998).

Λοῦκαν was believed to have come from a companion of Paul and was, therefore, the only choice suitable for an "exclusive Paulinist." From this it is also clear that Marcion's basic decision was not a canonical one: it was not about the gospel books themselves, but about the Apostles with whom the books were linked. And thus, Marcion happened to become also an early witness to the tradition, well circulated by the years 125–130, that the gospels of Matthew and Mark were of apostolic origin, going back to Peter and the Twelve, and that Luke's gospel was the work of a Pauline disciple.[20]

Moreover, Marcion was also in agreement with the Church at large about an important principle: one accepts or rejects a gospel on the basis of its apostolic credentials. Marcion rejects all gospels other than Luke's not because he rejects their apostolic origin, but because he rejects all Apostles other than Paul. When the churches of Asia Minor and the church of Rome broke ties with Marcion, they manifested their acceptance of both Paul and Peter along with the rest of the Twelve, against Marcion, who adhered to only one Apostle and one gospel. This well illustrates the meaning of the anti-Marcionite position held by both Irenaeus and Tertullian: in their argumentation on behalf of the four-gospel canon, they consistently emphasized the agreement that connects Peter and the Twelve with Paul, that is, the unity that links all authors of the canonical books both with Jesus and with each other.[21]

How authentic was Marcion's so-called Paulinism, admired by men even as late as Adolf von Harnack, in the nineteenth century?[22]

20. Most commentaries and introductions miss or undervalue the implications of Marcion's position and make their readers think that the earliest attribution of the third gospel comes from the late second century. So, for example, Raymond Brown: "By the latter half of the second century (title of [the papyrus] P75, Irenaeus, the Muratorian fragment) this book was being attributed to Luke, the companion of Paul." *An Introduction to the New Testament* (New York: Doubleday, 1997), 267. The sources which Brown quotes here are about a half century later than Marcion.

21. Cf. Hans-Joachim Schulz, *Die apostolische Herkunft der Evangelien* [The Apostolic Provenance of the Gospels] (Freiburg in Br.: Herder, 1995).

22. *Marcion: Das Evangelium von fremden Gott, Eine Monographie zur Grundlegung der katholischen Kirche* [The Gospel of the Unknown God: A Monograph on the Foundation of the Catholic Church], 2nd ed. (Leipzig: J. C. Hinrichs, 1924). A modern critique can be found in David L. Balás, "Marcion Revisited: A 'Post-Harnack' Perspec-

Did Marcion correctly represent Galatians 1:8–9 when he insisted that there is but "one gospel"?[23] Is it correct to say that Marcion's misinterpretation of Paul comes from his misunderstanding of the word εὐαγγέλιον, as he replaced its Pauline meaning (=salvific message of Jesus Christ)[24] with its later, second-century meaning (that is, an account about Jesus' words and deeds)?[25] Again, our answer must be nuanced.

First, Paul's position on the "oneness" of the "εὐαγγέλιον" is not as unambiguous as it sounds. In Galatians, Paul does not really state that there can be only one presentation of the gospel, for he allows for some diversity and multiplicity in the way the Church must "evangelize." In fact, in Galatians 2:9 he distinguishes between the "εὐαγγέλιον ἀκροβυστίας" and the "εὐαγγέλιον περιτομῆς," as two different presentations of the good news of Jesus Christ, one by himself and the other by Peter. In other words, Paul is ready to recognize Peter as the leader of the mission to the circumcised as long as he, Paul, is recognized as the leader of the mission to the Gentiles. He identifies both forms of the message as the same "εὐαγγέλιον" of Jesus Christ, and obviously he implies the validity of each of the two versions of presenting the gospel. Thus the unity of the gospel

tive," in *Texts and Testaments*, ed. E. W. March, 95–108 (San Antonio, Tex.: Trinity University Press, 1980).

23. "But even if we, or an angel from heaven, should preach to you a gospel contrary to that which we preached to you, let him be accursed. As I have said before, now I say again, If any one preaches to you a gospel contrary to that which you received, let him be accursed" (RSV). The translation is a bit problematic, because the text uses the participle εὐαγγελιζόμενον, not the noun εὐαγγέλιον. Nor does Paul speak about a *gospel* "contrary" to what he preached, but "preaching as good news something else [ἄλλον]" than what he preached. However, it is justifiable to suppose that the direct object of the action εὐαγγελίζεσθαι is intended to be the εὐαγγέλιον. In this sense, Paul allows only one single authentic message which, however, may involve a variety of presentations.

24. "But in a vast majority of passages *euaggelion* denotes the content of his [Paul's] apostolic message." J. Fitzmyer, *To Advance the Gospel* (Grand Rapids, Mich.: Eerdmans, 1981), 150. For Paul, "'the message of Christ' and 'the gospel' are the same." However, P. Stuhlmacher, "The Pauline Gospel," in *The Gospel and the Gospels*, ed. P. Stuhlmacher, 150 (Grand Rapids, Mich.: Eerdmans, 1991), shows that this specific interpretation of the Pauline usage of the term εὐαγγέλιον comes from A. Harnack and may need further scrutiny.

25. This would then be Marcion's basic misunderstanding: identifying Paul's reference to "my gospel" as a reference to the content of a book: the Gospel of Luke.

is not defined by the sameness of its formulation everywhere nor by the identity of the behavior expected in connection with it, but by the sameness of "the one who worked through Peter for the mission to the circumcised" and of the one "who worked through me [Paul] also for the Gentiles" (2:8). This means the sameness of Christ and the sameness of the Spirit, not the sameness of observance with regard to the Mosaic Law.[26]

Second, we must ask if, indeed, the Pauline meaning of the word εὐαγγέλιον is as radically different from the meaning it had in the second century as is usually claimed.[27] It is well known that early in the second century the narrative accounts of Jesus' words and deeds began to receive the title εὐαγγέλιον, followed by the preposition κατά, as in κατὰ Ματθαῖον, Μάρκον, Λοῦκαν, and Ἰωάννην. Biblical experts routinely assume that εὐαγγέλιον in such contexts signifies not a message but a book, and that this change in the word's meaning happened in the first half of the second century.

We want to argue that the latter meaning (εὐαγγέλιον as a narrative account) is a close and direct derivative from its original sense (meaning the salvific message) and that its secondary sense already existed in the first century. Our most important witnesses are the parallel accounts of "the anointing in Bethany" found in both Matthew and Mark (Mk 14:9 with par. in Mt 26:13):

> Truly I tell you, wherever the good news (εὐαγγέλιον) is proclaimed in the whole world, what she has done will be told in remembrance of her.[28]

First, in support of this thesis, the Dominical saying quoted above presupposes that the proclamation of the "good news" is accompa-

---

26. This argument follows rather closely Tertullian's reasoning in *Adversus Marcionem* IV, 3, 2–4. Tertullian states that Peter and Paul proclaimed the same εὐαγγέλιον but the way of life which they followed (their *"convictus"*) was different. Tertullian also argues that both Paul and his disciple, Luke, were posterior to Peter and the Twelve, thus Peter and the Twelve cannot be accused of falsifying Jesus' teaching. After all, Marcion recognized that Paul's understanding of the gospel was correct and that Paul was posterior to Peter. Finally, if Marcion accuses the Apostles of Jesus for having falsified his gospel, he should accuse Jesus himself, for it is he who taught his Apostles.

27. Cf. Stuhlmacher, "The Pauline Gospel," 171–72.

28. The Matthean parallel has "these good news" or "τοῦτο εὐαγγέλιον."

nied by "narrative accounts," that is, by stories told about Jesus, just like the story of the anointing in Bethany.[29] Second, the sentence assumes that, by these narratives, the persons mentioned in them become permanently memorialized in the Church. Third, in making the prediction that this particular story will be narrated "wherever the gospel is proclaimed," the author obviously assumes that some (but not all) other stories may also need to be narrated in all the different renditions of Jesus' life and ministry.

Thus in both Matthew and Mark we are confronted with the evangelist's assumption that the choice of episodes to accompany the proclamation of the "εὐαγγέλιον" is not (or not yet) fully standardized and inclusion of one or another specific story among the other narrative episodes may be a matter of choice, which a preacher (or Apostle) could make. Some episodes are narrated in one place, and some are narrated in others. Yet Jesus' logion in the narrative of the anointing makes this point: every presentation of his gospel message ("everywhere in the world") will de facto include the "anointing in Bethany." While in this text the word εὐαγγέλιον does not mean a book; it means that the gospel message is inseparable from concomitant narration of stories, and so, at least by connotation, these narratives are linked with the meaning of εὐαγγέλιον. In this way, one can see how and why, in a short time, the word εὐαγγέλιον came to mean the salvific message as contained in a chain of stories about Jesus. Thereafter the meaning of the word broadened and widened until it ended up meaning both the message and the concomitant stories or, eventually, just the literary product containing the stories. Some of the stories like those accompanying the proclamation, or like those about Jesus' death and glorification, must have been regarded from the earliest times as indispensable parts of the proclamation.[30] From here it takes but a small step to see how the anointing at Bethany could have become a "compulsory episode"

29. The verb used is "λαληθήσεται" meaning not just "mentioning" but a "narrating" (*erzählen*).

30. Such an interpretation opens the road to interpret the "ἀρχὴ τοῦ εὐαγγελίου" (Mk 1:1) in reference to the whole book of Mark.

to be narrated all over the world, "wherever the gospel was being preached."

The conclusions reached above reveal a connection between the creation of the gospel titles and the formation of the four-gospel canon. Considering such a connotation we can easily understand the use of the preposition κατά. This preposition was rarely used to designate the author of an ancient Greek text; its use, however, was needed in order to combine the de facto plurality of the gospel books with the vision of Galatians. By using κατά, the titles both assert the oneness of the gospel and recognize its multiplicity in various literary compositions. At the same time, such titles also bring about a new emphasis that the proclamation of Jesus' good news is necessarily linked to narratives with some episodes included or absent, some selected at random, others predetermined—yet all done, one might say, with a divinely prescribed consistency.

In such a perspective, the word εὐαγγέλιον appears eminently appropriate for naming books that contain the narrative episodes about Jesus and uniformly end with comparatively lengthy passion narratives.[31] This new meaning of the word did not arise by accident or random change in usage, but as the product of theological reflection and maturation which guided the development of the gospel tradition from its oral phases to its subsequent literary consolidation.

There can be little doubt that the formation of the four-gospel canon concluded a process several decades in development. It was achieved by Christian churches after they came into possession of several compositions that all claimed apostolic origins, and began using them simultaneously. These compositions quickly replaced the oral narratives that accompanied the proclamation of the apostolic kerygma. Due to the link between those narratives and the kerygma, each literary work about Jesus' words and deeds began to be referred to as εὐαγγέλιον. Yet, on account of the reception of the Pauline corpus, and quite possibly under the influence of the onslaught of Mar-

---

31. I allude here to the classical remark made by M. Kähler in 1892 that "the Gospels are passion narratives with an extended introduction."

cionism, there remained significant caution against using the word εὐαγγέλιον in the plural; in fact, the various renditions of the life and ministry became referred to as the one εὐαγγέλιον according to the various apostolic witnesses, each offering a different but not discordant version of the Jesus tradition.

We may, therefore, conclude that the title "εὐαγγέλιον κατὰ" responded to the second-century Church's need to construct a conceptual framework for designating a limited number of literary works about Jesus' words and deeds. Only with their assured apostolic provenance could they be exclusively authorized and inclusively imposed for use in and by the Church. However, the actual decision by which these "apostolic gospels" were accepted and their use made compulsory is not directly documented.

One may ascribe a good degree of probability to William R. Farmer's conjecture that this decision took place when St. Polycarp and a delegation from Asia Minor met with Pope Anicetus in Rome to resolve the Quartodeciman controversy around the year 151.[32] By then the Quartodecimal dispute about when to celebrate Easter must have been simmering for decades. It brought into a seemingly unsolvable conflict the Christians of Asia Minor and those of Rome. In Asia the celebration of Easter was determined according to the date of the Passover established by the Jewish calendar, while in Rome Easter was celebrated always on Sunday, regardless of the day of the week on which the Jewish Passover fell. The Asians appealed to the authority of the Apostle John; the Romans claimed to follow a tradition received from Peter. The memory of this meeting was preserved by Eusebius.[33] Thus the issue at hand in the controversy was quite similar to the crisis brought about around the same time by Marcion: a conflict between competing apostolic traditions.

---

32. W. R. Farmer, "A Study in the Development of the New Testament Canon," in *The Formation of the New Testament Canon*, by W. R. Farmer and Denis M. Farkasfalvy, 71 (New York: Paulist Press, 1983).

33. Irenaeus alludes to it: *Is enim [sc. Polycarpus] est qui sub Aniceto cum advenisset in Urbem multos ex his quos praediximus haereticos convertisset in Ecclesiam Dei* [For he is the one, who, when coming to Rome under Anicetus, converted the above mentioned heretics to the Church of God].

When Polycarp made his trip to Rome, the scandal which had been caused by Marcion in Rome around the year 144 and his subsequent excommunication were still fresh in the Church's memory. The conflicting reports of the synoptics and of the fourth gospel on the date of the Passover testify that the Quartodeciman conflict was, indeed, deeply embedded in local traditions, and that the conflict was not only about liturgy and church discipline, but also about claims of apostolic and scriptural authority. As Eusebius reports, using a text by Irenaeus, although Polycarp and Anicetus could not resolve their conflict about the date of Easter, they remained in communion with each other and jointly celebrated the Eucharist. Through this joint act they gave evidence of their recognition of each other's traditions, which were attested to by the one gospel, whose variant renditions (according to Matthew, Mark, and Luke, on the one hand, and according to John, on the other) were in use in the respective churches. Exactly because Anicetus and Polycarp recognized the authority of both the synoptic and the Johannine traditions, it is quite probable that the solution settled upon for maintaining the unity of the Church was intimately linked to a joint acceptance of the four-gospel canon. As a result of such a joint acceptance, Polycarp and Anicetus would have agreed that all churches must respect each and all of the four gospels, as well as the apostolic tradition which each represents. It is quite plausible that at that historic meeting, Irenaeus too, still a presbyter of the church of Lyons, was present.[34] This would explain why Irenaeus became as ardent and eloquent a promoter of the four-gospel canon as he appears to be in his *Adversus Haereses*, written some thirty years later.[35]

34. Irenaeus's familiarity with the situation of the church of Rome is commonly admitted. The trip he made to Rome under Pope Eleutherius concerning the Montanist crisis offers some probability that some twenty years earlier he was present in Rome at the arrival of St. Polycarp.

35. It is not unlikely that Irenaeus's concise formulation of the fourfold gospel canon in *Adversus Haereses* III, 3 contains a transcription of the text on which Polycarp and Anicetus agreed: "Matthew among the Hebrews published the written form of the gospel [*scripturam evangelii*] while Peter and Paul orally preached the gospel [*evangelizarent*] in Rome and laid the foundations of the Church. After their departure [*excessus*, for the Greek term ξοδος] Mark, a disciple and interpreter of Peter, himself

The most remarkable feature of the four-gospel canon is its ecumenical character and potential. During its short period of incubation—the first half of the second century—the early Church was in danger of embarking onto the waves of history without solid structures and provisions for stability. To achieve a firm doctrinal basis it needed its doctrinal deposit—the tradition it received from and about the Lord—in a clearly defined, written form. The appearance of several written renderings of Jesus' words and deeds, all with a claim to authenticity (that is, apostolic origin), might have advanced the threat of disintegrating Christianity into a mushrooming multiplicity of beliefs and practices.

In fact, with the onset of the Gnostic movement, the fragmentation of Christianity had effectively begun. The churches tried to respond to every novelty by constant reference to an orally transmitted "rule of faith," which they supported by arguments based on "the prophets and the Apostles," that is, by the Scriptures of old and a variety of apostolic traditions, transmitted in oral or written records. But there were uncertainties, which are well reflected in the fragments of Papias. He reports about diverse Greek versions of the Gospel of Matthew, all of which lay claim to an origin in a Semitic apostolic composition. Moreover, he tries to shield Mark against charges of lack of order and incompleteness by referring to the apostolic witness of Peter. Such is the situation also behind the remarks of an ancient presbyter, quoted by Clement of Alexandria, who gave advice about how to tell apart the older (original) from newer (interpolated) versions of a gospel and to distinguish the authentic from

---

transmitted to us in writing what had been proclaimed. And Luke, a follower [*sectator*] of Paul deposited in a book the Gospel that was preached by him. Thereafter, John, the disciple of the Lord, who leaned over his breast also published a Gospel, while living in Ephesus of Asia." The text shows a "Roman perspective" in special reference to Mark: "He wrote *for us*." Applied solely to Mark, this cannot come from Irenaeus. But similarly there is a built-in recommendation of John's gospel by an allusion to Jn 13:23 and 25 (the "breast of the Savior"), manifesting an awareness of this apostolic witness's privileged intimacy with Jesus, a perspective typical for Asia Minor. The simultaneous presence of these two perspectives (Roman and Asian) supports the suggestion that this very text represents a verbatim agreement between Rome and Asia Minor: Anicetus and Polycarp.

what is falsified.[36] Finally, it is under such circumstances that Papias quotes his presbyter in favor of the "living voice" of oral tradition with an open mistrust for written documents—probably because they can be manipulated and passed on under fictitious names.[37]

The acceptance of four distinct apostolic gospels, each edited as a separate version of the one gospel and each attributed to a historically identifiable personality of a defunct Christian generation, was a bold, but appropriate and efficient, step. It succeeded in not only rescuing a large variety of ancient traditions but also in curbing the growth of the Gnostic movements.

From the retrospective point of view of modern Christianity, the four-gospel canon achieved two important goals: it declared the oneness of Jesus Christ, and posited the assumption that basic harmony reigns among the various canonical presentations about Jesus. It did not do so obviously by historical or exegetical demonstration; nor did it mean setting a goal to be reached by merely human endeavor and research. Rather, it meant a postulate and a claim that the same Spirit who animates the Church, validates the sacraments, and maintains the links of faith and charity among the local churches, has enabled each gospel tradition and each author to give an authentic representation of the truth of Jesus' salvific work, and makes the Church ever capable of discovering the same reality presented in a fourfold way through the gospels. The four-gospel canon allowed the Church to retain its unity with a limited and controlled dose of diversity. To put it another way, it demanded that unity be regarded as an ongoing task. By accepting a fourfold canon, the Church opted for diversity coexistent with unity rather than for a uniformity of exclusion and reduction.

A good example of what the four-gospel canon achieved can be found in the two-thousand-year-old question of the date of the Last Supper. As we have seen, the Quartodeciman dispute had not been resolved, yet Polycarp and Anicetus still retained their unity. Simi-

36. Denis Farkasfalvy, "The Presbyters' Witness on the Order of the Gospel as Reported by Clement of Alexandria," *Catholic Biblical Quarterly* 54 (1992): 260–70.

37. Farkasfalvy, "The Papias Fragment on Mark and Matthew," 92–106.

larly, the twentieth-century scholarly debates over the Johannine and synoptic timetables of the passion narratives produced no clear-cut solutions, and the Magisterium saw no reason to intervene by accepting either tradition at the exclusion of the other. Such tolerance about calendar may appear considerably easier in the twentieth century than it was in the second century. The four-gospel canon demands respect for both traditions. But it still teaches the Church that, being a historically conditioned process, the transmission of apostolic tradition includes schematization and simplification of the data that may well lead to the loss of material exactness in factual details about such things as precise chronology. On the positive side, it shows also the priority of the issues of faith and theology over circumstantial details. For the Church ended up objecting to the dissociation of the celebration of Easter from either the Resurrection or the Crucifixion and thereby it excluded neither the novelty of Jesus as "new creation" nor his identity with the Paschal Lamb. With the four-gospel canon in place, exegetical tasks became immensely more difficult, but the theology of the Christian Passover retained its riches.

The Collection of the Apostolic Letters

The collection of the Pauline letters was the result of an extended process. According to most scholars, it organically evolved from the production of posthumous letters and new editions of the primitive collection into a philologically revised ensemble of works.[38] Parallel to this process was the closure of the Pauline collection of letters and their final and stable sequencing. Marcion edited his own version of the Pauline corpus and called it *Apostolikon,* opting for Paul as the only true Apostle. But by AD 140 Paul's image as a literary

38. "During the second century there were two distinct editions of the collected letters of Paul. One was the edition used by Marcion, which consisted of ten letters of Paul arranged in the order Galatians, Romans, 1–2 Corinthians, 1–2 Thessalonians, Laodiceans (=Ephesians), Colossians, Philippians and Philemon. The other edition lies behind most early Greek manuscripts, including the earliest extant manuscript of Paul's collected letters, P 46, which is dated about 200 C.E." Gamble, *Books and Readers in the Early Church,* 59.

author was not a novelty. Its recognition by the Catholic Church is well documented by St. Polycarp in his letter to the Philippians, even earlier (by 125 at the latest) by a reference to "all letters" of Paul in Second Peter, in the letters of Ignatius (around 110), and in quotations of Paul as early as Clement of Rome, writing to the Corinthians around 97.

The central issue in the Marcionite crisis, Paul's relationship to Peter and the Twelve, was in one sense answered by a significantly synthetic development: the acceptance of Luke's two volumes, his gospel and Acts. This set of works shows continuity and basic agreement between, on the one hand, Peter, the leader of the Twelve and the chief witness of Jesus' earthly life, and, on the other hand, the Apostle Paul, whose missionary career peaks at the end of the work as he brings the gospel message to Rome, where he is received in full communion by a previously established Christian Church.

That the unity of the apostolic message and the agreement between Peter and Paul were matters of dispute is sufficiently documented in Galatians. While he was himself critical of Peter's hesitant behavior in the matter of Jewish ritual observances, Paul tried to transcend the conflict by insisting on the oneness of the gospel, and, shortly thereafter, in First Corinthians, by forbidding the use of the various apostolic names for competing factions among Christians: some were declaring loyalty to Peter in opposition to Paul, others promoting Paul in opposition to Peter (1 Cor 1:12). Thus, Marcion's position lacked legitimacy and stood in demonstrable discontinuity with the historical Paul. The leading Church Fathers of the early second century (Justin Martyr, Irenaeus, Clement of Alexandria, and Tertullian) rejected this position and accepted in its stead the views and guidelines expressed in the pastoral letters.

The non-Pauline apostolic letters (the catholic letters of James, Peter, and John) were collected at about the same time and, according to the witness of the earliest manuscripts, were soon attached to the Acts of the Apostles to form a separate collection. The separation of Acts from the Gospel of Luke (if they ever were edited together) took place under little-known conditions. Although the third gospel was certainly written by the same author who wrote Acts, it might have begun its circulation separately and won the approval of the Church only as inserted into a four-gospel canon. This is illustrated by a papyrus from the third century (P75) in which the Gospel of Luke is not followed by Acts but stands immediately before the Gospel of John. Even more significant is the fact that the textual history of Acts is quite different from that of Luke, which indicates that from earliest times Luke's gospel was copied separately from Acts and received wider and faster diffusion.

The origins of the Epistle to the Hebrews are shrouded in mystery, but its secondary ending shows an early effort to attribute it to Paul. Its inclusion in the Pauline collection must have happened after the order of the rest was firmly established. Nor was its Pauline authenticity ever formally asserted either by the binding decision of Church authorities or by insertion of an address formula. At the same time, the frequent use of Hebrews by Clement of Rome (AD 97) indicates a very early date and a probable Roman origin.

The only prophetic book of the New Testament, the Book of Revelation, is linked to the New Testament canon in three ways. Its attribution to the Apostle John is attested by Justin Martyr, a claim that is not easily dismissed.[39] Its first part consists of seven letters to seven churches in Asia Minor and thus, at first sight, it has some formal resemblance to a collection of apostolic letters. But the introduction to the letters (Rv 1:8–20) is a revelatory discourse by the risen Lord, elaborating upon both the apocalyptic discourses of the synoptic gospels and some of Christ's self-revelatory discourses of the fourth gospel. In this way the Book of Revelation fittingly ends the canon, by bringing gospels, apostolic letters, and the Johannine heritage to one single conclusion. It is the only New Testament book that insists on its own inspired and canonical character: "I certify this to all who hear the words of the prophecy of this book: If anyone adds

---

39. Regardless of Eusebius's accusation that in his references Papias mixed "two Johns," both from Ephesus, it seems that Papias attributed Revelation to John the Apostle. If so, our earliest witness to the Johannine origin of the book is only a couple of decades later than the composition of the book itself.

to these events, God will extend upon him the calamities recorded in this book. If anyone removes any of the messages of this book of prophecy, God will remove his participation at the tree of life and from the holy city, as spelled out in this book" (Rv 22:18–19).

The Old Testament in the Christian Canon

Regarding the Old Testament a particularly grave crisis came about in the second century. In addition to rejecting all Apostles other than Paul, Marcion also rejected the Old Testament in its entirety. The fact that for a short while Marcion enjoyed the trust of the local congregation of Rome may indicate that in the early second century a number of Christians might have perceived the Church's Jewish background as a liability. After AD 135, as the second Jewish war against the uprising of Bar Kochba came to a close, the spread of an anti-Jewish sentiment throughout the Empire was not surprising. Marcion, however, stated his opposition to the Old Testament in rather extreme terms: not only did he reject the old Scriptures, but he refused to accept the entire outline of a universal salvation plan beginning with Abraham and continuing through "his descendants." Instead he proposed a radical dualism, speaking of two gods, the wrathful god of the Old Testament (the Creator or *"demiourgos"*), set in opposition to a saving god who is the Father of Jesus Christ. He considered them two opposite and ultimate causes, one of all evil and the other of all good. According to Marcion the two Testaments contain many contradictions ("antitheses") and are irreconcilable.[40] He taught that the "God of our Lord Jesus Christ" had been unknown (ἄγνωστος θεός) before he sent his Son to free us from the slavery of an evil god, the creator of the material world who enslaved us under his law, the Law of Moses.[41]

40. Marcion's chief work bore the title Ἀντιθέσεις or "Contradictions." The occurrence of this term in 1 Tm 6:20 may not be mere coincidence: "O Timothy, guard what has been entrusted to you. Avoid godless chatter and the contradictions of what is falsely called wisdom [γνῶσις]." However, Marcion's choice as his work's title might have been borrowed as a Gnostic staple.

41. On ἄγνωστος θεός, cf. Acts 17:3. There is no proof that Marcion is quoting this verse, or that Acts 17:3 intends to refer to the teaching of Marcion.

By rejecting the Hebrew Bible and establishing a Christian Bible, consisting of a single gospel and the Pauline epistles, Marcion introduced an exegetical method by which the Christian writings were explored in light of their contradictions to the Jewish Scriptures. Moreover, his method of antithetic analysis was also a principle of textual emendation: he introduced changes in the texts of both Luke's gospel and the Pauline epistles, trying to make his whole canon theologically more homogeneous and compatible with his theology. Although he tried to eliminate or transform all that seemed to support the Scriptures of the Jews, Tertullian quickly observed that his system remained full of inconsistencies and that his basic anti-Jewish principles contradicted even those Pauline texts he had retained.[42]

Behind the Marcionite crisis we can detect not only a rising anti-Jewish sentiment in the general population of the Roman Empire, but also shifts of attitude toward Judaism within the Church as the proportion of converted Gentiles increased and the Church became the home of a fundamentally "Gentile" Christianity.

Marcion's dualistic understanding of the world deriving from two gods reveals another aspect of his identity. In spite of his tendency to reduce and limit the Scriptures to one gospel and a set of Pauline epistles, he soon seemed closely to resemble the majority of the Gnostics who, in fact, favored similar views about the material world. Both Justin Martyr and Irenaeus considered Marcion's dualism—seeing in the material world the work of an "evil god"—a typically Gnostic view. Tertullian attacked the Marcionite scriptur-

42. The claim that Marcion was a forerunner of biblical criticism, because he thought of the pastoral epistles as not authentic, is highly anachronistic. According to all evidence Marcion changed and mutilated texts according to his doctrinal priorities rather than working with manuscript evidences or applying literary criteria for dealing with variant readings. His rejection of Matthew was based on anti-Jewish bias, an unacceptable approach for recovering the authentic teachings of Jesus. Similarly, he chose Luke because of his mistaken notion that in Gal 1:11 Paul referred to the Gospel of Luke. The claim formulated by Harnack about Marcion as a forerunner of Luther and of the Protestant reformation is based on false premises and has lost its popularity in recent scholarship. See David L. Balás, "Marcion Revisited: A 'Post-Harnack' Perspective," in *Texts and Testaments,* ed. E. W. March, 95–108 (San Antonio, Tex.: Trinity University Press, 1980).

al canon directly, by showing that even from the little Marcion retained from Luke's gospel and Paul's letters, one can prove that Paul identified the God of Jesus Christ with the Creator of the world, and that Jesus was truly and fully human.

The Synthesis of Irenaeus

The teachings of the anti-Gnostic leadership of the Church received their earliest systematic presentation in Irenaeus's book *Against Heresies* (*Adversus Haereses*) written sometime around AD 185.[43]

His approach is based on a theology of salvation history which superimposes an order of salvation on the order of creation. One and the same God created the world, called Abraham, chose Moses, sent the prophets, appeared in Jesus Christ, and gave Christ's Apostles their mission. The history of salvation follows one single plan, though it is divided into several phases. Earlier phases must be understood in the light of the later ones. Where the Gnostics detected contradictions and inconsistencies, Irenaeus saw imperfections of earlier phases slowly being corrected and perfected in later phases. The whole of salvation history is under God's pedagogy; therefore we can observe gradual transitions from one phase to the next. Simple and imperfect beginnings lead to fullness and perfection in Christ. Just as the Old Testament is imperfect, because it points beyond itself to the perfection of the New, so the New Testament is incomplete, pointing beyond itself to the fullness of time: the eschatological vision.

In just this way, at the beginnings of patristic exegesis, the key to the Scriptures was provided by the discovery of salvation history. With Christ being both the peak and the fullness of this history, one needs to ask of every part of Scripture how it refers to Christ. From such a perspective the various books of various times and ages are to be regarded not only as complementary but as partial and imperfect

43. Denis Farkasfalvy, "Theology of Scripture in St. Irenaeus," *Revue bénédictine* 78 (1968): 319–33. Bingham, *Irenaeus' Use of Matthew's Gospel.*

presentations of one single common topic: Christ, in whom God is fully revealed.

Yet even Christ's coming takes place in history. His incarnation is prepared for and anticipated in the Old Testament and is followed by his passion and glorification. Moreover, his glorified humanity is further extended to all human beings throughout history in the Church's ministry of preaching and administering the sacraments. All phases of salvation history and all books of Scripture are united by the source of their inspiration, the same Spirit who reveals the same Divine Word made flesh. All prophets were inspired by the same Spirit, by whose fullness Christ was anointed. He in turn poured out his Spirit upon his Apostles and the Church from his glorified body. Christ is "the hidden treasure" (see Mt 13:44) which lies buried in the rich soil of the biblical word. It was the same Spirit that guided all "prophets and Apostles" to understand, proclaim, and explain the mystery of Christ in their preaching and their writings. This same Spirit continues his activity in the Church, making the sacraments effective and causing the faithful to believe and to understand the meaning of the writings of "the prophets and the Apostles."

When referring to the Scriptures as authored by "prophets and Apostles," the conjunction of these two terms obtains from Irenaeus a more specific theological meaning. It does not necessarily mean that the holy books were dictated by a scriptural prophet (one of the twelve in the Old Testament) or by an Apostle (one of the figures listed among the Twelve in Matthew, Mark, Luke, or Acts, to whom Paul is added). Rather, this coupling means that all the Scriptures refer to Christ by either anticipation or recollection. According to Irenaeus, the whole Old Testament is prophetic because it sprang from a foreknowledge of Christ granted in advance, although such knowledge was perceived and articulated in an imperfect way. Irenaeus consciously bases his notion of prophecy on that of John's gospel, stating that Abraham "saw" Christ "and rejoiced," and that Moses foretold Jesus, for "if you believe Moses, you believe me, just as well."[44] The

44. Jn 8:56 quoted in *Adversus Haereses* 4.1.2, and Jn 5:46 in *Adversus Haereses* 4.3.1.

latter Johannine verse is taken by Irenaeus literally, meaning that the words of Moses are equal in power and authority with those of Christ, since the Spirit that inspired Moses was the Spirit of the Lord. On the other hand, Irenaeus understands the New Testament as derived from the Apostles' experience of Christ: they were "spectators [that is, eyewitnesses] and ministers of the Word of Truth."[45] Irenaeus was the first Church Father consistently to maintain the analogy between the prophets and the Apostles and to build on it the parallelism between the Old and the New Testaments as two collections of holy books. In this way he opened the path for applying, again by analogy, the concept of prophetic inspiration to the whole of the Bible.

In Irenaeus's anti-Gnostic arsenal the concept of apostolicity is most important. Only what is authentically apostolic can give authentic historical witness to the incarnate Son of God. Consequently, only those who inherited the Church's true apostolic legacy, the bishops of the Church, can bear witness to it validly as the legitimate successors of the Apostles. The Church is the only body legitimately in possession of God's Spirit and, as such, the Church continues Christ's work in the world by exercising the gift of apostolic succession through the activities of bishops, the Apostles' successors, chosen and ordained in an unbroken chain of subsequent generations. Thus, for identifying and interpreting the books of the Bible, Irenaeus relies on the Church because the Church was founded by the Apostles, is governed by the successors of the Apostles, and is in possession of the Spirit, as it continues both to preach the word of Christ and to celebrate the sacraments entrusted to them by Christ and made effective by his ongoing presence.

On a more technical level, Irenaeus developed a new exegetical approach, a model further developed by the Church after him. This new method of exegesis was prompted by an innovation of the late decades of the first century: the codex. The use of the codex rapidly spread in the course of the second century, obtaining wider and wider use everywhere, but especially in the Christian Church.[46] The co-

45. Acts 1:2 in *Adversus Haereses* Preface 2.
46. See "Transition from Roll to Codex," in Gamble, *Books and Readers in the Early Church*, 49–66.

dex was apparently less costly than the scroll of leather, parchment, or papyrus used earlier. While Jewish tradition continued to prefer the scroll to the codex, there is strong archeological evidence that early on the Christian preference was for the codex.[47] This new technology made it possible to include in one large volume all the four gospels or the whole Pauline collection. More importantly, by being copied into codices, the scriptural texts became randomly accessible: one was able to page through a whole codex to check on the exactness of a quotation, on parallel texts, and on various small details in the wording much more quickly than was possible when the text was on scrolls. Earlier, the so-called "proof texts" were either looked up in florilegia (collections of quotations) or had to be remembered.

The growing popularity of the codex might best explain the new style of exegesis quite explicitly present already in Irenaeus. This new exegesis thrived on the juxtaposition of quotations from various independent texts, demanded verbally accurate quotations, carefully caught inexact usage, confronted variant readings, and accused opponents of slight but nefarious alteration of certain key terms. In fact, quoting a passage or verse verbatim and disputing minute details became an important issue not only for all Church Fathers but also for the Gnostics. Thus, it was in the second century that the textual form of the New Testament moved to the center of attention in Christian theology and apologetics. Also, it was then that, partly because the codex was less expensive, the New Testament began to be copied in larger and larger quantities and started on the path toward its unprecedented and unmatched bestseller status.

Due to a new awareness of the importance of verbal exactness, the Church of the second century engaged in its own kind of "textual criticism." Irenaeus had already identified a good number of Pauline texts and gospel quotations that the Marcionites, for doctrinal purposes, turned to variants or excised. Tertullian, while disapproving of the Marcionite canon as a whole, also complained about gratuitous changes in the biblical texts, coming, as it seems, from a sys-

47. Colin H. Roberts and T. C. Skeat, *The Birth of the Codex* (London: Oxford University Press, 1983).

tematic revision of some texts by Marcion himself.[48] Even if in some cases the Marcionite reading of a passage might have represented an unintentional or legitimate variant in the textual tradition, Marcion had no scruples about changing the text in order to accommodate it to his own doctrinal positions.[49] In any case, the third century appears to be the first major period in the Church's history when critical concerns began to play a major role in the transmission of the biblical text and its interpretation.

The short but violent persecution sponsored by Decius (250–251) considered it a high priority—for the first time in history—to confiscate and destroy the Church's books; biblical codices, lectionaries, and other liturgical texts were destroyed in large numbers, thereby testifying to the importance of the written word in the Church's life. During the next major persecution, at the end of the third century, the bureaucrats of Diocletian proceeded even more systematically with the destruction of Christian literature. After these persecutions the *"traditores"*—those who delivered the sacred books to the authorities—constituted a special category of lapsed Christians, a sign that depriving the Church of its sacred books was an important issue for both the persecutors and the persecuted. Handing over the sacred books was perceived both as a sinful act of disloyalty and as an act hurting the Church by depriving it of its Sacred Scriptures. All this makes us better understand Origen's activities: during the third century, he invested immense labor in providing the Church with correct biblical texts. His exegetical commentaries and school notes often address variant readings with proposals to resolve textual obscurities by pointing out the differences in the manuscripts and the various alternatives for translating them.

After the Gnostic crisis had ebbed, Irenaeus's synthesis of salva-

---

48. See Tertullian's *Adversus Marcionem*, 5 vols. (*Sources Chrétiennes* 365, 368, 399, 456, 483; with critical comments by R. Joseph Hoffmann, *Marcion: On the Restitution of Christianity*.

49. According to Joseph Hoffmann, such changes happened most clearly in the text of Marcion's gospel, because, for Marcion, "the *evangelion* as written text stands in need of constant correction"—a fact with which Tertullian gleefully reproached Marcion, and which Marcion did not deny (ibid., 110).

tion history remained a permanent part of the tradition of Christian theology. Even after Origen and Tertullian, who also used the philosophical tools of their age for interpreting the Bible and elaborating doctrinal systems, Irenaeus's vision of salvation history persisted—and does so up to our day—as a lasting source of inspiration and a paradigmatic ideal.

It would be an exaggeration, however, to claim that Irenaeus or even Origen created a truly novel outlook. In fact, Irenaeus did not want be an innovator. What he accomplished was a conscious expansion of a canonical reading of New Testament books, combining on every important question the four gospels and Paul's letters, especially John's gospel and Paul's epistle to the Romans, in search of a doctrinal synthesis. His thought presents the most important link between the books of the New Testament and the patristic age. He made it possible for Tertullian and Origen to formulate the theological ideal of the "true gnosis": a deeper knowledge achieved by the spiritual man, which for them implied, first of all, faithfulness to apostolic orthodoxy enshrined in the Scriptures.

We can say that the first blossoming of Christian theology was occasioned by the Gnostic crisis. It was during this conflict that the ideal of a Christian theologian and exegete was first formed and expressed. And, of course, one must add that at this time theology and exegesis were inseparable not only from each other but also from Christian spirituality, a threefold unity which remained in existence until the end of the Middle Ages.[50]

Nevertheless, Catholic Christians and Gnostics never agreed on certain foundational issues which, in today's language, mostly belong to the theology of revelation. Gnostics claimed to possess a "secret tradition," passed down to them by some of the Apostles or apostolic figures of the early Church. This claim motivated the Gnostics to produce and cultivate various apocryphal and pseudo-apostolic writings.[51] The

---

50. The *terminus ad quem* envisaged here is, of course, not easy to determine. One may state, however, that until the beginnings of scholasticism (thus for almost a thousand years) the basic model of theology remained unchanged.

51. The collection of Gnostic writings found in Nag Hammadi contains a number

quick appearance of such "gospels," epistles, and "acts" prompted the Church Fathers to identify more closely, and occasionally even to list, the authentic written documents of the Christian faith, that is, the "apostolic Scriptures" which they recognized.

These debates about apocryphal apostolic sources always implied the general question of how to distinguish between orthodoxy and heresy. Irenaeus's position combined both doctrinal and historical criteria for orthodoxy. According to him no person or book represented the orthodox apostolic faith unless it articulated a belief in the Old Testament, the four-gospel canon, and all true apostolic writings and traditions. On this last point Irenaeus taught that any true apostolic tradition had to be in harmony with the so-called *Regula Fidei,* the "rule of faith," and with the teachings of those bishops who legitimately succeeded the Apostles as leaders of the communities founded by the first Apostles. The *Regula Fidei* permitted a certain variety in its wording, but its outline always included the following unvarying doctrinal points: adherence to only one God and Creator, and to his only Son, who was truly made flesh, truly suffered, truly died, and truly rose from death.[52] When he identified the apostolic churches in which the authentic faith was preserved, Irenaeus listed in the first place the church of Rome, adding also the churches of Antioch, Alexandria, Ephesus, and Corinth. He documented the apostolic succession in these places by presenting lists of the names of bishops who succeeded to the Apostles in these churches. Thus Irenaeus never conceived the canon of the New Testament independently from the living tradition of the Church. For him the Scriptures were documents in live use. They were being copied, catalogued, and stored in archives, but also read, transmitted, preached, and interpreted.

It was also in the second and third centuries that theological de-

---

of books originating in the second or third centuries, including the Gospels of Thomas, Peter, Philip, and Mary, the Gospel of Truth, etc., of which only the Gospel of Peter seems to be an approximation of the literary genre represented by the canonical gospels. But the Gospel of Peter transmits a Gnostic Christology.

52. By the third century the *Regula Fidei* attained a finalized formulation in what is known and used unchangingly as the Apostles' Creed.

bates became not only focused more and more explicitly on scriptural texts but also formulated in more precise exegetical terms. Though this is not to say that the early Church would have introduced at any point in time what became known later as the Protestant principle of *"sola scriptura,"* but beginning in the second century, Scripture began to gain primacy in the Church's apologetic tools and was preponderantly used to prove the apostolic origin of a doctrinal position. On the one hand, Scripture was considered an authentic depository of the apostolic tradition—in its verbal form it represented the solidified and finalized teaching of the Apostles. On the other hand, the expressions of the living tradition of the Church—catechetical instruction and the various forms of instruction included in worship—were organized around the use of scriptural readings and quotations, as well as their ongoing interpretation. It was in such a vivid context that patristic exegesis began to blossom in the following centuries.

VI. PATRISTIC EXEGESIS AFTER IRENAEUS

Origen and His Contemporaries

The theologians of the third century opened a new era in the history of Christian thought.[1] First of all, they began to exploit systematically and methodically the riches of the Old and New Testaments by using them as source material both for apologetics (the defense of the faith against Jews and heretics) and for doctrinal systematization.[2] The new developments can be summarized as follows.

As indicated above, now in every debate against Jews or Gnostics, it became increasingly important for the exegete to determine the precise form of the biblical text. This apologetically motivated interest in a precise and faithful rendition of the text prompted Origen to create his famous *Hexapla,* an edition of the Old Testament according to six textual forms in six columns representing the various Hebrew and Greek literal meanings of the Jewish Bible.

Furthermore, it was Origen who first created an exegetical sys-

---

1. For a concise overview of patristic exegesis, with a complete list of the extant patristic commentaries, see David Balás and Jeffrey Bingham, "The Patristic Exegesis of the Bible," in *The International Bible Commentary,* ed. William R. Farmer, 64–115 (Collegeville, Minn.: Liturgical Press, 1998).

2. "Jews and pagans" must not be considered as traditional enemies of Christianity but, sociologically, as the two groups from whose ranks the Church recruited its membership and, therefore, from which it needed to differentiate itself from more and more. Ever since Paul's Epistle to the Romans, any presentation of Christian teaching had to list and examine its agreements and disagreements by confronting two groups: Jews and Gentiles. Thus early Church Fathers would typically write works *adversus Judaeos* and *adversus paganos* or *Graecos.*

tem of interpretation, which he included in the fourth book of his *Peri Archon* ("On First Principles") in the form of theoretical principles for Christian biblical exegesis. As Henri de Lubac's book on Origen's exegesis has shown, the system of the "fourfold sense" of Scripture comes from him.[3] This system became the backbone of Christian biblical interpretation for over a thousand years and dominated exegesis until the late Middle Ages.[4]

According to Origen the first task for the exegete is to find the passages' literal or historical sense, which is to be explored by the tools of textual research, grammar, and literary analysis. The accusation that Origen neglected or at times even denied the validity of the literal sense is based more on misunderstandings and misinterpretations than on his system's actual shortcomings. Only in the case of patently non-historical narratives like a parable or a tale of edification would Origen, or for that matter any ancient author, speak of the absence of historical meaning. Yet even in such cases, one must speak of a "literal sense," that is, the meaning of the text discoverable by the tools of grammar. This meaning can be equally obtained by every reader, Jew, pagan, and Christian alike. Moreover the literal meaning must be the same—or ambiguous in the same way—to all readers. It was for the sake of understanding the literal sense that Origen consulted Jewish teachers and exegetes, all experts in the Hebrew. Had Origen undervalued or neglected the importance of the literal meaning, he would not have invested so much work in text-critical studies, nor would he have discussed countless questions of textual variations, geographic locations, and biblical names and personalities.

However, in two ways Origen's understanding of the historical or literal sense differs from what a biblical scholar would today call

3. Henri de Lubac, *History and Spirit: The Understanding of Scripture according to Origen,* trans. A. E. Nash (San Francisco: Ignatius Press, 2008).

4. In his monumental *Exégèse médiévale* (Paris: Aubier, 1960–1964), de Lubac shows that in both theory and practice, Origen must be credited with the theology of Christian exegesis. An abridged presentation of the patristic theology of Holy Scripture is found in a selection of de Lubac's writings under the title *Scripture in the Tradition* (New York: Crossroad, 2000).

the "historical-critical" meaning of the text. On the one hand, living in antiquity and well before the age of the Enlightenment, Origen lacked what we call today a specific "historical consciousness," an awareness of the complex and continuous development that characterizes human life and culture. Our present-day understanding of history is based on this historical awareness, which generally permeates our understanding of human existence and thought. Moreover, in modern (basically "post-Enlightenment") Western culture, history is done critically. Historical criticism evaluates every human report about the past—even historical remembrance—as a source limited and at least partially biased due to human subjectivity. Modern critical historiography wants to determine how heavily a historical report is influenced and eventually distorted by an observer's or author's philosophical presuppositions and prejudices, which he usually shares, at least in part, with his immediate predecessors and contemporaries.

As in matters of science, so also in matters of history, Origen's thought—as well as that of all his followers in ancient and medieval times—could be characterized as "naïve realism." Pre-critical thinkers took historical narratives at face value and reached back over centuries of cultural developments with no preoccupations about cultural differences. Yet Origen also lacked the bias of historical empiricism, which limits and may even dominate the thought of modern historians. His understanding of biblical accounts did not aim at reconstructing "the facts" and not asking questions about their meaning. Rather, he approached "factual information" about the past (the historical meaning of the text) for the sake of recovering the religious and theological sense conveyed by the text.

Before we pronounce judgment on Origen's exegesis, we must realize that his outlook was closer to the point of view of the biblical authors than that of a modern historian (or exegete). As a rule, ancient and medieval people saw no other purpose in exploring the past than to learn about its meaning. They recalled the past for the sake of finding guidelines for the future, rather than for the sake of obtaining an objective reconstruction of what "really happened" and connecting the chains of historical causes and effects. Thus, while in the so-called historical-critical exegesis of our times, reconstructing the mindset of the author ("what the Bible meant") is more or less the ultimate goal and even the final stage of exegesis, for Origen, a historical and literal understanding of the text constituted only an initial stage for the exegetical process, and needed to be further extended so as to discover the more remote and hidden layers of meaning.[5]

In Origen's system, the second meaning is called *"allegorical"* or "typological." In the language of the Church Fathers, this is often referred to as a spiritual or symbolic meaning, an interpretation that connects the text with the mystery of Christ. In the case of an Old Testament text, the exegete would discover such a connection by pointing out what links a particular event, story, or literary or theological theme to other parts of the history of salvation, which culminates as a whole in Christ's life, death, and resurrection. The "meaning" of the text, therefore, goes beyond the literal sense. The exegete aims at discovering the Christological relevance of a passage, which may be discovered in a diversity of ways: by verbal similarities, by thematic analogies or symbolism, by historical or geographic connections, and so on. A text taken from the New Testament would usually offer a direct Christological link on the literal level, even if that meaning is not directly connected either with an event of Jesus' life or some teaching recorded in the Gospels. Thus, also in the case of the New Testament, the allegorical interpretation demands going beyond external, visible, and tangible facts concerning Jesus of Nazareth, and implies that by faith the reader must penetrate the mystery of the Word made Man. The allegorical meaning is the cornerstone of Origen's exegetical approach. Its strength consists in its potential to provide Christian relevance for every biblical text.

5. Here we touch upon the distinction between "what the Bible means" and "what the Bible meant," made popular by Raymond E. Brown, *The Critical Meaning of the Bible* (New York: Paulist Press, 1981), 23–44. Even with the qualifiers he later introduces, Brown's considerations are a slippery slope. Distinguishing between "what Scripture means for the authors and what it means for the Church" (41) and speaking about the "tension" between them does not bring more clarity. The issue is rooted in the question about human "authorial intent" being elevated and instrumentally used by God's transcendental action for conveying what he wants the Bible to express.

What is debatable is its application, the concrete way in which the Origenian exegete assesses the Christological relevance of a particular text. Yet one must not forget the continuity which links Origen's program to the apostolic preaching. Ultimately, it wants to achieve nothing other than reading all the Scriptures in the light of the Christian faith in the risen Christ.

In even narrower historical terms, Origen's system is built upon an expansion of the synthesis established by Irenaeus, but the sheer volume of his output and the philosophical foundations of his thought raise Origen significantly above Irenaeus and all other patristic exegetes. He is the most influential biblicist of the first fifteen hundred years of Christianity and, according to many, the greatest exegete of all times. As did Irenaeus, he too developed and used his interpretation of the Bible as the most important weapon in the Church's battle against Gnosticism. Using his system of interpretation, Origen considered each and every passage of Scripture as material for reflection upon Christian faith, and in so doing, he sought to remain equally distant from both a Jewish understanding and a Gnostic interpretation of the Bible. Yet, Origen excels Irenaeus from one additional point of view. He cultivated the "true gnosis," combining the exploration of the Scriptures with meditation on the issues of spiritual experience, and, therefore, he is the first and most influential exegete to use the Bible as a resource for the spiritual life. Origen knew that one of the most attractive features of Gnosticism was its appeal to the men and women of late antiquity who were seeking to promote spiritual life. As did many of his Gnostic contemporaries, he used Scripture to enhance, by the tools of religion and philosophy, the human potential for reflection and interiority in an age when the public life of the Hellenistic cities seemed to offer less and less guidance to the human quest for eternal values.

For modern historians and exegetes, allegory, the most important tool in Origen's use of the Bible, often appears to be set on shaky foundations. It is often considered the single feature of Origen's system that makes his thought seem alien to our age and it is, in fact, an easy target of criticism by historians and literary critics. According to the objections frequently raised against Origen, the search for allegory is just a tool of manipulation, open to arbitrary use by hasty superimposition of a Christian meaning through forced analogy, far-fetched symbolism, or false etymology. Although for at least fifty years contemporary interest in patristic exegesis and especially in Origen has been on a constant rise, the majority of biblical scholars handle him guardedly and with suspicion. Many express serious reservations as they review his "fanciful" Christological applications of the biblical texts, and warn against any "return" to such a model. But in patristic studies, scholarship has long discarded the assumption that Origen's Christian allegory essentially follows an Alexandrian model, developed in late Hellenistic thought, which sought to turn anthropomorphic myths of the Greeks into philosophical tales about the gods (the realm of the divine) by using lofty symbolism. Thus, most experts in patristic studies today see only a superficial similarity between Origen and Philo.[6] Instead, they deduce Origen's biblical exegesis ultimately from the apostolic exegesis of the Old Testament, including Paul's use of allegory (cf. Gal 4:24), and the Matthean "fulfillment" theology promoted by Justin Martyr's Logos theology.

However, among biblical scholars, even Catholics, Origen's reputation remains tarnished, not so much on account of his purported heresy, but rather because of his "Hellenization of Christianity" through the use of allegory in exegesis. As recently as 2002 the Pontifical Biblical Commission published a document, *The Jewish People and Their Sacred Scriptures in the Christian Bible,* in which, for the sake of stating the "supremacy of the historical-critical method," patristic allegory received harsh criticism, with most of the blame being put on Origen.[7] Step by step, the document narrates how "the Hellenistic world" began interpreting the classical texts by allegorizing them. Jews living in the Diaspora "utilized this method, espe-

---

6. See Francis Martin, *Sacred Scripture: The Disclosure of the Word* (Naples, Fla.: Sapientia, 2006), 252–60; Georges T. Montague, *Understanding the Bible* (Mahwah, N.J.: Paulist Press, 2007), 32–39, 51–53.

7. Vatican City: Libreria Editrice Vaticana, 2003. Quoted phrase is from no. 20, 46.

cially to justify certain prescriptions of the Law which taken literally would appear nonsensical to the Hellenistic world." Due to his Hellenistic education Philo of Alexandria began to apply the same method to the Old Testament by often "overshadowing" the original meaning of the text, but "his exegesis was not accepted in Judaism." Nevertheless "the Church Fathers and the medieval authors" succumbed and "made a systematic use of it for the entire Bible." The document mentions some "nonsensical" examples, all quoted from Origen, to reach the regrettable conclusion that, due to the use of allegory, "interpretation became arbitrary" and church exegesis entered an era of "irreversible decline."[8] One of two chief examples quoted by the document of the excesses of allegory is Origen's interpretation of the scarlet thread of Rahab in the Book of Joshua (2:18). Attached to her window and thereby a visual sign saving the inhabitants, the red ribbon becomes for Origen a symbol of the blood of Christ, as it saves the Church (all who are in the house of a previous "harlot") from perishing.

Ironically, the commission could not have found a better example to prove the contrary of what it had intended. For in his allegorical interpretation, Origen follows not Philo but Justin Martyr, who had presented a similar symbolic understanding of Rahab's story some hundred years before Origen.[9] But the roots are even older: Rahab appears to offer similar symbolism in the Letter of Clement of Rome to the Corinthians around the year 97.[10] It seems that in two texts of the New Testament, in the Epistle to the Hebrews (11:31) and the Epistle of James (2:25), the praise of Rahab's faith was also used as a symbol (or, if one prefers, "type" or "allegory") for the salvation offered to the Gentiles, symbolically a "harlot" whom God chooses and cleanses to turn her into his spouse, the Church. Rahab's image appearing in these early Christian texts is further linked with two further themes broadly used in the apostolic exegesis: that of the story of the prophet Hosea's wife (Hos 1:2; 2:7; 3:3) and the Paschal Lamb whose blood smeared on the doors of the Israelites saved them

8. Ibid., no. 20, 44–46. 9. *Dialogue with Trypho* 111:3–4.
10. *First Clement* 12:8.

from the wrath of judgment (Ex 12:22–23). One might say that the exegesis of Rahab's story is one of the best examples for justifying patristic allegory, because of its close connection not to Philo, but to the roots of the Christian message.

The third meaning in Origen's scheme is called the *"tropological"* or moral meaning. It follows from the nature of Christian truth that it always leads to moral challenge, but in Origen's thought we find a further nuance. According to his understanding of the ethical life, moral considerations also imply a return to the self for a reassessment of one's self-understanding and so also of one's relations to other human beings. For Origen, therefore, the Bible's moral meaning springs forth from the way the knowledge of Christ comes about and develops always in close confrontation with the self, and prompts the believer to renew his social relations in the light he has received from Christ. This must take place in exegesis as well. Every text that speaks of Christ must lead to questions concerning moral conduct. Of course, several objections about this point in Origen's system can be raised, but they all boil down to one question. Is Origen's moral teaching genuinely biblical, or is it ambiguously placed between Hellenistic models of ethics and biblical moral teaching? The answer cannot be given without ambiguity, and for this reason we shall return to it again a little later.

The fourth meaning is the *"eschatological"* or *"anagogical"* (ἀναγωγή) sense, a meaning that concerns the final outcome of salvation history. This issue appears fairly simple: since the final purpose of all salvation history is the resurrection of the body and the attainment of the world to come, it would seem logical that every insight into the meaning of Scripture leads us to a better assessment of what lies ahead at the end of time and reinforces our hope of eternal life.

In the Origenian tradition the second, third, and fourth meanings of Scripture have often been called comprehensively "the spiritual meaning" of the scriptural text. This expression often reveals some connection with a Platonic dualism of the "letter" (that is, literal meaning) and the "spirit" (the spiritual meaning). Consequently, "literal" (or "historical") and "spiritual" are antithetical terms, and they reveal the philosophical presupposition that all created reality is twofold: material (corruptible, transitory, and changing) and spiritual (incorruptible, lasting, and unchanging). In other words the "biblical dualism" of Origen (letter and spirit) is linked to a metaphysical dualism (matter and spirit) and also to an anthropological dualism (body and soul/spirit). This dualism, of course, is not radical and absolute, for it does not regard spirit and body as irreconcilable opposites linked essentially to good and evil and engaged in a cosmic battle. Rather, the relation of "letter" and "spirit" is itself double-sided. On the one hand, the terms denote radically opposed realities; on the other hand, they come from the same Creator and ultimately serve a common purpose. The "letter" of Scripture, which belongs to the tangible and the visible order, manifests—and thus serves—a deeper, spiritual meaning, while the "spiritual meaning" belongs to the world of the invisible and otherworldly. The letter and its innerworldly meaning (the literal sense) serve as sign and symbol, making the spiritual content manifest and accessible to the flesh. The letter both veils and reveals. Being "flesh," the sign cannot fully and adequately represent what it signifies, yet it nonetheless transfers to the level of the corporeal senses meanings of a higher order, which would be otherwise inaccessible and elusive to the human being whose intellect must always depart from information received through the senses.

Origen and the majority of the Church Fathers are indebted to a Platonic (or at least Platonizing) epistemology which regards the reports of sense perceptions and their understanding by the mind in terms of signs and symbols, images and analogies, rather than in terms of concepts formed in the mind by a process of abstraction. Consequently, due to its epistemological presuppositions, ancient exegesis does not seek, as its ultimate goal, to form clear and distinct concepts, nor does it aim at expressing in adequate and fully articulated terms the spiritual meaning uncovered. Rather, its ultimate goal is to provide an experiential encounter between the soul and the divine Word.

Beginning with Origen, throughout the patristic age, and into the greater half of the Middle Ages, one frequently meets the view that the goal of exegesis cannot be reached without the actual presence of the Spirit, for it is only through grace-given and faith-based encounters with the Word that the human subject can complete its journey from human word to divine meaning. Exegesis is the last phase of the revelatory process: the mind conforms to the divine Logos to appropriate the truth discovered in the text, while the will embraces the truth by consent and conformity as it appropriates the moral meaning. Thus the reader adheres to the Logos in the very act by which he understands the text. *"Amor ipse intellectus est,"* a famous phrase of Gregory the Great, one of the great followers of Origen's spiritual exegesis, succinctly summarizes such an exegetical experience.[11] This kind of exegesis distinguishes but does not isolate or separate intellect and will *in concreto* within the process of appropriating the spiritual meaning. Gregory's sentence, coined under Origen's influence, might be also the best illustration of how the "tropological" (moral) sense obtains its privileged place, as well as how the interpretation of the Bible is exercised with constant display of anthropological concerns which are applied to the individual's interior life.

Henri de Lubac devoted a chapter in his study of medieval exegesis to Bernard, Gregory, and Origen, to show that these three extraordinary practitioners of the four senses of the Bible stand in conscious succession and, through their disciples and their influence, determine the approach to the Bible for an astonishingly long period, almost a thousand years.[12] What we have presented reflects, quite specifically, the exegesis of these three great persons, but of course (as de Lubac hastens to point out), Ambrose, Jerome, and Augustine are also deeply indebted to Origen, the entire monastic exegesis of the Middle Ages is largely dependent on Gregory the Great, and Bernard's influence is vividly sensed up to and beyond late me-

11. *Hom. In Evang.* 27, 4 (PL 76, 1207), quoted explicitly by Saint Bernard in his *Sermones de Diversis* 29, 1, vol. VI–1 of *Sancti Bernardi Opera Omnia*, ed. J. Leclercq (Rome: Editiones Cistercienses, 1970), 201.

12. Henri de Lubac, *Medieval Exegesis*, trans. Mark Sebanc, vol. 1 (Grand Rapids, Mich.: Eerdmans, 2000), 153–62.

dieval times, because even writers as recent as Pascal and Blondel depended on him.[13] In our own day—as recently as the second half of the twentieth century—studies of St. Bernard went through a true renaissance, so that he continues to exercise his influence.[14]

For these ancient authors, true understanding of the biblical word comes about when the reader meets the personal Word of God and the content of the Bible becomes part of the reader's self-understanding. The meaning of the text is revealed not only through the letter, as if from outside, but simultaneously by the Spirit too, influencing the reader from within. The individual believer meets the Spirit who inspired the text: it is the same Spirit who moves him to conversion, to a life committed to faith and love. In this way the meaning of the text is integrated into the soul's reflection upon itself. The images and words of the text lead to inner illumination both rational and intuitive, by both reasoning and inner experience. The meaning of the text is ultimately conveyed by the Holy Spirit as an experience of the self mirroring the meaning expressed in the text.[15]

Therefore, one of the most important components of Origen's exegesis is a strongly emphasized mystical bent. The final point of the exegetical process is not a rational system of concepts and thoughts, but a spiritual encounter between God and the human soul communicating through the sacred text. Therefore, interpretation always involves prayerful attention to the "inner man" and the actual presence of God's Spirit enlightening the believer. The interpreter aims not to reach a merely intellectual comprehension of the text but to

13. Ibid., 160–61. De Lubac speaks of "the Gregorian Middle Ages," meaning Gregory the Great and not Gregory VII, ibid., 117–25. See, in addition, J. Chatillon, "L'influence de saint Bernard sur la scolastique" [The Influence of Saint Bernard on Scholasticism], *Saint Bernard théologien, Analecta S. Ordinis Cisterciensis* 9, 3–4 (1953): 268–88; and A. Forest, "Saint Bernard et notre temps," ibid.: 290–96.

14. See Denis Farkasfalvy, "Bernard the Theologian: Forty Years of Research," *Communio* 17, 4 (1990): 580–94.

15. The monastic exegesis of the twelfth century, reaching its peak in the spiritual exegesis of St. Bernard, is particularly sensitive to this aspect of Origen's heritage. Bernard believes that the reader *recognizes* in himself what he reads about in the biblical text. For him a major task of exegesis is to coordinate text with a spiritual experience, or, more precisely, to correlate the experience of the inspired author with that of the inspired reader.

experience the reality about which the text speaks, and thereby to encounter God, the ultimate speaker in each biblical passage.

Origen saw in the fourfold structure of the biblical meanings a reflection of human nature: "As the human being is made up of body, soul, and spirit, so is also Holy Scripture."[16] One cannot transcend the literal meaning without transcending the limits of one's own bodily senses. At times, one must admit, Origen's language was so strongly influenced by his Platonic sources that he seems to state that the exploration of the spiritual meaning of Scripture is little more than an intellectual ascent into the lofty regions of the human spirit. This aspect of his thought explains why in his texts at times the fourfold structure of biblical meanings, defined according to the pattern of salvation history (history, allegory, tropology, eschatology) collapses into a threefold pattern, in which the order is changed: letter, tropology, and allegory (the last of which is eventually extended to eschatology).[17]

The system of the threefold structure is patterned primarily on the triplet of a Platonist anthropology: body—soul—spirit. In this system, the analysis of the text by grammatical and literary means is followed by a symbolic interpretation, by which the text is made relevant to a human being's interior life. Often this second step is a bit ambiguous, for at times only in the subsequent step (in extracting the moral meaning) does it lead to specifically Christian (Christological and eschatological) considerations. When following this threefold order of scriptural senses, Origen was more likely to pursue a Platonic agenda without sufficient Christological control. It is in such cases that he tends to introduce a spiritual message that might resemble Gnostic speculations. This kind of exegetical endeavor owes more to the Hellenistic quest for liberating man from the body than to the gospel's message, with the latter's focus on saving

16. *Peri Archon* IV, 2, 4.

17. De Lubac speaks of "two formulas" and "the inversions" of the order of the spiritual senses: *Medieval Exegesis,* vol. 2, 90–115. This is considerably more nuanced than de Lubac's position on Origen's exegesis in an earlier book, in which he distinguished only three scriptural senses: *History and Spirit: The Understanding of Scripture according to Origen,* trans. A. E. Nash (San Francisco: Ignatius Press, 2008), 159–71.

the whole human being, body and soul, flesh and spirit, all together. Later tradition inherited from Origen both systems, the threefold and the fourfold, and preserved a certain ambiguity by eventually yielding to the Platonic anthropology presupposed by the three-step system. With a rebirth of Neo-Platonism at the end of the Middle Ages, the danger of mixing Christian mysticism with Platonic elements became less remote. Indeed, it became more prevalent under the growing influence of the anonymous (probably sixth-century) Greek writer today called Pseudo-Dionysius.[18] From the end of the twelfth century onward, his texts greatly affected medieval theologians and spiritual writers.

The Golden Age of Patristic Exegesis

Although the outline of Origen's exegetical system presented above is cursory at best, it may sufficiently convey the spirit in which the exegesis he had initiated kept on flourishing without interruption even beyond the end of the twelfth century. The "spiritual" meaning of the Bible, which Origen systematically explored for the first time, had many variant forms, but Origen's influence upon Christian exegesis stood unrivaled for at least a thousand years, not only in the East and in the school of Alexandria to which Origen himself belonged, but also in its rival, the school of Antioch, and in fact in the entire Christian tradition. In the Antiochian school more caution was raised both about the use of allegory and about Origen's personal heritage. Origen's name came under serious attack less than a century after his death. Yet his basic assumptions were hardly ever questioned. The Antiochian exegetes were just as devoted to the search for the text's "spiritual meaning" as he was.[19]

In this way all the great figures of patristic exegesis directly or indirectly fell under the influence of Origen. The Cappadocian Fathers (Basil the Great, his brother Gregory of Nyssa, and their friend,

18. His works were falsely attributed to Dionysius the Areopagite, a man whom St. Paul converted in Athens (Acts 17:34).
19. See Martin, *Sacred Scripture*, 260–62.

Gregory of Nazianzus) were greatly influenced by Origen, and they transmitted much of his legacy through their own writings. So did John Chrysostom, who belonged to the Antiochian school, as well as the great figures of the West, Ambrose, Jerome, and Augustine. When writing a commentary on the Gospel of Luke, Ambrose directly copied Origen. Although he was in later years a passionate anti-Origenist, Jerome had for years admired and imitated Origen and had undertaken the translation of several of his works. Although Augustine relied much on his own philosophical reflections based on another branch of Christian Platonism, in exegesis he still tried to develop Origen's thought further. The "golden age" of patristics—we mean mostly the Church Fathers of the fourth century—was the direct heir of Origen's exegetical program, seeking Christ on every page of the Bible.

Thus it was under Origen's influence that the great scriptural commentaries of the patristic age came about: Ambrose's *Commentary on Luke* and *Explanation of Psalm 118,* Augustine's *Expositions of the Psalms* and *Tractates on the Gospel of John,* John Chrysostom's *Homilies on Matthew,* Gregory of Nyssa's *Life of Moses* and *Commentary on the Song of Songs,* Jerome's commentaries, including those on Isaiah, Matthew, and the Minor Prophets. Of a later age but of equally influential importance were the scriptural commentaries of Gregory the Great: *Homilies on the Gospels, Moralia in Job, Commentaries on Ezekiel,* and *Commentaries on the Song of Songs.*

Patristic Thought on Inspiration and Scriptural Canon

In addition to his development of Christian exegesis, Origen made an important contribution to the theology of inspiration by inserting the material of previous Christian tradition into a systematic pattern of thought. He describes the authors of the Old Testament as prophetic figures who were given a proleptic (anticipatory, literally "forward springing") understanding of the Christological content of their prophecies, but had to express the prophetic message under the veil of images and symbols. We must not attempt to appropriate this concept in a modern historical sense, and thereby accuse it of naiveté: it does not suggest that Moses or Solomon or Isaiah knew the Christian dogmas but consciously kept quiet about them, expressing them only in hidden and symbolic ways. Rather, Origen (and his followers) thought of prophetic revelation as analogous to a mystical experience. He regarded such anticipatory knowledge of the God of Jesus Christ by "the Patriarchs and the Prophets" as true encounters with the Triune God and his salvific plan, but encounters shrouded in mystery and thus accompanied by an intuitive and, therefore, non-discursive, non-conceptual knowledge.

Following in the footsteps of Irenaeus, Origen interpreted the words of Jesus in John's gospel about Abraham—"Abraham, your father, rejoiced to see my day; he saw it and rejoiced" (8:56)—to mean that Abraham truly encountered his messianic Offspring and received a share in the messianic gifts of salvation. In the same vein, Irenaeus referred to Jesus' statement from John's gospel about Moses, "He wrote about me" (5:45), in order to explain that the scriptural authors knew about the mystery of the Son, if not with conceptual clarity, at least through the medium of intuitive religious experience. Origen's teaching agrees with and is partly based upon Irenaeus's anti-Gnostic message about the unity of the two Testaments. Irenaeus already explicitly held that all authentic knowledge and experience of God had to be an anticipation of the gifts of Christ because the Son is the only way to the Father (see Mt 11:25–30). This principle contains, therefore, nothing radically new, yet what was new in Origen was his wide-ranging application of the principle to every part of the Bible as well as his combining them with philosophical (mostly Platonic) principles of anthropology and epistemology.

Origen and the Church Fathers who followed him saw in the New Testament the sum total of the "apostolic writings" recognized as such by the Church. Furthermore, they held that the New Testament Scriptures contained a spiritual meaning exactly because they took their origins from the Apostles, who had been the first to receive the fullness of the Holy Spirit. For Origen the main consequence of biblical inspiration is the presence of a spiritual meaning under the letter. This spiritual meaning found its way into all biblical texts through their inspired authors (the prophets and the Apostles), who were led into a deeper knowledge of God's thoughts and were moved by the Spirit to express it in oral and/or written form. The task of the exegete is to explore the inspired text and to reach, under the guidance of the Spirit—the same Spirit that had influenced the author—an analogous spiritual experience, thus rediscovering the spiritual (that is, Spirit-induced) meaning.

In terms of this inner, spiritual experience, there is a two-tiered analogy between the inspired author and the inspired exegete. The first involves the level of the material universe, that is, the "letter" of the Bible (or the history which it expresses) and the second involves the level of spiritual existence, where author and exegete are linked to God's Holy Spirit, who elicits analogous insights and experiences in the writer and the reader, in the human author and interpreter of the scriptural text. Thus the exegete is a spiritual disciple of the prophets and the Apostles. In Origen, therefore, the model of spiritual exegesis is intimately linked with a particular model of biblical inspiration. This basic model remained central for the Church's biblical culture until the beginning of the Renaissance.

By Origen's time, the list of inspired books was consciously formulated and protected. The oldest such Christian canon of the Old Testament still extant comes from Melito, bishop of Sardis (died 190), while the oldest list of the books of the New Testament is the Fragment of Muratori, also from the end of the second century. However, the earliest formal decisions about a full scriptural canon that we know of only took place as late as the fourth and fifth centuries. The first such decision under a bishop of Rome was at a local (not ecumenical) synod of Rome in 384 convened by Pope Damasus. It lists in full the canonical books, including both Old and New Testaments. It contains forty-five books of the Old Testament canon, including the deutero-canonical books which later the Protestant reformers refused to admit into the canon. Its order follows that of the Septuagint, that is, its sequence ends with the "Prophets," not with the "Writings" as in the Jewish canon. It contains all the twenty-seven books of the New

Testament canon which are today shared by Catholic, Protestant, and Orthodox Christians. With a slight variation in the order of the books, it lists the Pauline letters right after the gospels, and names the Acts of the Apostles after the Catholic epistles. It concludes with the Book of Revelation.

The doubts about the canon that emerged sporadically during the patristic era need not be exaggerated. They surfaced in connection with heresies that seemed to base their separatist doctrines on one or another book. For example, the Montanists of the third century, in their literal interpretation of the Book of Revelation, created doubts about its apostolic origin and canonical status, but could not prevail over the Church's established conviction, which maintained both its Johannine origin and its place in the canon. Similarly the Epistle to the Hebrews, when included among the Pauline letters, provoked reaction, starting with Dionysius of Alexandria, who on a stylistic basis doubted the Pauline authorship of the book. Nevertheless, such controversies only raised concerns or at most challenged the authority of a particular book; none of these challenges led to the rejection of any of these books from the canon. The brevity of Second and Third John, as well as doubts whether their author, "the presbyter," was identical with John the Apostle, prompted similar doubts about their apostolic status, but they too have never been excluded from the canon. On the other hand, the respect surrounding First Clement, the anonymous Epistle of Barnabas, the *Didache,* and some other ancient Christian books, led to their inclusion in some of the comprehensive biblical codices, like the Codex Vaticanus (fourth century) and the Codex Alexandrinus (fifth century). But this was not enough to establish a place in the canon for them. The sorting out of the canonical books from among the apocryphal books—which had been disqualified on account of their heretical doctrine, late origin, or legendary content— was finally completed by the fourth century. The canon of Scriptures became so firmly rooted in the Church's tradition and practice that until the time of the Reformation this issue rarely brought forth major dispute or even required much attention.

What caused the Church of the fourth century to continue wrestling with the norms of orthodoxy was not the problem of the canon, but the question of applying philosophical concepts and terms to define the precise meaning of the apostolic faith. As is well known, the fourth and fifth centuries gave rise to a long chain of controversies, heresies, and excommunications in matters of Trinitarian and Christological doctrine. In all these exchanges, both sides on the various issues accepted the same inspired texts, but disagreed on their interpretation. At the end of each Trinitarian and Christological dispute, the Church formulated its final position by using both biblical and non-biblical terms, the latter being borrowed from philosophy, incorporating words like "essence" or "substance" (οὐσία), "person" (πρόσωπον), and "nature" φύσις). These newly formulated positions signaled the victory of a certain type of exegesis that was open to the intellectual life of Hellenism, willing to engage in philosophical discourse, and ready to use philosophy to digest, order, and systematize the biblical data. By such decisions, the ecumenical councils took the position that Christian theology had nothing to fear from entering into thought systems developed outside of Christianity in order to appropriate concepts and insights found valuable for the faith.

We might also say that, following these ecumenical councils, Christians declared that it was legitimate to use and transform Hellenistic concepts to express Christian content, and, for that matter, to take over elements of ancient cultural tradition. Thus, in the patristic era, Christian thought not only advanced a program of Christological exegesis for each page of the Bible, but also declared its intention to appropriate all valid features of mankind's intellectual heritage. By doing so, Christianity completed the process which had begun with the apostolic Church: it ended its formerly exclusive immersion in the cultural realm that formed the Bible and embraced cultural universalism as the logical extension of the missionary universalism of the gospel (see Mt 28:18–20; Col 1:5–6). From the point of view of cultural history, by these decisions about creedal statements the Church formally linked together two cultural spheres that had already run the course of mutual interpenetration for several centuries: biblical thought and Hellenistic culture.

In their exegetical work the Church Fathers showed little familiarity with most of the critical problems that occupy center stage in modern biblical research. Even so, they paid much attention to the faithful preservation of the authentic text of the Bible. The best illustration is, of course, Origen's *Hexapla*, but text criticism was not limited only to him. For the Latin Church the most important textual problem was to produce a faithful translation with respectable literary quality for the entire Bible, a work to which St. Jerome dedicated much of his life. While earlier Latin translations of the Bible (generally referred to as the "old" Latin version, or the *Vetus Latina*) depended on the Septuagint, Jerome emphasized throughout his life the importance of what he called *"Hebraica veritas."*[20] By this he meant the normative use of the Hebrew text for the Old Testament over against its Greek translation in the Septuagint. By editing the Vulgate on the basis of the Hebrew text, he became, and remained, the foremost interpretive authority of the Western Church.

One of the key features of patristic biblical exegesis was the breadth of its perspective, which enabled it to serve diverse readers and audiences. The greatest figures among the patristic exegetes considered it their task to excel on all levels, by commenting, on the one hand, on sophisticated theological questions, and serving the daily needs of ordinary Christians on the other. The Cappadocians, along with Ambrose, Augustine, and the two "Great" popes, Leo I and Gregory I, served both as theologians and pastors of their flock. As a result, besides biblical commentaries, they left behind sermons addressing the widest communities of the faithful, delivering deep and insightful thoughts that even today do not fail to impress and edify the most varied circles of readers. Their short biblical homilies can at once nourish the simplest believers with accessible food and provide the most learned with theological explorations of great depth. Throughout the Middle Ages, spiritual writers kept on quoting a saying by Gregory the Great, a marvelously formulated guideline,

20. Bruce M. Metzger, *The Bible in Translation* (Grand Rapids, Mich.: Baker Academic, 2001), 29–32.

which itself expresses deep truth in simple language: "Scripture is like an immense sea in which a little lamb might safely walk, and yet even an elephant is forced to swim."[21] In the Bible the simplest faithful—the little lamb—may safely find instruction, while the heaviest champions of the intellect must struggle to penetrate the mysteries of divine revelation without being engulfed by them.

21. *Letter to Leander*, introductory to the *Moralia in Job* (PL 75, 615a).

VII. SCRIPTURE IN THE MIDDLE AGES

The Role of the Bible in the Middle Ages

In the patristic era both theology and Christian life were based on the interpretation of the Bible. In the liturgy and in theological disputes the reading of biblical texts guaranteed close contact with the written records of revelation issuing from the preaching of God's inspired word by "prophets and Apostles." At the same time, the Church learned that the letter by itself is sterile and dead, and thus the Church's living tradition must remain the context for interpretation; in other words, interpretation must be under the influence of the Spirit and under the teaching authority of the successors of the Apostles. The content of Scripture was not conceived of as some abstract theoretical system of truth, but as a spiritual reality reproduced in the minds and souls of the faithful under the actual influence of the Holy Spirit. The preservation and the interpretation of the sacred writings were linked to all other facets of church life: sacramental practice, the hierarchy's activities of teaching and governing the faithful with power received through apostolic succession, and, to no little extent, the spiritual experiences of Christians at large.

During the Middle Ages the Church continued reading, listening to, and interpreting the biblical word in this context. As all Europe became Christian, the Bible also became the core and backbone of culture. Biblical texts exercised a decisive influence upon every aspect of learning. The arts focused on biblical topics. The Latin Bible, the Vulgate, left an indelible mark on medieval Latin, the language of learning and international contacts as well as of church life. The Vulgate also made a major impact on the nascent languages of modern Europe and even on their slowly unfolding vernacular literature. The stories, images, and symbols of the Bible became part of the basic treasure of Western culture, and much of this literature appeared in every aspect of daily life: new concepts and formulas, proverbs and popular sayings. In every walk of life, if one wished to function in an intellectual role, one had to appropriate a great deal of biblical knowledge. For centuries—actually up to and even beyond the Renaissance—Christian Europe was held together by long-lasting ties of cultural unity, which kept Europe's culture together even after its political unity had disintegrated. Ultimately, what held the culture of Christian Europe together was the general vision of salvation history—the basic story line of the Bible—which explained every human being's origin, place, role, and destination, and provided practically all educated people with the same experience of the world's order, coherence, and purpose.[1]

In the Middle Ages, theology was regarded as nothing more than interpreting the *Sacra Pagina,* that is, the biblical text. St. Thomas Aquinas in his *Summa Theologiae* uses the terms *sacra doctrina* and *sacra scriptura* in a mutually inclusive sense and considers the explanation of the Bible as the central task of theology.[2]

In one respect, however, the medieval use of the Bible is patently different from that of the Church Fathers. The separation of Western culture from the use of the Greek language brought about some important changes, comparable only to the loss of contact with the original Hebrew texts that occurred during the early patristic age.

1. See the classic work by Beryl Smalley, *The Study of the Bible in the Middle Ages* (Oxford: Blackwell, 1952), and a broad collection of essays about the role of the Bible in the Middle Ages in *Le Moyen Age et la Bible,* ed. P. Riché and G. Lobichon (Paris: Beauchesne, 1984).

2. This tendency begins with Abelard and becomes the explicit program of exegesis at the medieval universities in the thirteenth century, as is documented by Jacques Verger, "L'exégese de l'Université," in *Le Moyen Age et la Bible,* 217–18. Verger mentions the conjectural statistics of the commentators, according to whom, in St. Thomas's *Summa,* from among a total of about 38,000 quotations, only about 4,300 come from Aristotle but about 8,000 from Christian authors and 25,000 from the Bible.

After the collapse of the Roman Empire, in the new Carolingian culture, both exegesis and theological discourse grew apart from the Septuagint and, in general, from the original texts of the New Testament. Augustine might have been the first major Christian theologian whose knowledge of Greek was deficient. After him, more often than not, Latin exegetes followed the text of the Vulgate and, as a rule, were unequipped to deal with the Greek text. In spite of all its imperfection and obscurity, the Latin text had to be used as the point of departure for all exegetical endeavors. Textual problems in the original languages of the biblical books naturally fell into oblivion. In the Latin Church ancient textual variants survived only by exception or by accident, either in translated patristic texts or in some passages of the *Vetus Latina* preserved in the liturgy.[3] Yet the original text was not fully forgotten. Even the meaning of many Hebrew words—at least their popular etymology—remained known from the continued use of St. Jerome's *Nomina Hebraica*.

Medieval exegetes, even if little acquainted with problems of textual criticism, were often aware that the Church Fathers used for a given passage variant textual forms and attached important theological ideas to the variants. So, for example, an ancient variant of Lamentations 4:20 kept on being translated in sermons and treatises with the following wording deriving from the Septuagint: *"Spiritus ante faciem nostram Christus Dominus; sub umbra illius vivimus inter Gentes"* ("Before our face the Spirit is Christ the Lord; under his shadow we live among the pagans").[4] Even if the literal meaning of this variant text appeared obscure, a sophisticated Christological meaning was attached to it already in the early second century,

3. So, for example, several of the introits and offertory and communion antiphons sung in Gregorian chant preserved the Old Latin texts of the Psalms, especially in the oldest parts of the missal, like masses in Lent.

4. Today one translates the Hebrew text of this verse in the following way: "The breath of our nostrils, the Lord's Anointed was taken in their pits, he of whom we said: 'Under his shadow we live among the nations'" (RSV). About the history of this text see Jean Daniélou, "Christos Kyrios," *Recherches de sciences religieuses* 39 (1952): 338–52. Daniélou claims that this biblical variant and its exegesis go back to apostolic times and were preserved in a variant reading different from both the Massoretic text and the Septuagint.

which became widely known and was used by many Church Fathers, like Origen, Ambrose, and Gregory the Great. It returned with frequency in the works of St. Bernard of Clairvaux, and under his influence appeared in the Cistercian tradition.[5]

Another example is an old variant of Genesis 4:7 found in the Septuagint and translated in a somewhat strange way by the *Vetus Latina*. In that form it became widely known probably on account of its use in the penitential liturgy of the third century.[6] Among other places, it shows up in St. Ambrose's texts, whence it could have been disseminated widely.[7] According to this variant, after the murder of Abel, Cain (and thus everybody guilty of a grave sin) was addressed by God: *"Peccasti? Quiesce."* ("Did you sin? Calm down.") Its application to a penitent was probably this: should you be guilty of a grave sin, you must first withdraw from church life and stay in the rank of public sinners. The way St. Bernard quotes it leaves no doubt that the reader is supposed to recognize the text as a well-known biblical line: "Behold again a voice comes from the clouds and says: Have you sinned? Calm down."[8] But, of course, in Bernard's time public penance did not exist any longer, so the textual variant's meaning was "spiritualized": the converted sinner must not throw himself into exaggerated acts of mortification but must first abstain from further sins.[9] So, in spite of the fact that the Vulgate, following the Hebrew text, offers a substantially different translation of the verse, the variant reading that follows the Septuagint survived in the Latin tradition for at least a thousand years.

One is tempted to say that, for the patristic and medieval tradition of the West, the verbal accuracy of a biblical quotation was less important than it had been for Origen and his immediate disciples; consequently, medieval authors became less interested in text-critical

---

5. Jean Daniélou, "Saint Bernard et les Pères Grecs" [Saint Bernard and the Greek Fathers], in *Saint Bernard théologien, Analecta S. Ordinis Cisterciensis* 9, 3–4 (1953): 46–55.

6. *Apostolic Constitutions* II, 15.

7. *De paenitentia* II, 11, *Sources chrétiennes* vols. 79, 196.

8. The Septuagint has the statement built into a divine oracle from heaven: "κύριος εἶπεν . . . ἥμαρτες ἡσύχασον."

9. *De conversione ad clericos* 8 (*Sancti Bernardi Opera Omnia* IV, 80). The critical edition by Jean Leclercq does not identify this scriptural allusion.

questions or in the inadequacies of biblical translations, including, of course, the Vulgate. But this might not have been entirely so. Although philological studies did, indeed, decline, Augustine's theory about the multiple meanings of a text continued to be upheld and even gained ground in the early Middle Ages. Students of the biblical texts remained interested in textual variants but not necessarily with the intention of eliminating them for an amended text. Rather, the variants were regarded as parallel paths offering access to the deeper riches of the biblical text and were handled not as competitors from among which one had to choose, but as complements entitled as such to "equal opportunity" in representing the original text.

We must, however, avoid underestimating the perspicacity of the medieval exegete. One is again and again surprised at how stubbornly the demand for "authenticity" resurfaces in the course of history, as various reform movements make their appearance in the history of the Church. First the Carolingian reform of the ninth century, then the so-called Gregorian reform of the eleventh, which then blossomed into a true "renaissance" of patristic culture during the twelfth century, all show a high concern for authenticity. It prompted reforms in the liturgy and led to re-examination of the Church's books, including the biblical texts. An interesting figure in this medieval quest for authenticity is one of the founders as well as the organizer of early Cîteaux, St. Stephen Harding, the most important initiator of the influential Cistercian movement of the twelfth century. While, on the one hand, he sent monks to Metz to find authentic documents for renewing Gregorian chant, he also launched a re-edition of the Vulgate. The product of this labor, a gorgeously illustrated copy of the Bible—the so-called Bible of St. Bernard (truly of St. Stephen Harding)—survived the destruction of Cîteaux in the French Revolution and was eventually preserved in the Municipal Library of Dijon. In it we can follow the efforts of Stephen Harding to revise various parts of the Latin Old Testament in consultation with Jewish rabbis about the precise meaning of numerous Hebrew words and phrases.[10] Another

10. See A. Lang, "Die Bibel Stephan Hardings" [The Bible of Stephen Harding], *Cistercienser-Chronik* 51 (1939): 250–56.

example is found fifty years later in the efforts of Andrew of St. Victor, who tried to establish the exact meaning of certain passages by working with Jewish experts on the original Hebrew text.[11]

From the patristic era, without interruption, Origen continued to influence Latin medieval exegetes. While Origen's works were systematically destroyed in the East on account of accusations of heresy, Latin translations of many of his texts, made by St. Jerome and Rufinus, continued to be copied and read throughout the Latin Middle Ages. A catalogue of the monastic library of Clairvaux, dated from the end of the twelfth century, shows that the monastery of St. Bernard possessed all of Origen's works that were available in Latin.

The Continuation of Patristic Exegesis

In the Middle Ages the Origenian scheme of patristic exegesis remained practically intact. All Scripture was read as a reflection on Christ. This Christological meaning was explored by a habitual use of allegory. The allegorical meaning was extended into moral and eschatological themes, "tropology" and "anagogy." In medieval monasticism the last two meanings obtained new emphasis. The preponderance of the "moral" meaning became a characteristic feature of a new branch of interpretation: monastic exegesis, which produced innumerable commentaries and sermons on topics of cloistered life, the practice of humility, obedience, celibate chastity, and the observance of monastic customs. What we call today "spirituality" or "the theology of spiritual life" found frequent expression in the literary form of monastic "homilies," real or fictitious sermons and chains of sermons commenting on favorite scriptural texts verse by verse.[12]

11. Smalley calls him "a Hebraist of the twelfth century" in *The Study of the Bible in the Middle Ages*, 112–85.

12. The medieval monastic sermons represent less the preaching than the writing of the monks. Although the monastic schedule provided for frequent preaching by the abbot, the exact wording of the sermons did not survive except as outlines or literary elaborations, based on memory. Contrary to the audiences of St. Augustine, in medieval monasteries the skill of shorthand was not known. But more importantly sermons or homilies like those of St. Bernard's *Super Missus Est* or many of the liturgical sermons like those of Isaac of Stella must be regarded as chapters of an ongoing commentary fictitiously framed as a chain of sermons for a feast.

In this practice they followed Origen, Augustine, and Gregory the Great, along with anonymous sources spuriously attributed to these famous authors. One of the most preferred scriptural texts, on which numerous allegorical commentaries were written previously, was the Song of Songs. In a similar way we find series of sermons on gospel texts, Pauline epistles, or the texts of the prophets. Thus, even in its choice of topics, medieval monasticism remained in direct contact with patristic exegesis. But now the audiences (who were readers more often than hearers) represented different social groups. The sermons of Augustine or Ambrose or of the Cappadocian Fathers regularly addressed lay communities of the late Roman Empire, receiving instruction from their bishops. The monastic sermon was directed to more select groups: the ascetically trained monastic communities of the eleventh and twelfth centuries.

A significant novelty was the appearance of the mendicant orders (Franciscans and Dominicans) evangelizing the cities. The history of these orders shows their indebtedness to medieval exegesis. When on his preaching journeys seeking to convert the Albigensians (dualistic heretics in southern France), St. Dominic carried with him in two small volumes the most important scriptural texts: the Gospel of Matthew and the epistles of St. Paul. Clearly, he was preaching in an environment where the exact quotation of Scripture was considered highly important.

Under the influence of the mendicants, theology and biblical exegesis took a new turn. Adopting the new methods of learning taught in urban schools and universities, theology shifted toward a new orientation. Now called scholasticism, this new brand of learning, which was more closely joined to philosophy, adopted a new approach to exegesis. While remaining deeply rooted in the Church Fathers, scholastic exegesis was also intimately connected with the revival of classical philosophy and, specifically, with a newly acquired interest in Greek philosophical resources. Scholastic exegesis did not shy away from allegory, yet it paid more attention to the literal meaning and focused less on the moral sense. Rather than providing guidance for the individual in his quest for sanctity, the scholastic exegete tried to build objective systems of teaching in which public revelation was explored by the use of reason—of course, under the guidance of faith and the enlightening grace of the Holy Spirit. Typically, the scholastic exegete, more focused on providing concepts and proofs for building a theological system, shows less interest in promoting the distinctive spirituality of a religious community, the particular way of life which separates them from the world. The scholastic exegete was likewise less interested in imitating the ornate style of the ancient Church Fathers who, as children of their times, were highly skilled in oratorical style and well trained in ancient rhetoric. The objective of a scholastic exegete was closer to teaching than to exhortation; the scriptural commentaries produced by scholasticism read more like class lectures than like festive homilies or poetic exhortations addressing the emotions.

The scholastic exegete was quite aware that his approach to theology carried two dimensions: since it involved both reason and faith, it read from both the "book of nature" and the "book of Scripture." Yet his approach was never rationalistic; the goal of learning was to lead from faith to faith, offering foundational (philosophical) truth for supporting and explaining the act of faith, or elaborating on the content of faith by means of rational discourse. Thus, though the ultimate goal of exegesis remained the same as before—to enable the individual's inner encounter with God—the mystical components of this ultimate goal were being pushed further out onto the horizon so that, at times, they appeared marginalized. Contrary to what some surveys of the history of exegesis might suggest, for St. Thomas the fourfold meaning of the Bible remained as foundational as it had been in previous centuries.[13] In the *Summa Theologiae* (I, 1, 10) Thomas demonstrates the place that spiritual exegesis obtained in the scholastic system: while the literary sense of the text must be investigated in the first place and must be unambiguously identified, in the Bible the reality signified by the text has further significance, which the ex-

13. See Francis Martin, *Sacred Scripture: The Disclosure of the Word* (Naples, Fla.: Sapientia, 2006), 266–69.

egete is invited to explore. This further or extended meaning is found in the context of the mystery of Christ and this mystery's moral and eschatological implications. The various "further" meanings should not make for ambiguity in the text, but rather should only indicate its rich and multifaceted character. St. Thomas himself practiced spiritual exegesis in his somewhat less known and only partially edited scriptural commentaries. It is no mere coincidence that he died in the Cistercian monastery of Fossanuova, while commenting to the monks on the text of the Song of Songs.

Medieval Theology of Inspiration and Interpretation

Medieval theologians did not create a new theology of biblical inspiration or a new theological hermeneutics, nor did they examine either of these topics in themselves but always together with other subjects. They made frequent reference to inspiration in the context of revelation: they said that Scripture was rooted in a supernatural knowledge of which the human mind by itself is incapable. In this light the medieval and, especially, the scholastic theologian was not as much interested in how the Bible was produced as in how the relationship between human mind and divine enlightenment, between natural and supernatural knowledge, was to be conceived. Therefore, St. Thomas himself does not treat the question of biblical inspiration in the way modern theologians do. Rather, he studies in a detailed fashion both the concept and the different kinds of prophetic knowledge, since he considers a large part of the Bible to be the product of prophetic inspiration.[14] Consequently, Thomists and neo-Thomists like to use Thomas's thought on prophecy for developing a scholastic theology of biblical inspiration. The Thomistic doctrine of bibli-

14. See *Summa Theologiae* II–II, 171–77, with Hans Urs von Balthasar's commentary, *Thomas von Aquin: Besondere Gnadengaben und die zwei Wege des menschlichen Lebens: Kommentar zur Summa Theologica II–II, 171–182* [Thomas Aquinas: Special Charisms and the Two Ways of Human Life: Commentary on the Summa Theologica II–II, 171–82], vol. 23 of *Die Deutsche Thomas-Ausgabe,* ed. H. M. Christmann (Vienna: Pustet, 1958); or from the more limited perspective of modern scholasticism the essays by Pierre Benoit, O.P., *Inspiration and the Bible,* trans. J. Murphy-O'Connor and M. Keverne (New York: Sheed and Ward, 1965).

cal inspiration, however, is more about what St. Thomas would have thought on biblical inspiration than about what he actually taught on the subject.[15] Yet, in scholastic theories of inspiration, "instrumental causality" *(causa instrumentalis),* by which St. Thomas habitually explains the interplay of divine and human causes, rightfully began to take central importance.

According to this view, God must be seen as the "principal cause" *(causa principalis)* of the sacred texts. Since God is responsible for all the results of his inspirational influence, he must be considered to be fully the "author" of each and every text, and of each text as a whole, with all its particular characteristics. But this divine causality (authorship) is mediated by the instruments he uses, instruments that are time-bound and possibly deficient, namely, the human authors who act with their personal and time-bound limitations when writing their texts according to the conditions of their own times and cultures. The text is the product of both the divine Author and a human one; the two are not in conflict because of the subordination implied by the scheme of instrumentality. St. Thomas depicts the functioning of a divine cause influencing the human intellect and will, while keeping in evidence all of what he teaches elsewhere about the cooperation of a free finite human subject and the infinite and absolute divine First Cause. The idea that the inspired human authors are like "instruments in God's hands" had already been formed and affirmed by many Church Fathers. Yet the images and comparisons which they had used left open the question of what kind of instrumentality they had in mind. Is the human author used as an instrument in the way a pen, a chisel, or a musical instrument would produce its effect in the hands of a scribe, an artist, or a musician? Or is the instrument mechanically transmitting the instructions which it receives from above? Is the human author like the pipe of an aqueduct, passively allowing water to run through it? Or is it like the flute that produces sound exactly as the artist determines

15. Theological textbooks of the early twentieth century often pretended to be articulating St. Thomas's actual teaching, but Aquinas never asked the question of how divine and human actions had jointly produced the Bible.

it?[16] The merit of St. Thomas's system consisted in philosophically deepening the idea of instrumental causality and showing that in the case of biblical inspiration the Absolute Divine Cause fully and totally dominates the instrument by causing it to cause what God intends, while at the same time allowing it to remain a free human agent.

A Retrospective View

Among modern theologians, medieval exegesis prompts a double response of admiration and criticism. Contemporary theologians can admire the rich, multifaceted use of the biblical texts, the unity of exegesis and theology, and the uniting of spirituality and doctrine, but in more than a few points they may be baffled by the liberties medieval theologians take in exegesis. The points of criticism are the following.

Although medieval exegetes often showed interest in linguistic, critical, and literary issues and thus concern themselves (usually at the beginning of the exegetical discourse) with the context *(consequentia)* or the internal logic and structure *(ordo et rationes)* of a passage, they often seem to have taken such matters much too lightly or with a measure of negligence. Clearly, their concern was to build theological systems, or to explore the human experience of spiritual life, or just to discover intricate and spirited relationships between various biblical passages, terms, and expressions.

For a contemporary reader of medieval texts there are two specific areas of discomfort. On the one hand, exegesis becomes overburdened by symbolism and allegory; on the other hand, the exegetical language is so filled with key-terms and cryptic references to various allegorical systems that it begins to resemble a code language of signs and symbols. Looking back at medieval culture, modern-day readers of ancient exegetical texts may feel disoriented. One is not always sure of the grounds on which biblical passages are transposed into a system of theological reference. Even when reading them with

16. The two meanings ("pipe" and "flute") of the Latin word *fistula* are not always distinguishable in ancient Latin texts.

a concordance of the Vulgate in hand, we might experience difficulties in following the cross-references of words and images that weave a tapestry of concepts, symbols, biblical expressions, and technical terms into a maze of hints or allusions, sometimes immersed in puzzling cultural tidbits.[17]

In medieval exegesis the relationship between interpretation and philosophical reflection is often unclear. Lacking a sense for the historical dimension of reality (at least in the modern sense of the term), the medieval exegete may not realize that he must not force upon the biblical text the concepts and the terminology of another culture or age. Medieval exegesis is, therefore, like a kaleidoscope. It is full of shiny items, including many true gems, but also objects that are like glass beads or false gold, appealing to the eye but without lasting value.

Following in the footsteps of patristic exegesis, medieval authors also believed that the ultimate content of the sacred text is the spiritual reality to which it refers, which can be fully explored only under the influence of grace and in the intimacy of a believer's soul. Thus the exegete considered his own work as an inspired activity, undertaken by the same Spirit who inspired the biblical author. These two kinds of inspiration are not conceived of as identical, but analogous. However, in exploring the analogy, the exegetes might use the same images and symbols to describe the inspiration of the author as that of the reader. Terms like "revelation" and "inspiration" are not restricted to their specific technical sense, that is, the original acts by which the constitutive events of salvation history were caused and enshrined in the Scriptures. Rather, both terms are applied not only to what "the prophets and Apostles" experienced, but also to what a later exegete of their texts might discover or feel (*sentitur,* meaning "to sense") when interpreting the Bible. From this perspective it is very difficult to distinguish a personal, subjective experience while reading the Bible from what, for the sake of all mankind, has

17. One example may suffice. In the eighty-six sermons of St. Bernard on the *Song of Songs,* the critical edition has identified more than five thousand scriptural quotations. This means one biblical reference for every two or three lines. The result is that, as some writers concluded, St. Bernard "speaks the Bible," turning his comments into little more than chains of biblical phrases and quotations.

happened only once as a foundational event of salvation history. Of course, what happened initially is documented in the Bible for the sake of establishing a paradigm normative for all subsequent ages.[18]

The Renaissance and the Reformation managed to shake the very foundations of medieval culture and theology. At that time the unsolved issues of medieval exegesis erupted and greatly contributed to the intellectual and spiritual crisis which followed. It became clear that the theoretical foundation of medieval biblical interpretation was insufficient for a new age, in which the demand for "objective" truth as opposed to its "subjective" perception became the central issue—a methodological issue evolving mostly from a newly discovered concept of nature, which in turn led to the development of the natural sciences. The humanists of the Renaissance rediscovered and deepened the linguistic, textual, and critical issues that had been simmering since the time of Origen. At the same time, the leaders of the Reformation began their fight for the supremacy of individual interpretation, appealing to the masses, for whom they provided translations of the biblical texts in the vernacular. They went out to champion as the only authentic way leading to salvation the rights of personal interpretation under the direct influence of the Holy Spirit. In response came the movement of the Counter-Reformation, spearheaded by the Council of Trent, which defined the basic questions of the faith about the Christian Bible: the nature and source of its inspiration, the full list of the scriptural canon, and the role of the Church's Tradition and Magisterium in biblical interpretation.

18. The idea finds its marvelous classical expression by St. Bernard: *"Hoc semel contulit universitati: hoc quotidie singuli in nobis actitari sentimus"* [This happened once for all mankind, this each one of us experiences to be happening inside of us every day] *Sermo super Cantica* 16, 2, vol. 1 of *Sancti Bernardi Opera Omnia,* ed. J. Leclercq (Rome: Editiones Cistercienses, 1958), 90. But we discover, at the same time, the flip side of the concept explained by de Lubac under the subtitle *"Quotidie"* (that is, "each day," contrasted in the ancient texts with *"semel,"* or once) in his *Medieval Exegesis,* vol. 2, 134–43.

VIII. THE BIBLE AND BIBLICAL THEOLOGY IN THE MODERN CHURCH

The End of Medieval Exegesis

Much of the Middle Ages (at least as early as the ninth century) could be characterized as a chain of repeated "renaissances" or "returns to the sources," which meant, in terms of Christian history, efforts to return to both the cultural standards of classical antiquity and the apostolic sources of the faith. An early example of such movements is the "Carolingian renaissance," a movement promoted by the imperial court of Charlemagne and his successors. Another example is found in the reform of the monasteries of the eleventh and twelfth centuries after the Gregorian Reform and, subsequently, in the various waves of early scholasticism flourishing at medieval universities.

A major break with the past, however, is represented by the fifteenth century's humanistic renaissance. In contrast to the biblical renewals of earlier movements, there appeared at this time a new eagerness to cultivate the original Hebrew and Greek texts of the Bible and to demand a new theological discourse based on the authentic form and meaning of the texts, well understood and thoroughly analyzed by linguistic and grammatical tools. This new preoccupation with the biblical languages brought to an end the monopoly of the Vulgate and the monolingual world of the medieval Latin biblical culture. The new movement was welcomed with enthusiasm by many Catholics. The first Greek printed edition of the New Testament was prepared by Erasmus and appeared in print in 1516, just one year before the Reformation; the first printed Hebrew Old Testament, that of Cardinal Ximenez, was published in 1522. Both were fruits grown from trees planted by the humanists of the fifteenth century.

Renaissance and Reformation: Impact on the Study of the Bible

The next logical step taken by the Reformers was the translation of the Bible into the vernacular tongues of Europe. Partly due to the invention of typography and its quick application to the Bible, these new texts literally inundated the Christian world of the modern age, bringing the Bible to the masses. Since they were made from the original Hebrew and Greek texts, they claimed superiority prima facie—regardless of their particular merit—over the Vulgate. As the Reformers and their Catholic opponents became engaged in fierce confessional disputes about a whole series of doctrinal issues, the variance of the Vulgate from the Hebrew or Greek text became a theological and confessional issue to be used for proving or disproving doctrinal matters. The study of the Church Fathers also acquired a new apologetic edge, since both the Reformers and their opponents tried to prove that their doctrine coincided with that of the early Church in its pure and uncorrupted form.

Nonetheless, the spiritual exegesis practiced in the Middle Ages still continued to play an important role. Although allegorical exegesis was, in principle, not admitted in apologetic debate,[1] both sides remained convinced that Christian interpretation needed the guidance of the Holy Spirit. But while the Catholic side operated on the assumption that the guidance of the Spirit reached the faithful also through the teaching office of the Church (the Magisterium), Protestants considered the Spirit's guidance to be at work only in the private realm of the conscience. Thus for the Reformers, the old

---

1. This was not a new practice. St. Thomas himself states that in a doctrinal dispute (*argumentum*) one can use only the literal sense. For such, the allegorical sense (*ea quae secundum allegoriam sunt*) is to be excluded. After that, to show that this is a traditional principle, he quotes St. Augustine (*Summa Theologiae* I, 1, 10 ad 1).

practice of spiritual exegesis involving the subjectivity of a person's inner experience offered evidence for supporting the newly stated Protestant principle *sola scriptura*. This principle eventually became central to the Reformers' use of Scripture, and when fully articulated and consistently applied, it became a basic postulate of their theological method. To be demonstrated validly in this new historical context, all articles of faith had to be shown to be literally and explicitly present in the biblical text, and, in addition, the truths of faith needed to be "discovered" or "recognized" in the text by the individual believer within the realm of his own faith experience. Therefore, each person needed direct access to the truth of the Bible through personal exposure to the inspired biblical text by means of a vernacular translation, the only one which each believer could personally understand. The new Christian confessions all proclaimed that the only road to the revealed truth was by direct exposure, or, in other words, a personal reading of the Bible. Thus the Bible became a necessary tool of salvation not only for the Church in general but for every individual. The possession by a majority of individual believers of a reliable and precise translation of the biblical text and thus its distribution to the masses became a fundamental requirement. Once this condition had been achieved, the individual Christian was equipped to pass judgment over any theological utterance coming from tradition.

Of course, these convictions did not keep the leading figures in the various new confessions from formulating and imposing on their followers their own formulation of the faith and also, therefore, their interpretations of the various biblical passages. Nor did the Reformers refrain from attributing a measure of authority to their interpretive assertions, which they promulgated by their preaching and teaching, and to the various "confessional" formulas with which they defined their position on the main issues. Even so, in principle all authority had to be derived from the Bible as interpreted in the individual's interior realm.

The Reformers continued to follow most of the traditional teaching on inspiration. They considered the Bible to have had God as its author, who created it under the influence of the Holy Spirit; as such it was an infallible source of faith, lacking any error. In matters of the canon of the New Testament, they also remained in agreement with the Catholic Church. However, for the Old Testament, they soon begin to adopt, in agreement with the Jewish canon, a shorter list of canonical books. This position took its origin from a complex state of affairs that was the aftereffect of the process by which the Christian canon of the Old Testament developed. This process began as early as the patristic period. The Reformers' position was a result of the ambiguity with which the Church Fathers handled the relationship between the Greek Septuagint and the Hebrew text of the Jewish Scriptures. These had coexisted from the earliest times in the Church and had produced slightly diverse book lists in different local churches.[2] Ironically, the Reformers attacking the Vulgate eventually rallied to the side of Jerome, the translator of the Vulgate, who had militantly promoted the truth of the Hebrew text and thus the Jewish canon. But though Jerome's claim to *Hebraica veritas* prompted him to create the Vulgate, with its frequent departures from the Septuagint, he never rejected the additional books of the Septuagint—those books which had been originally written in Greek. On this point the Reformers remained bitterly opposed to Jerome's Vulgate, and did not want to accept any book whose original text was in Greek.[3] In response to the Reformation, the Council of Trent defended and promoted the use of the Vulgate as a text sanctioned by more than a thousand years of the Church's possession,

2. Problems existed on the practical level from apostolic times. The Greek Bible was used as "scripture" by the first Christian missionaries when addressing the population of the cities steeped in the Hellenistic culture of the Roman Empire. Yet for Palestinian Jews speaking Aramaic, and also for the ethnic population of Syria, the Hebrew text was easier to understand. Similarly, a pre-Christian Aramaic *targum* (translation) of the Hebrew Scriptures would, in general, be more convenient for converts with a Semitic background.

3. The reluctance to accept the Septuagint was also the result of doctrinal bias. Very clear was the case with the Books of the Maccabees, which praise and recommend the custom of praying for the dead, and making a monetary collection for the purpose of offering sacrifices for the deceased (2 Mc 12:44–46). This topic touched a very sensitive nerve of the Reformation and had to be kept out of the canon.

and defined the canon according to the more inclusive and longer list of Old Testament books, as found in the Septuagint.

Although a more detailed account would be too complex, it is important to make three methodological remarks.[4]

First, the Fathers of the Council of Trent were convinced that, in the matter of the canon, they were expressing the Church's long-standing position. In fact, they had no other choice, because a century earlier, at the Council of Florence, Catholics and the Greek Orthodox Church affirmed that their shared Old Testament canon coincided with that of the Septuagint.

Second, the Council's decision is a good example not only of the need for a functioning teaching authority within the Church but also for the practice of restraint: the Church should engage her teaching authority only when a need clearly emerges and a crisis must be resolved by such an intervention.

Third, the correspondence of the canons of the Catholic Church and of the Eastern churches, historically speaking, proves that it was the Reformation that stepped out of the continuity of tradition; thus, the Reformers carried the burden of proof for rejecting the books considered as Scripture in the Septuagint. Yet soon after the influence of Protestantism began to reach Eastern Orthodoxy, doubts arose among the Orthodox about the Old Testament canon. Moreover, because of an absence of "functioning magisterium," further doubts about the canon of the Old Testament persisted without ever being fully resolved in some of the Orthodox churches, specifically in the Russian Orthodox church.

4. For a summary about the status of these so-called "deuterocanonical writings" I quote Reginald Fuller: "The books and parts of books by the above title are called Apocrypha by the churches of the Reformation. With one or two exceptions, they are extant only in Greek and do not form part of the Hebrew canon. They are recognized as inspired and canonical Scripture by the Catholic (and predominantly) by the Eastern Churches that accepted the Greek LXX as their Old Testament. These books are Tobit, Judith, Esther (Greek additions), Wisdom of Solomon, Sirach (Ecclesiasticus), Baruch 1–5, Letter of Jeremiah (Baruch 6), Daniel 3 (Song of the Three), Daniel 13 (Susanna), Daniel 14 (Bel), 1 and 2 Maccabees." See Reginald C. Fuller, "The Deuterocanonical Writings," in *The International Bible Commentary,* ed. William R. Farmer, 179 (Collegeville, Minn.: Liturgical Press, 1998).

In spite of their faithfulness to the doctrine of inspiration, the Reformers never successfully resolved the inconsistency of their teaching about the canon. In principle they could not accept the idea that the definition of the canon would be the task of the Church's teaching authority; that would have meant putting Tradition and Magisterium above Scripture. On the other hand, they needed an answer to the question, how do we know which books are inspired? Their answer, ultimately, was to turn to subjective criteria. When confronted with choices about the Scriptures, the believer was expected to rely on the grace of faith working concomitantly with one's own inner enlightenment about the inspired character of the canonical books. Thus the individual's faith response to the message of Scripture began to be regarded as inclusive of some personal, subjective evidence about the inspired character of each sacred book.

The Catholic Reform and the Bible

During the crisis of the Reformation, the use of the Bible in the Catholic Church underwent many changes. The Council of Trent took up the task of declaring the basic principles to which Church Tradition adhered regarding the Bible.[5] Then, in the aftermath of the Council, important steps were taken for improving, standardizing, and publishing the biblical texts used in the Church. On the one hand, due to the intellectual standards of Catholic humanism formulated long before the Reformation, the Council resisted the will of its conservative wing to forbid the study of the original Greek and Hebrew texts. On the other hand, it unified and standardized the use of the Vulgate in the liturgy and in theology, thus laying the foundation for the post-Tridentine Church's Latin biblicism, all of which was focused on the Vulgate's text. Moreover, Catholic Counter-Reformers did not hesitate to produce their own vernacular Bible translations, all of which were, however, based on a standardized edition of the Vulgate. For English-

5. See the texts of the Council's decisions about the Scriptures in Denzinger-Schönmetzer, *Enchiridion Symbolorum*, 36th ed. (Freiburg in Br.: Herder, 1976), nn. 1501–5.

speaking Catholics this impetus toward the vernacular produced several versions, including the Douay-Rheims, based on the Vulgate. Contrary to the widespread but outright false notion that the Council of Trent forbade or suppressed the reading of the Bible, the decisions of the Council actually resulted in effectively promoting the reading of the Bible by the faithful. In fact, the Counter-Reformation sponsored Catholic Bible translations in all European languages, most of which were carried out in the course of the seventeenth century. They all followed the policies set by the Council of Trent that mandated that Catholic Bibles be published with exegetical notes and explanatory comments, thus providing the faithful with the guidelines of interpretation. In reaction, most Protestant Bibles abstained from using subdivisions, subtitles, exegetical notes, or even introductions, and continue to do so up to the present time.

At Trent the main issue concerning the Bible was its relationship to Tradition. While the Council never claimed that some elements of the faith not found in the Bible must, therefore, be received from Tradition alone, it stated that Tradition must be regarded as a source of revealed truth, equal in importance and dignity with Scripture. Consequently, since the sources of divine revelation cannot be reduced to Scripture alone, in this sense the Council of Trent rejected the principle of *sola scriptura*.

In the apologetic literature of post-Tridentine theology the Council's position was sometimes exaggerated into the statement that some revealed truths are found in Scriptures, and some in Tradition, claiming that the Council possibly imposed not only a formal but also a material distinction between the two sources. Such a statement would make it heretical to hold that each of the two sources (Scripture and Tradition) covers the entire range of Revelation. More unfortunate was the way in which interconfessional disputes deteriorated de facto into argumentations about biblical passages. Ironically, while often claiming "the material insufficiency"—as it was called—of Scripture as the source of all revelation, Catholics often accepted the challenge of proving dogmatic issues from the Scriptures alone, without reading them in the context of Tradition. But then, when "exegetically cornered," they were prone to take the "safety exit" by appealing to Tradition, thus backing off from submitting their doctrinal position to an ultimate scriptural scrutiny. However, obviously, appealing to Tradition has never become an all-purpose problem-solver.

The teaching of Trent was correctly applied by Catholics whenever they refused to accept individual interpretation—even if it appeared to be scientifically most competent—as the highest authority in teaching doctrine or morals. While Protestants claimed the sovereignty of the word of God as documented in the written biblical text (edited, translated, and published by themselves), Catholics were not allowed to separate the authority of the Bible from the teaching authority of a hierarchically structured and guided Church, entrusted with the role of preserving, propagating, and interpreting the biblical texts. As a long-term result, "faith" was seen by the Reformers as a private response to God's written word, while Catholics thought of it as a response to the Church's proclamation of the gospel. The Council of Trent defended inseparable unity between Scripture and Tradition, while simultaneously demanding a biblical renewal in the Church and remaining attached to its fifteen-hundred-year-old identity as the guardian and interpreter of the Scriptures.

The Bible in the Post-Tridentine Church

The century following the Council of Trent brought about important changes in the relationship of theology and exegesis among Catholics. In the new situation of a divided Western Christianity, apologetic issues obtained primary importance. Textual criticism and the knowledge of biblical languages became very important, especially because the Reformers regarded the Vulgate as teeming with mistranslations and errors, while the Council of Trent gave its full support to the Vulgate. Both Catholics and Protestants engaged feverishly in decrying each other's translations and interpretation. Nevertheless, amidst all disputes, the Bible remained the most important bridge doctrinally connecting Catholics and Protestants: confessional disputes constantly involved quoting the Bible. As was mentioned above, in doctrinal disputes the allegorical meaning of the Bible was not acceptable and thus all denominations restricted their use of allegory to the devotional and exhortative use of the biblical text. Consequently, the "four senses" of the Bible lost their status and were soon forgotten, leaving the literal and historical sense to obtain exclusive rights in theology. As a result, in theological studies, Scripture came to be regarded by all confessions as little more than a collection of "proof texts" and a source from which one extracted doctrine in the form of propositional statements. This one-sided insistence on using the Bible to prove (and disprove) doctrinal issues laid the foundation for a new approach to the Bible, which could be called "confessional exegesis": the practice of finding proof texts for supporting the most important doctrinal points of one's own brand of Christianity, like justification by faith alone, or the real presence, meritorious acts, purgatory, or original sin, to name but a few.

Until the arrival of historical criticism—itself an offspring of the eighteenth century's Enlightenment—Catholics and Protestants shared a common understanding of history. In European culture at large, the biblical narratives were accepted at face value and were reconciled with other historical sources, as well as among themselves by simple harmonization or even by an appeal to the miraculous, rather than to the previous custom of applying allegorical interpretation.

While the increase of linguistic and literary studies upgraded biblical exegesis, confessional exegesis meant a definite impoverishment for Protestants and Catholics alike. This epoch, however, saw the birth of some impressive Catholic commentaries. Most remarkable are the works of two Jesuits, Juan Maldonado (1534–1583) and Cornelio de Lapide (1567–1637). Their commentaries show perceptive penetration of the biblical text's grammatical and structural features and a great interest in doctrinal matters. Their method reflects philological precision, careful organization of the data, and, in theology, a positive use of faith and tradition.

Only in the course of the eighteenth century did the true offspring of the Renaissance, the rational study of the Bible, come to maturity. While the roots go back to the humanists of the fifteenth century, only with the accumulation of a critical mass of linguistic and historical knowledge did a rationalist approach prevail and become a significant challenge to the traditional interpretation of the Bible. One must also realize again the importance of the philosophical roots. The great rationalist philosophers of the eighteenth century had, in fact, all shown keen interest in employing historical or scientific tools in a rationalistic critique of the Bible. The French Oratorian priest Richard Simon (1638–1712) was the first important Catholic scholar to engage in this combat, using the new critical approach to the Scriptures either to defeat the rationalists or to adjust traditional views on the Bible to rationalistic principles. Although some of his works were censured by the Church, he remained a Catholic up to the end of his life.

According to commonly held public opinion, the first clash between Scripture and science was the Galileo affair (1616–1633). In fact, although the objections raised against Galileo's heliocentric positions involved biblical arguments, at his time biblical exegesis and theology had not yet come under significant attack from science. But at the end of the seventeenth century, the issue of contradiction between the biblical description of the physical universe and the rapidly evolving scientific discoveries became a hot topic of debate and grew in intensity during the eighteenth and nineteenth centuries. More important, in these two centuries, both the development of archeology as a field of scientific study and the viewing of ancient history in the light of such discoveries made it clear that the Bible could not be used as a handbook for the study of ancient history and with even less confidence could one use the first chapters of Genesis as a historical description of the origins of the human race. Thus the realization emerged that the biblical texts, if they were to be used as a source of historiography, must be subjected to the same standards of historical criticism as any other source material.

In the nineteenth and twentieth centuries, the development of scientific and historical research pushed the theologians of the Bible further down the path of apologetics in defense of the biblical representations of nature and history. Whereas after the Reformation biblical texts were scrutinized for proving or disproving theological statements, now, following the Enlightenment, the historical and scientific truthfulness of the Bible stood as the focus of the debates. Theologians were often lured into the questionable enterprise of providing a rationale for an archaic view of nature and the naïve representation of geography or history, which many parts of the Bible, indeed, seemed to presuppose. In their apologetics they often accepted the supposition that in order to be truthful, the statements of the Bible had to contain correct answers—or be at least compatible with the correct answers—to questions which science and history have only recently begun to ask. It is in this context that, under the influence of Enlightenment and rationalism, the historical and critical method of biblical interpretation began its career, applying to the biblical texts the methods used until then only for other sources of historiography.

In the early period of rationalism only some selected biblical texts were scrutinized under the light of secular science and obtained new interpretations in later phases. For example, various theories about the sources of the Pentateuch were developed and speculations were launched about the natural causes of the miraculous events of the Exodus. In the latter half of the nineteenth century there appeared an even higher degree of ambition to create broad and comprehensive theories of human history, whose intent was to encompass and transcend most of the biblical material. The philosophers of the nineteenth century sought a rational understanding of the Bible as a whole and wanted to insert it (together with a comprehensive theory about the origins of Christianity) into their general understanding of mankind's religious history. They wanted ultimately to create a purely rationalistic synthesis that would eliminate the need to recognize anything supernatural or miraculous in the process of history. Instead, they would explain all phenomena by physical, psychological, sociological, or other natural causes. It was an age for constructing broad, comprehensive, and bold systems, often using rather sweeping generalizations based on myopic and one-sided analytical studies, which were, in turn, based on one or another new scientific discovery. Thinkers like Hegel, Marx, and Freud offered their understanding of many biblical texts and used them as popular examples for illustrating their theories, thereby greatly influencing modern biblical interpretation; they were among those who sought new avenues for validating, albeit outside the religious framework, the ancient biblical message amidst a constantly changing cultural context.

Up until the middle of the twentieth century, while Catholic circles remained negative and defensive toward any efforts to bring about a new and secularized biblical science, some of the best Catholic thinkers did attempt to respond to these new tendencies more positively and started some dialogue with the rationalists.

Already at the end of the sixteenth century, a Jesuit in the Netherlands named Lessius began to explore the possibility of considering the biblical texts in a new way, as the result of merely human industry. Is it not possible, he asked, that the various biblical books came about under normal human circumstances in the same way other contemporary writings were composed and, therefore, was it not only in light of a later approval by the Church that they obtained their "inspired" character? This and similar theological hypotheses tried to legitimize the perception that the Scriptures had a "human face" and were, in fact, nothing more than the product of a limited human intellect. One of the concerns of such authors as Lessius was, of course, to reconcile the faith of both simple believers and theologians to the human deficiencies of the texts which, in their view, reflected mostly time-bound insights and views characteristic of their human authors. At first, these efforts received little approval.

The same reaction met those efforts which, under the pretext of limiting the inspired content of the Bible to areas that concern faith and morals only, while dispossessing other biblical passages, seen as irrelevant for enhancing religious belief, of any claim to special qualifications, including inerrancy. Such a view was already expressed by the Englishman Henry Holden in a book published in 1658, but it was only in the nineteenth century, under the influence of Cardinal Newman, that it caught the attention of a wider circle of theologians.

In the intellectual climate of Europe at the time of Newman, the inerrancy of the Bible stood at the focal point of most attacks directed against biblical faith. Almost all the objections were argued from the side of science and history. In its response, contemporary apologetics began to search for a definition of inspiration that would equally respect the divine origins of the Bible and the validity of the modern advancements in scientific and historical research. Newman's basic understanding was simple and logical: it would be fair and reasonable to criticize the Bible on a rationalistic basis only if it had been written under the standards of modern science or historiography. Newman made the mistake, however, of materially limiting the influence of inspiration and inerrancy to those parts of the Bible which spoke of "faith and morality." He tried to isolate the biblical statements of religious relevance and exempt the rest of the texts—the so-called *obiter dicta,* or statements made on the side—from standards of inerrancy. In his encyclical *Providentissimus Deus,* Leo XIII rejected the theory of the *obiter dicta* in the same way that Vatican I had previously condemned Lessius's doctrine of "retroactive inspiration."[6]

The difficulties raised by historical criticism kept on multiplying until they finally resulted in a broad and general crisis, later called by the collective name "modernism," that was painful and often confusing for modern Catholic biblical scholarship. The modernists tried to establish complete separation between truth statements based on scientific knowledge and those expressing the truth of the faith. In this way the modernists pretended to subscribe fully to the fashionable affirmations of modern science and history while adhering to all articles of faith. When they separated historical and scientific knowledge from matters of faith, they denied a priori any potential conflict between the two realms. The various papal documents by Pius X against the modernists led to the apostasy of some of the most brilliant Catholic exegetes, like the Frenchman Alfred Loisy, a Catholic priest and a prolific writer. At the same time, it became difficult for some Catholic biblical scholars to remain in the Church

6. See in ibid., nn. 1787 and 1950–51.

while applying the historical and critical method to the study of the Bible. The Pontifical Biblical Commission, established at the end of Leo XIII's pontificate (1903), became the principal tool of papal vigilance overseeing Catholic scriptural research, intervening regularly in practically all biblical issues, usually acting in favor of traditional doctrine and warning against innovations in the biblical disputes of the day.

However, the promises of a new era also began to appear in the form of a new institute, the École Biblique in Jerusalem, founded in 1890 by French Dominicans under the leadership of J.-M. Lagrange. He first began to work with Old Testament texts in order to apply to biblical studies the insights obtained from ancient texts newly discovered by Middle Eastern archeology. However, he also undertook to study, in the light of St. Thomas's writings, the theology of inspiration and the general issues of Catholic biblical hermeneutics. The journal of his institute, the *Revue biblique,* and its series of publications under the title *Études bibliques* became the most important instrument for disseminating a new approach to Catholic biblical research. Soon Lagrange switched to New Testament studies and began publishing commentaries on each of the four gospels as well as on the Epistle to the Romans. These works presented a new kind of Catholic scholarship, both open to all legitimate gains in scientific learning and fully loyal to the faith as well as to the classical heritage of Thomism, to which Lagrange remained devoted. His publications also revealed a growing interest in the study of patristic and medieval exegesis.

During the decades that followed the initial period of modernism, we can observe a slow transition in Catholic theology from a defensive style of apologetics to a more open and positive approach that welcomed a variety of new trends in modern thought. Lagrange's new style of scholarship received a major boost from the encyclical *Divino Afflante Spiritu* by Pius XII, a document which, soon after its publication, was hailed as a long-awaited recognition and promotion of modern Catholic biblical scholarship. Published in 1943 during the turbulent time of World War II, it succeeded soon after the war in providing leadership for Catholic biblical scholarship to overcome the tone of defensiveness and to start using the solid results of modern criticism not just for the sake of remaining up-to-date, but for the sake of exploring the doctrinal depths of biblical teaching.

As a result, in cooperation with a patristic and liturgical renewal, a new trend was born in the Church leading to a new, biblically grounded type of Catholic theology, which gradually yielded the intellectual and spiritual fermentation that stimulated the decrees of the Second Vatican Council. Not only in the Dogmatic Constitution *Dei Verbum* on divine revelation but also in the treatment of other theological issues, the Council reflected the results of this new biblicism, which the French theologians of the 1950s and 1960s frequently called the *"mouvement biblique,"* animating a *"nouvelle théologie."* Theology began to pay close attention to the biblical sources of Catholic doctrine as well as to the results of modern biblical research.

IX. INSPIRATION AND INTERPRETATION AT VATICAN II

The Dogmatic Constitution *Dei Verbum*

The Dogmatic Constitution *Dei Verbum* was the product of a lengthy struggle. Even its final version is not the mature conclusion of the process which produced it. Here we must neither discuss its detailed history nor trace the path which the theology of revelation and inspiration traveled between the two Vatican Councils. We shall, however, engage partly in some historical inquiry to demonstrate the following double thesis:

First, *Dei Verbum* has successfully restored the proper context in which Tradition developed and nurtured the theology of inspiration, inerrancy, and the ecclesial use of Scripture.

Second, although in its chapters 3 through 5 *Dei Verbum* applied a renewed theology of revelation to which the topics mentioned above belong, its effort to bring about a synthesis resulted only in a sketchy and incomplete text that still awaits completion.

The Place of Biblical Inspiration in *Dei Verbum*

Obtaining the Proper Context

The original schema of what later became the Dogmatic Constitution *Dei Verbum* was the product of a certain "Roman theology" which was well known from theological manuals used in the Roman pontifical universities in the first half of the twentieth century. These were textbooks assigned to courses compulsory for candidates to the priesthood, carrying the title *Introductio Generalis in Sacram Scripturam*.[1] The famous encyclical *Divino Afflante Spiritu* of Pius XII was basically a product of the same Roman school of theology in its final and best phase. A comparison of the topical outline of the encyclical with the leading textbooks is instructive. Their common point of departure is a proof of the "existence of inspiration," which presents the Bible as essentially a collection of texts written under the inspiration of the Holy Spirit.[2] This is followed up in two directions. First, the "extent" of inspiration is shown to include every text of the Catholic Bible.[3] Second, there follows the treatment of the "essence" or "nature" of inspiration as a divine influence on the sacred writers of the biblical books, the "hagiographers," which engaged their minds and wills so that the literary works they produced could truly be characterized as both "having God as their author" and having human authors as God's instruments.[4] To conclude the first part of such a textbook, this double authorship, human and divine, is discussed in terms of the scholastic concept of "instrumental causality" borrowed from the chapters of St. Thomas's *Summa* about prophecy, and then applied to literary authorship.[5]

The treatise's second part continues with the study of inerrancy as the "most important effect of inspiration," covering every text in

1. One of the best representatives of such books is H. Höpfl and B. Gut, *Introductio Generalis in Sacram Scripturam* (Rome: Arnado, 1950), further expanded and edited first by Adalbert Metzinger, then by Louis Leloir, and used until the late 1960s. Similar books were compiled by J.-M. Lagrange, A. Merk, J.-M. Vosté, A. Bea, S. Tromp, and others. Bea and Tromp played a major role in writing the first schema of *Dei Verbum*.

2. *De exsistentia inspirationis* begins on page 1 in Höpfl and Gut, *Introductio Generalis*. The same content appears in nn. 1–2 in Pius XII's encyclical *Divino Afflante Spiritu*.

3. This issue follows in the encyclical under no. 3. In the textbook by Höpfl and Gut, the chapter *De extensione inspirationis* begins only on page 63, as this textbook gives logical priority to the nature of inspiration.

4. The section *De natura inspirationis* begins in Höpfl and Gut, *Introductio Generalis*, on page 40, while the encyclical starts speaking of the influence of the Holy Spirit on the authors in no. 5.

5. See ibid., 49. In the encyclical *Divino Afflante Spiritu*, St. Thomas's doctrine of instrumental causality is markedly absent. Instead, quotations from the Church Fathers illustrate the idea of "divine words in human language" (no. 41) and the concept of "divine condescension."

its entirety, including those with a non-religious content referring to history, geography, natural sciences, and descriptive observations.

The encyclical *Divino Afflante Spiritu,* published in 1943, was rightly praised for two decades as the Magna Charta of Catholic biblical scholarship, since it encouraged linguistic, archeological, and critical studies of texts, focusing on the literal sense while also emphasizing the importance of the Church Fathers' exegetical tradition. It kept the theology of inspiration and inerrancy, however, locked in the narrow perspective of the Roman textbooks. *Divino Afflante Spiritu* was issued on the fiftieth anniversary of Leo XIII's encyclical *Providentissimus Deus,* and closely reiterated the main theses of the earlier papal document. Nevertheless, the more recent encyclical also exuded admiration and enthusiasm for modern biblical studies and, in support of the patristic renewal slowly expanding in the 1930s and 1940s, encouraged the study of ancient exegesis, though without proposing any specific guidance for combining the two approaches.[6]

High hopes were pinned on the novel concept of the "literary genre," which *Divino Afflante Spiritu* strongly promoted. Catholic exegetes began to emphasize that, due to their specific literary genres, most biblical texts could not be held to standards of modern science and historiography. In both the pulpit and the classroom, the importance of this development cannot be underestimated.

The study of the literary genre brought further benefits as Catholics began to realize that the majority of the biblical texts consist of religious poetry as well as prose, and that they often follow ancient literary conventions governing persuasive, ethical, or legislative compositions. For a large number of the biblical texts, therefore, a rationalistic application of "inerrancy" (following the concept of "historicity" from modern historiography) began to appear pointless. *Divino Afflante Spiritu* successfully opened the doors to a Catholic "biblical movement" which quickly gained momentum.[7]

But the first preparatory schemas of the Council on the biblical

6. It explicitly speaks of "theological" and "spiritual" (even "mystical") interpretation built upon the "analogy of faith" (no. 24).

7. Roger Aubert, *La théologie catholique au milieu du XXe siècle* [Catholic Theology in the Middle of the Twentieth Century] (Paris: Aubier, 1956).

matters of inspiration and inerrancy offered little hope for significant progress. In an attempt to deal with the considerable backlog from the Council of Trent and Vatican I, the first five schemata tried in vain to place Tradition (and thus the Magisterium) above Scripture by controlling its interpretation, thus resolving the potential conflicts between the "two sources of revelation," Scripture and Tradition, by subordinating the former to the latter. In their response, the Council Fathers rejected the documents from the preparatory committee and soon brought the conciliar debate to the brink of a stalemate. Such an action was averted when in November 1962, through an intervention by Pope John XXIII, the project was removed from the agenda. Almost two years passed until an initiative issued by Pope Paul VI (March 7, 1964) brought these topics back under a new title, *De revelatione*, with a newly appointed subcommittee in charge.[8] This group began to draft a new schema with fresh insights.

Now, for a second time, the theology of revelation took center stage in the Council, integrating some of the topics treated previously and marginalizing others. The new schema approached revelation according to the patristic perspective of a comprehensive "economy of salvation."[9] This approach appeared successful, for the new schema easily transcended the dualism of "Scripture vs. Tradition" which had previously marred all post-Tridentine debates about this issue. *Dei Verbum* states at its beginning: "The divine economy is realized by deeds and words" (I.2). From this perspective not even

8. This new group included, among others, Lucien Cerfaux, Carlo Colombo, Yves Congar, Aloys Grillmeyer, Charles Moeller, Karl Rahner, Joseph Ratzinger, and Otto Semmelroth.

9. The alliance of two powerful intellectual trends in the Church, the "biblical movement" and the "patristic movement," became chiefly responsible for animating the theology of Vatican II. They enabled the Church to participate in the modern-day advances of historical and linguistic studies. One may also say that the rediscovery of the Greek Church Fathers (among them, most importantly, Irenaeus, Origen, and the Cappadocians) made the most powerful and longest lasting impact on modern Catholic theology, including specifically the theology of revelation and a new outlook on exegesis. It became clear that as early as the second century a brilliant vision of Christian theology had begun to unfold: the vision of a "sacred oeconomia" (history of salvation and revelation), capable of presenting a "gradual development" of revelation in which both the element of human imperfections and the feature of God's gracious condescension are equally important components of God's self-disclosure.

the "verbal" form of revelation appears central and primary. Rather, revelation becomes a comprehensive concept: it includes all forms and means of communication by which God has chosen to manifest himself to the human race. Even more important, *Dei Verbum* rectified the approach by which the papal encyclicals of Pius XII, *Divino Afflante Spiritu* and *Humani Generis,* had begun their discourse by speaking of the inspired authors *(hagiographi)* of the sacred books. *Dei Verbum* correctly emphasized that, in the first place, revelation takes place as history (and not just in history), so that revelation cannot be reduced to verbal and conceptual expressions, let alone to written texts. Secondly, *Dei Verbum* did not allow the notion of "revealed truth" to be reduced or restricted to propositional statements. Instead, revealed truth was presented as a complex set of historical events and developments which, in fact, not only have certain specifically cognitive aspects and find expression in narrative texts and theological statements, but also include other aspects of the religious experience which often give birth to alternative forms of verbal expression, such as poetry, legislation, prophecy, prayer, etc.—all of which appear in the Bible.[10]

The conciliar document's opening paragraph contains a summary of "sacred history"—the way the Bible deals with history—as a narrative of the biblical past. Such treatment of the past is frequently repeated in patristic authors, but with no regard to modern historical consciousness. By this procedure the document was allowed to incorporate smoothly further patristic doctrine on revelation and inspiration. *Dei Verbum* made no attempt, however, to bridge the gap separating the pre-critical view of history from contemporary thought. On matters such as human evolution, hominization, and the emergence of culture and religious practices in pre-historical times, it did not even try to compare biblical content with contemporary categories of history, as was done, for example, by William Albright's classic, albeit outdated, work, *From the Stone Age to Christianity.*[11]

10. Of course, this way of transcending *Divino Afflante Spiritu* brought about, at the same time as a result, the study of the literary genres, which the same encyclical had strongly encouraged.

11. Baltimore: John Hopkins University Press, 1957.

The document cautiously preferred to repeat traditional language and avoided a confrontation between biblical history and modern anthropology.[12]

Biblical Inspiration in the New Context of Revelation

The final version of *Dei Verbum* inserted the traditional doctrine of biblical inspiration into the context of a renewed notion of revelation. Although this traditional doctrine remained basically unchanged, the new context almost automatically enriched it. This appears most clearly in chapter 2, where the text moves from the notion of the "divine economy"—events and experiences happening to God's People, that is, both Israel and the nascent Church—to the topic of "the transmission of divine revelation." The concept of "transmission" was broad enough to include both the oral and the written transmission of divine self-disclosure and thus, from the beginning, *Dei Verbum* emphasized the unity of, rather than the distinction between, Scripture and Tradition. Yet, by a curious but intentional shortcut, the document passes over in a single sentence the first phase of sacred history and, with regard to the Old Testament, does not even distinguish between oral and written traditions: "In his gracious goodness, God has seen to it that what He had revealed for the salvation of all nations would abide perpetually in its full integrity and be handed on to all generations" (no. 7).

One might even be led to think that, without mentioning the Scriptures of the Jewish people, this sentence emphasizes right from the beginning the transmission of revelation through Christ and his Apostles, for it continues immediately with the following:

> Therefore, Christ the Lord, in whom the entire revelation of God the most high is summed up (cf. 2 Cor 1:20; 3:16; 4:6), commanded the Apostles to preach the Gospel which had been promised beforehand by the prophets and which He Himself has fulfilled in his own person and promulgated with his own lips. (no. 7)

12. One might say that the Council's caution was eventually vindicated if we recall that the enthusiasm which surrounded the works of Teilhard de Chardin, having reached its peak just before and during the Council, soon after died down.

In any case, the concept of revelation presented here is strongly Christocentric. All revelatory instances of the Old Testament are summarized as mediated through "the prophets" in a comprehensive sense, referring to all those who preceded and anticipated Christ until he, at the peak of revelation, pronounced the Good News "with his own lips" and transmitted it thereafter through his chosen Apostles to all future generations. In this scheme, patterned after the categories "prophets and Apostles," the longitudinal or temporal dimension of the salvation-history outline is complemented by a scheme of mediation in which there is but one mediator and revealer, the Son, who engages further spokesmen and mediators in every age and time.[13] Christ's omnipresence in every phase of the economy of salvation makes each phase transcend its historical limitation in two ways, first by overcoming finitude and, thereby, receiving temporal extension and, second, by being released from lock-step temporal succession. Furthermore, since Christ is both human and divine, his actions obtain a supra-temporal relevance and availability by their theandrical constitution; they even exercise supra-temporal causality (most clearly in the sacraments, but analogously in every kind of proclamation of the word) by bringing about and endowing with efficacy the salvific encounters between God and man always and everywhere.

Christ, the "prophets" of the Old Testament, and the Apostles form a sort of "triptych," a triple structure of revelatory mediation in which the terms "prophets" and "Apostles" take on a generalized and quasi-technical meaning. On the one hand, the term "prophets" signifies those who are the recipients of revelation in Israel and, ultimately, the authoritative sources of the Old Testament Scriptures; on the other hand, the term "Apostles" refers to the immediate recipients of Jesus' mission, the chosen eyewitnesses who took the word of

13. The scheme follows a patristic outline which we studied above, but more closely it reflects Congar's criticism of Rahner's theology of inspiration in which, for all practical purposes, "early Church" replaces the human mediators of the "word." This criticism of Congar's was expressed in a book published at the beginning of Vatican II, *La Tradition et les traditions* (Paris: Fayard, 1960). This was the point about which Congar criticized Pierre Grelot's attempts at a new theology of inspiration after the Council.

revelation from his mouth and became the fountainhead of the apostolic tradition from which the Scriptures of the New Testament also originate. Understood in this way, the economy of salvation cannot be reduced to a historical process conceived as a one-dimensional accumulation of subsequent installments. Rather, it is a chain of anticipations leading to their peak and summit in Christ, happening all at once at the Incarnation of the Logos, but then being extended to and distributed over all subsequent times and places.

Only at this point does *Dei Verbum* introduce explicitly "the Scriptures." Although the document previously made references to "Moses" (no. 3) and "the prophets" (also in no. 3 and later in no. 7), these were mentioned only in the role of "speaking" God's word as if by an oral message.[14] Scripture as such is mentioned explicitly for the first time in article 7, in reference to the full message of Christ's revelation: "The commission was fulfilled, too, by those Apostles and apostolic men who, under the inspiration of the Holy Spirit, have put into writing the message of salvation" (no. 7).[15]

It is no accident that, in this way, the first mention of Scripture and biblical inspiration takes place in reference to the apostolic tradition, so that the document begins its theology of inspiration in reference to the New Testament. The document in its entirety understands all the Scriptures as derived from Christ, their fountainhead. Thus later, in the fourth chapter, the texts of the Old Testament are treated as "the economy of salvation fore-announced, narrated, and explained" (*praeannuntiata, enarrata atque explicata,* no. 14), possibly one of the least understood and appreciated aspects of the document. As the patristic heritage had always seen it, the purpose and

14. One must admit that both the biblical text and Tradition frequently use verbs like "says" or "said" when quoting a written text. But it appears intentional that the concept of inspiration is brought up only after surveying the whole of revelation, including its fullness in Christ.

15. The division of the authors into *apostoli* and *(viri) apostolici* (apostles and apostolic men) is expressed by Tertullian, referring to Matthew and John as *apostoli,* and Luke and Mark as *apostolici: "Denique nobis fidem ex apostolis Johannes et Matthaeus insinuant, ex apostolicis Lucas et Marcus instaurant"* (Finally from among the apostles, Matthew and John convey us the faith, from among the apostolic men, Luke and Mark establish it). *Adversus Marcionem* IV, 2.2.

meaning of the Old Testament lies in its prophetic character. Only by pointing to Christ does it possess permanent value for mankind's universal salvation history. The economy of salvation of the Old Testament "has its *raison d'être* chiefly in this" *(in hoc potissimum disposita erat),* that it might "prophetically announce and typologically signify the coming of Christ as the Redeemer of all and his messianic Kingdom" (no. 15).[16]

Because it is based on a patristic theology of revelation, the concept of biblical inspiration presented in *Dei Verbum* stands head and shoulders above that of *Divino Afflante Spiritu* and the Roman textbooks of the 1950s. The latter, in their opening chapters *"De exsistentia inspirationis,"* sampled arguments from Scripture and Tradition in order to "prove" that Scripture was inspired, a method which did not involve—the textbooks argued—logical fallacy because, at this point, the Bible was used only as a historical source without any supposition of its inspired character. However, using the Bible as a historical source to prove that the Bible was believed to be inspired was a confusing procedure. After all, no book can be quoted as a witness to its own reception. At best one was able to illustrate in this way that certain passages in the biblical books referred to other passages of the same collection of books as inspired, and that in both Judaism and Christianity there was a general concept of "the Scriptures," the precise content of which remained unclear until the completion of the canon by the Church's Magisterium.

Dei Verbum used a different approach, beginning, like many other

16. In his book *Inspiration in the Bible* (New York: Herder, 1961), Karl Rahner states: "It follows that by willing and creating the Apostolic Church and its constitutive elements with a formal, absolute, salvation-historic and eschatological will, God wills and creates the Scriptures in such a way that He becomes their inspiring originator and author." Immediately after the formulation of this thesis, Rahner makes it clear that this "definition of inspiration" applies to the Old Testament just as well. He does not mean that Scripture would become Scripture only in retrospect by canonization (as if canonicity could replace the notion of inspiration), but that the process by which Scripture comes about *(Schriftwerdung)* integrally extends itself to the formation of the canon. Therefore, also in the case of the Old Testament, the fact of biblical inspiration is revealed with certitude and full clarity only at the coming of Christ. Only then does the prophetic message preparing his coming become manifest, and the identity of the inspired books becomes established by the ministry of the Church.

documents of Vatican II, with the self-understanding of the Church. From its beginnings, as a "community of salvation," the Church understood itself to be in possession of "the Scriptures," due to its belief that Christ's life, message, death, and resurrection had taken place "according to the Scriptures" (cf. 1 Cor 15:3–4). This awareness was linked with the apostolic tradition, itself conceived as a received teaching "about what was from the beginning" (ἀπ' ἀρχῆς) (cf. 1 Jn 1:1) and transmitted by those who were original eyewitnesses, again "ἀπ' ἀρχῆς" (cf. Lk 1:1).[17] This understanding of the Scriptures implies faith in their inspiration, but a faith which is quite different in both context and content from what one can glean from scattered and casual remarks about various biblical passages asserting or alluding to the existence of inspiration.[18]

In the textbooks which preceded *Dei Verbum* the relationship of Tradition and Scripture and their relationship to the Magisterium remained unclarified. In the system which they projected, the only sufficient and truly efficient criterion of truth was the Magisterium, since it was not clear if either Scripture or Tradition were definable without recourse to decisions by the Magisterium. In the vision that *Dei Verbum* proposes, a clear effort is made to tip the balance in favor of the "apostolic Church." The apostolic Church is seen as a historically closed and unchangeable reality, enshrined in the twenty-seven books of the New Testament as in a divinely created literary deposit of revealed truth, but also extended into time through the ministry of the Church, which continues dispensing the salvific treasures of Christ's teachings, as well as his sacrificial death and everlasting risen life. In this vision, revelation is conceived of as a broad, multidimensional reality, and Scripture constitutes only one component

17. These two uses of the expression ἀπ' ἀρχῆς in the New Testament demonstrate well what the "original" apostolic message meant for Luke and John. That this foundational preaching needs to be written down so that the Church may obtain solid certainty (ἀσφάλεια) is emphasized by Luke (1:4).

18. *Dei Verbum* has, therefore, succeeded in pointing out the specific characteristics of the Christian belief in the Scriptures, making one better understand both that Christian theology about God's Word necessarily differs in some essential points from Jewish thought, and that Jewish and Christian canons cannot coincide in content and meaning.

of this reality. Scripture is the written documentation of salvation history, which in the ongoing ministry of the Church, coexists with the flow of tradition and the ecclesial expansion of Christ's presence on earth.

After the first two chapters, written with a basically patristic orientation, chapter 3 of *Dei Verbum* delineates a theology of inspiration that becomes increasingly entangled in a set of modern concerns which lie outside the patristic perspective. We now need to examine these concerns before we turn to two different sets of statements about the two Testaments in chapters 4 and 5, each of which constitutes a skillful summary of traditional doctrine, yet appears to be, for several reasons, incomplete and unfinished.

Inspiration in Chapter 3 of *Dei Verbum*

While chapters 1 and 2 of *Dei Verbum* masterfully succeeded in replacing the opening chapter of the textbooks on "the existence and essence (or nature)" of inspiration, chapter 3 treats the material of the manuals under the heading *"De extensione inspirationis"* and simply repeats their teaching for the most part. The problems of inspiration had been left unresolved by Vatican I and were revisited by the encyclicals which followed *(Providentissimus Deus, Spiritus Paraclitus,* and *Divino Afflante Spiritu)*. Efforts were made by various theologians to limit the extent of inspiration to certain parts of the Bible, carving out texts and/or topics which would not have God as their author, and thus would not be covered by inerrancy. These included Cardinal Newman's famous proposal to eliminate the inspiration of the so-called *obiter dicta*—statements unessential to the purpose of the biblical authors because of their lack of religious relevance. Yet the Magisterium insisted that all biblical texts were covered by inspiration in their entirety and thus were fully endowed with inerrancy.

Chapter 3 begins with an insistence on the true authorship of the human writers who produced the biblical texts. That they were *"veri auctores"* excludes any mechanistically conceived authorship in which the human author would have neither freedom of decision, nor authorial purpose or goal, but would be just a blind instrument following the Divine Author. The human author's conscious and free participation in the process of inspiration had already been highly emphasized in *Divino Afflante Spiritu,* proposing caution in the interpretation of many patristic and medieval images that compared the human authors to inanimate instruments (pen, flute, pipe, etc.).

At the publication of *Divino Afflante Spiritu,* Augustin Cardinal Bea (probably the ghostwriter of the encyclical) published the view that the phrase *Deus auctor Scripturae* was the most important formula for inspiration.[19] A decade later, Karl Rahner raised serious objections to the indiscriminate use of this metaphor, and argued that God cannot be called a *Verfasser* (literary author), but only the *Urheber* (the originator) of a book. Yet Rahner admitted that in Latin the term *auctor* is ambiguous. Rahner's proposal was received positively by many (mostly German) theologians, but *Dei Verbum* did not follow up on his remarks about "divine authorship" for good reason: Rahner never examined whether tradition had called God *"auctor Scripturae"* in a literary sense.[20] Even now, forty years after *Dei Verbum,* it may not be quite clear to what extent and in what sense tradition speaks of *Deus auctor Scripturae.*[21]

Ironically, the authors of the first schema on revelation and the new subcommittee which replaced them readily agreed on the concept of a "double authorship," human and divine, for the Bible. Yet the term *veri auctores* for the human authors went unmatched by a reference to God, as the latter is not called *verus auctor,* perhaps be-

19. A. Bea, "'Deus auctor S. Scripturae.' Herkunft und Bedeutung der Formel" [God the Author of Sacred Scripture: Provenance and Significance of the Formula], *Angelicum* 20 (1943): 16–31.

20. Nor did he examine the shades of meaning that *auctor* possessed or, most importantly, what the corresponding terms meant in the Greek tradition.

21. Two aspects are usually overlooked in the discussion. First, the word *auctor* connotes authority, and the Bible is certainly seen as endowed with divine authority. Second, ancient usage (and spelling) has mixed the words *auctor* and *actor.* For example, in St. Bernard's fifty-sixth sermon on the Song of Songs, vol. 2 of *Sancti Bernardi Opera Omnia,* ed. J. Leclercq (Rome: Editiones Cistercienses, 1958), 114, Christ is said to be the *auctor* of the scriptural text, but the meaning of the word is *actor.* See Denis Farkasfalvy, *L'inspiration biblique dans la théologie de saint Bernard* [Biblical Inspiration in the Theology of Saint Bernard] (Rome: Herder, 1964), 34.

cause insistence on the "hagiographers" as true authors was so much the focus of attention that God's role as truly *auctor Scripturae* was hardly ever questioned.

In a book published too late to influence the Council, Luis Alonso Schökel showed that in patristic texts God is said to be "the author of Scripture" much less abundantly and unanimously than modern authors had usually assumed.[22] What did the medieval theologians think about it? St. Thomas Aquinas provides a rather stable usage when he speaks about God as the *"auctor principalis"* and the "hagiographer" as the *"auctor instrumentalis"* of Scripture.[23] One cannot, however, identify this Thomistic usage with speaking about a double literary authorship. What St. Thomas had in mind is probably the very same distinction between *Verfasser (auctor instrumentalis)* and *Urheber (auctor principalis)* for which Rahner had argued.[24] It seems that such a usage of the term *auctor* was applied analogously to God and the hagiographer, whence it gave rise to the concept of a "double authorship." The Council of Trent called God the *"auctor"* of Scripture in this sense: *"Omnes libros tam Veteris quam Novi Testamenti,*

22. *The Inspired Word* (Rome: Herder, 1967); this English edition, prepared by Francis Martin, is more complete than the original Spanish text, *La palabra inspirada* (Barcelona: Herder, 1966). Alonso Schökel even observes that the "literary analogy" of a "divine author" is fairly absent from ancient Church Fathers, with the possible exception of Justin Martyr, whose text, however, does not fit the modern-day concept of "someone writing through an intermediary." In ancient texts, reference to God as an "author" is at best a mixed metaphor, for the divine "author" is usually described as someone speaking but not necessarily "dictating," just communicating or making certain statements while the writing is done only by the *human* author. In all these texts it is not clear to what extent a patristic witness would impute literary authorship to both the divine and human agent. Moreover, when God is said to be "dictating" to a man who writes what he hears, it is not clear how far this metaphor is meant to go and to what extent the word *dictare* is meant to convey the sense of a modern dictation or refers to a wider sense of authorship as we have it in the German verb *dichten*. All these considerations add up to the realization that we need more detailed studies to answer the question, "What did the Church Fathers really say about God as the *auctor* of the Scriptures?"

23. *Summa Theologiae* I, 110; *Quodlibet* 6, 16; 14 ad 5.

24. H. Urs von Balthasar, *Thomas von Aquin: Besondere Gnadengaben und die zwei Wege des menschlichen Lebens: Kommentar zur Summa Theologica II–II, 171–182* [Thomas Aquinas: Special Charisms and the Two Ways of Human Life: Commentary on the Summa Theologica II–II, 171–182], vol. 23 of *Die Deutsche Thomas-Ausgabe*, ed. H. M. Christmann (Vienna: Pustet, 1958), 359.

cum utriusque unus Deus sit auctor. . .pari pietatis affectu ac reverentia [concilium] suscipit et veneratur" (from the year 1546, D 83).[25]

The texts of the Councils of Florence and Trent emphasize in their statement the one divine author of the two Testaments. At Vatican II this emphasis shifted. Originally, insistence on a reference to both Testaments came from a very ancient, anti-Gnostic, and specifically anti-Marcionite tradition, formulated for the first time by Irenaeus and Tertullian.[26] Tertullian used the word *auctoritas* and left no doubt that here not "literary authorship," but rather the one and same divine authority by which both Testaments are endowed was at issue. However, the meaning of *auctoritas* in Tertullian corresponds to what Irenaeus states about their origin: both the prophetic and the apostolic writings come from the same God and the same divine Spirit. Thus the Councils of Florence and Trent were most likely speaking of both issues: an equal authority and an identical authorship or source for both Testaments.[27] Yet none of these state-

25. "All books of the Old and New Testament are accepted and reverenced [by the Council] with equal sentiment and honor of piety, since the one and same God is the author of both." This text, which closely repeats the statement of the Decree of the Jacobites given at the Council of Florence in 1441 (D706), has also found its way into *Dei Verbum*.

26. We quote only a few samples:

"Quoniam autem dictis nostris consonat praedicatio apostolorum et Domini magisterium et Prophetarum adnuntiatio, et Apostolorum dictatio et Legilatoris ministratio, unum eundumque Deum Patrem laudantium" (Our statements here stand in harmony with the preaching of the Apostles, the teaching of the Lord, and the proclamation of the Prophets, as well as the writing of the Apostles and the promulgation of the Law). Irenaeus, *Adversus Haereses* II, 58, 2.

"How could the Scriptures have testified of Him [the Logos], unless all are from one and the same Father?" Irenaeus, *Adversus Haereses* IV, 20, 1.

"Tam enim apostolus Moyses quam apostoli prophetae, aequanda est auctoritas utriusque officii ab uno eodem domino apostolorum et prophetarum" (Moses is as much of an Apostle as the Apostles are prophets, and the authority of both offices is to be held equal on account of the one and same Lord over both the prophets and of the Apostles). Tertullian, *Adversus Marcionem* IV, 24, 8–9.

27. Raymond F. Collins begins his documentation of patristic material in support of the formula "God, the Author of the Scriptures" as a "classic expression" of the Church's teaching about inspiration, with the fifth century *Statuta Ecclesiae Antiqua* from Latin Africa (DS 325–329). He does not seem to realize that he is dealing there with Tertullian's anti-Marcionite formula, where the emphasis is on the sameness of the author of both Testaments *(uno auctore)* and no assertion is made about God as a literary author. *Introduction to the New Testament* (New York: Doubleday, 1982): 328–29.

ments affirm that God, to equip his salvation plan with written records, took up the "métier" or trade of a writer and "wrote a letter to Philemon," or compiled wise sayings (Proverbs), or became either a poet of love songs (Song of Songs) or a humorist (Jonah).[28]

Then, in a peculiarly convoluted sentence (the third sentence of article 11) the conciliar text combines the two kinds of authorship (human and divine) of Sacred Scripture. The Commission responsible for the final text intended to show that the two authors, undiminished in their respective roles and natures, joined forces to produce a common product. There was no way of avoiding a tension between the notion of "true (human) authors" fully using their talents and the Divine Author "employing" (one could even say "using") them so that, while writing as free agents, they would write exactly—no more or less—what the Divine Author wanted them to put down in writing.

So, after all, the schema confronted Rahner's concerns, at least by logical implication. In what sense can God be called an author? In the document, of course, God is not said to "commit anything to writing," and is not called a "literary author." However, he is said to guarantee that the human writers produce exactly what he intended them to write. While only the hagiographer is considered a "literary author," or *"Verfasser,"* the Divine Author is quite specifically responsible for everything that the text says or, more correctly, for the resulting text in its entirety. The problem created by this model should not be underestimated: the human being employed by God is thereby fully and specifically predetermined to do what God wants him to do. Can we therefore still say that he is making fully free decisions? We are able to answer in the affirmative as long as we understand that the divine cause, due to its transcendental character, does not reduce or restrict human freedom, but rather constitutes it; it neither diminishes human freedom nor is diminished by it.[29] While

28. These examples are meant to illustrate Rahner's statement: "If God is to be the literary author of the Scriptures, He is, if we may formulate it in this way, a categorical and not a transcendental cause."

29. Rahner has some very well-formulated sentences about the correct application of the concept of instrumentality to inspiration: "It is precisely not a question of the

the language of the document fully incorporates the use of "author" and "authorship" for both God and man, the text avoids stating that God is a literary author, and equally avoids employing the Thomistic categories of *causa principalis* and *causa instrumentalis*.

In spite of its nuanced restraint, this first paragraph of article 11 of *Dei Verbum* failed to make a major impact on post-Vatican II Catholic biblical scholarship. It was perceived as a statement locked in a traditional framework, irredeemably out of touch with contemporary scholarship's projections about the origins of the biblical books. In fact, the threefold scheme "God—hagiographer—inspired text" may well be applicable to the origins of certain texts, like the (authentic) Pauline letters. But for books like the gospels or the Pentateuch this scheme appears to be too simplistic.

According to modern biblical scholars' treatment of these and other texts of the Bible, the (transcendental) Divine Author coordinated a flow of events in which the text was shaped and transformed, and underwent redactional changes and corrections in successive mental, oral, and written phases, all with the participation of various human beings who may not even have known each other, yet influenced each other's work. In such an understanding, which of them are the *veri auctores,* the "true (literary) authors"? The question reveals a serious gap, separating *Dei Verbum*'s concept of inspiration from the modern scholar's conception of the birth of biblical texts.

But the ultimate problem may come from another direction: the discrepancy of the meanings of literary authorship. The modern concept of a literary author is too closely linked with the way modern literary works are produced, while the traditional doctrine was formulated in a vastly different cultural milieu. Ancient culture had the liberty of speaking of Moses, David, or Solomon in the Old Testament, and the four evangelists, or Peter, Paul, and John in the

---

instrumentality of a secretary in regard to the author, but of a human authorship which remains completely and absolutely unimpaired, which is permeated, embraced but not diminished by the divine authorship. Only in this sense is it an instrument of God. And it is an instrument in such a way that the instrumentality of the writer, linked with the divine authorship, does not only tolerate, but also demands the human authorship, and that there would be no point in divine authorship if man were but a secretary." *Inspiration in the Bible,* 15.

New Testament, invariably as "hagiographers" or "sacred writers" only because they employed a differently applicable, analogous sense of literary authorship. The concept of the "hagiographer" was never sufficiently concretized and, therefore, left the door open to broadly divergent applications.

In *Dei Verbum* the term "hagiographer" is used sparingly, and the document prefers to speak of "authors" rather than of "writers." All this caution, however, had little impact on Catholic biblicists, who needed a concept of inspiration pertinent to the process in which they learned to assess the origin of the biblical texts. Critical scholarship continued to move toward an increasingly anonymous model of the (literary) authors, merging more and more with the concept of "redactors" and "compiler(s)," even with the concept of so-called "traditionalists"—the preachers, teachers, and church leaders of various times who transmitted an oral tradition—who had no intention to produce lasting documents. Which of these people should be then identified with "the chosen persons" envisaged in *Dei Verbum*? Which are the men selected by God to put into writing "those and only those things which God wanted to be put in writing?"[30] Thus, understandably, the carefully crafted sentences of *Dei Verbum* had a weak effect on biblical scholarship after Vatican II.

Dei Verbum also failed to address the issue of verbal inspiration.[31] One can only guess that the general trend at the Council was to be more than cautious with the idea that God determined every iota in the Bible. As a result, however, the traditional formulas about verbal inspiration faded into a respectable retirement. In the end, most readers of the documents of Vatican II were likely to retain little more from the Council's doctrine of inspiration than the notion that after Vatican II, Catholics stopped thinking that the bibli-

30. No. 11. *Dei Verbum* contains no attempt to further a "collective" concept of inspiration, not even in the form in which Karl Rahner presented it in his book quoted above.

31. By definition, if the text is produced under the influence of divine inspiration, then God's influence on the writer must "trickle down" all the way to the text and affect the very words of Scripture. And, in fact, the amount of time and effort spent on text-critical issues seems to indicate a conviction that every bit of verbal nuance in the biblical texts matters.

cal texts were characteristically of divine authorship. They also grew oblivious of the fact that the double authorship applied not only to the meaning of the scriptural text but to Sacred Scripture itself.

The Treatment of Inerrancy in *Dei Verbum*

The topic of inerrancy made history at Vatican II. Since the First Vatican Council it had been like a time bomb waiting to explode; but when it did, it probably created more noise than damage. The manuals treated inerrancy as the chief and most important effect of inspiration, a misperception caused in reaction to many rationalist efforts to find erroneous statements in the Bible. In Christian apologetics, the concept of inerrancy became an exercise in blind denial, excluding any formal error from the canonical text. The progressive wing, which emerged during the first session of the Council as a mighty force, soon set out to terminate this anxious clinging to the concept of inerrancy and to replace it with a more relaxed view that allowed questions concerning the historical, geographic, and scientific accuracy of the Bible. Was it, after all, essential for the Bible to be absolutely free of human error? Would it not seem to be more appropriate for the human authors, as *veri auctores,* to show their limitations and be fallible in matters that would not compromise the transmission of divine truth into human concepts and language? The theologians rewriting the first draft of *Dei Verbum* soon answered this question by eliminating the term "inerrancy" and replacing it with "truth," claiming to introduce a "positive" approach to the topic. This approach, they said, was more consistent with the theology of revelation presented in the first two chapters.

A mere change in vocabulary, of course, can achieve little. Moreover, the inevitable follow-up question, "What kind of truth is meant?" cast shadows from the past, recalling the debates of Vatican I and the positions taken by Leo XIII in his *Providentissimus Deus,* in which he rejected earlier attempts to limit materially the extent of inspiration only to certain topics of the biblical text. Finally, the unimaginable happened: Franz Cardinal König of Vienna—one cardinal facing an ecumenical council—asserted publicly that the Bible contains errors; in retrospect, though, this intervention appears as a relatively minor event and barely merits the label of a scandal. Cardinal König's authority as an expert in oriental studies has now considerably faded, and his samples of "biblical errors," which had been acknowledged for a long time, were at best inconclusive. Even the veneer of his tactfully elegant Latin phrase (*"a veritate deficere,"* meaning "deficient with respect to the truth") has worn off. All that is remembered of his once powerful intervention is that he admitted, "The Bible contains errors."

At the time, of course, this statement caused the procedures to go off track, so that John XXIII stalled the document by taking it off the agenda. Ultimately, however, the topic was given another chance. At the last session of the Council, as a new debate took shape, the question of inerrancy resurfaced. This time, a new schema specified "the truth" which the Bible teaches unfailingly as being *"veritates salutares,"* or "truths which belong to [that is, which promote or effect] salvation." A significant minority reacted adversely, thinking that the formula was ambiguous. The objections raised in the first session reappeared: in spite of its cautious formulation, the new text also limited inerrancy (and thus inspiration) only to religious and moral statements. This time, however, since the progressives had taken control of the Council with a solid majority, the committee to which the issue returned stuck to its guns, hoping that *"veritates salutares"* would eventually pass into the final text.

Again it was the papacy that saved the Council from itself. Paul VI, admitting his own *"perplessità"* about the issue, ordered further study and reflection by sending the text to the Council's Theological Commission, and asking for a new formulation. His request resulted in a phrase that won almost unanimous approval: *"Veritatem quam Deus nostrae salutis causa litteris consignari voluit,"* meaning, "Truth that, for the sake of our salvation, God wanted to be put [namely, by the biblical authors] in writing."[32] This saved the document from ambiguity or even, possibly, from error. Ultimately, how-

32. This is the meaning of a last-minute change of the active *consignare* to the passive *consignari*.

ever, it provided no significant insights or true advancement of the issue under debate. On the one hand, the concept of "truth" in the document still remains undifferentiated and unspecified. Moreover at the request of a substantial minority the phrase *"sine errore"* was eventually reinserted, so that even the vocabulary of inerrancy in its traditional sense showed up again in the text. Therefore, those who refused to accept Cardinal König's contention that sometimes the biblical texts are "deficient in truth" had every reason to agree with the amended text.[33] On the other hand (and this is no small matter for the post-conciliar era), the convoluted grammar of the sentence opened the possibility for ambiguous translations and interpretations. Consequently, in several of its translations, *Dei Verbum* misleadingly appears to teach that inerrancy covers only those statements which regard our salvation. One may say that this misinterpretation caught on early in the reception of the Council, and is being propagated even by recognized and high-quality scholars.[34]

Despite more than a century of bickering over whether or not the Bible's antiquated notions about the physical world and the events of history are errors, the experts of the Council did not manage to reformulate the issue of inerrancy. For the Church Fathers and their medieval followers, the truth of the Bible was its Christological content, that is, a revealed truth offered to the reader, who was to receive it with faith. In their pre-critical approach to history and science, they easily embraced a biblical view of reality. The first two chap-

33. Vorgrimler's commentary translates König's phrase as "lacking accuracy," but the expression *deficit a veritate* is much stronger, for it contains the noun meaning "truth."

34. See, for example, Raymond E. Brown in his most influential *The Critical Meaning of the Bible* (New York: Paulist Press, 1981), 18–19. He suggests that the ambiguity came from a conscious "juxtaposition of more conservative older formulations with more open recent formulations." A curious footnote (p. 18, n. 41) is added which ridicules those "for whom it is a doctrinal issue that the Church never changes." The note recalls Galileo, who, when told that it was a doctrinal issue that the earth does not move, officially changed his position while whispering, *"E pur si muove"* (Nevertheless it moves). This is an unfortunate comment, for the Council deserved a better treatment. The story about Galileo is a legend (so much for historicity) and the Italian quotation is faulty (so much for the "original language"). Supposedly he said, *"Eppure si muove,"* but the statement is widely recognized as apocryphal. However, the insinuation that the Council was purposely misguiding the faithful is very disturbing.

ters of *Dei Verbum* improved on this view by regarding biblical history as an "economy of salvation." Yet a number of issues remained obscure. To see how, as the chief result of inspiration, the Christological truth of the Bible extends itself to each and every part of its text would have demanded a new hermeneutics for which the theologians of Vatican II were not yet prepared. The way in which this kind of revealed truth, the truth of the Bible, relates to the notion of scientific and historical truth which we pursue by modern scholarly research was not successfully explained. In this respect, the conciliar document constitutes no breakthrough. At best, it manages to diffuse some of the rationalistic challenges about *"veritates profanae"* (truths regarding secular issues) by proposing a new point of view, maybe even a new method, to be applied when probing the truthfulness of the Bible's propositional statements. *Dei Verbum* may also have indicated some paths by which the rationalist approach to the "truth of the Bible" may be transcended. It failed, however, to confront squarely the problem—implied in the "double authorship" of Holy Scripture—as actually rooted in the very structure of the economy of salvation: God chose to descend into the realm of human imperfection, where the light of truth is sparse and must exist in the penumbra of partial knowledge mixed with partial ignorance.

Inspiration and Incarnation

The patristic outline of salvation history puts into its center the Incarnation of the Son as the peak of God's self-disclosure, which essentially achieves the divine plan and creates the highest and most intimate union between God and man. All previous anticipations (like the institutions and texts of the Old Testament) and later extensions (like the sacraments and the apostolic writings of the New Testament) draw their meaning and validity from this central event of "God becoming flesh." It is not quite clear when and with what clarity the ancient Church saw an analogy between "God made man" in the Incarnation and "the Divine Logos becoming human word" by means of biblical inspiration. Is it in the "inspired author" (and reader) or in the "inspired text" that human and divine elements are linked? And in what sense is this linkage analogous to the hypostatic union, so that we may speak of biblical Monophysites and Nestorians?[35] It seems that the Church Fathers applied the analogy mostly to the inspired text, pointing out its "quasi-sacramental" qualities.[36] Due to a broader pre-scholastic use of the word *sacramentum,* we find explicit texts all the way up to the twelfth century in which the written word of the Bible is said to be "a sacrament."[37] On the level of the inspired author, however, parallelism between the grace of the Incarnation and the charism of inspiration can only be established with more difficulty. Even if *Dei Verbum* makes use of the patristic idea of divine "condescension" (συγκατάβασις), it is unclear how this analogy operates.[38] Does this parallelism illustrate God's humility in assuming the appearance of human words, or rather in the permanent union between himself and the physical world? In either case, does this truly mean a proper analogy with the hypostatic union (the Word becoming flesh), or is it just a metaphor externally related to the Word made flesh who dwelt among us?[39]

Rahner's use of the term *Schriftwerdung* might throw light on the

35. See Alonso Schökel, *The Inspired Word,* 52–53, with bibliography on 88.

36. One of the early studies was by J. H. Crehan, "The Analogy between *Dei Verbum Incarnatum* and *Dei Verbum scriptum* in the Fathers," *Journal of Theological Studies* 6 (1955): 87–90. Henri de Lubac was among the first to point out that Origen had initiated this parlance, with his influence permeating to most of the Church Fathers and the monastic Middle Ages. See "The Incorporations of the Logos," in *History and Spirit: The Understanding of Scripture according to Origen,* trans. A. E. Nash (San Francisco: Ignatius Press, 2008), 385–426.

37. So, for example, St. Bernard comments on the first verse of the Songs of Songs as *sermonis huius profundissimum sacramentum. Sermo super Cantica* 1, 4, vol. 1 of *Sancti Bernardi Opera Omnia,* 4.

38. The text quotes St. John Chrysostom, *Hom. in Gen 3:1,* 16, 2 (PG 53, 134).

39. In fact, we find in Origen and his followers texts which compare the letter of the scriptural word to the Flesh of the Word, but in the sense of a tool of manifestation or appearance (his vestments), and not nature taken up as his human nature was. See the following texts: by Origen, *"secundum litteram quae tamquam caro Verbi est et indumentum divinitatis eius"* (according to the letter which is, just like the flesh of the Word, the vestment of his Divinity) in *Hom. in Lev.* 1:1 (PG 12, 405a–b); by Ambrose: *"Et fortasse vestimenta Verbi sunt sermones Scripturarum"* (And maybe the vestments of the Word are the texts of the Scriptures), *Hom in Lc* 8:13 (CCL 14, 219); by Bernard: *"Vestimentum profecto spiritus littera est et caro Verbi"* (The vestment of the spirit is the letter and the flesh of Word Incarnate), *Ad milites Templi,* vol. 7 of *Sancti Bernardi Opera Omnia,* 13.

difficulties which arise from a direct comparison between inspiration and Incarnation.[40] For a correct understanding of the statement "the Word became flesh" (Jn 1:14), one needs to make clear that "the Logos" means the Son, the second Divine Person, and "flesh" means Jesus' individual human nature and, thus, that the *Menschwerdung* takes place on the personal level. Yet *Schriftwerdung* does not mean uniting the divine and the human authors in a similar process. Rather, it means that divine revelation becomes perceptible as a human message which is proclaimed and, at the end of the process, becomes written word, fixed and preserved with stable and unchangeable canonicity.

Further reflection leads us to discover that the process of *Schriftwerdung* is not so much a parallel to *Menschwerdung* as it is the continuation and extension of the latter into human writings and records of revelatory "words and deeds" of the Incarnate Word. *Schriftwerdung* is not a parallel or alternative mode for the Logos to plunge into the human realm (as if by an additional κατάβασις), but a mode of transmitting Christ, the one and only Incarnate Word, by means of both the spoken and written word. While in *Menschwerdung* the immutable God enters history in a flux of events peaking with a human being's individual life, in *Schriftwerdung* something of an opposite process takes place: this flow of history becomes crystallized, solidified, and codified in a fixed text and canon. Thus, the latter event resembles the resurrection of Jesus more than his conception and birth. *Schriftwerdung* belongs to the objective side of inspiration, of which modern treatises of biblical inspiration, focusing only on the use of St. Thomas's treatment of prophecy in the *Summa,* tend to lose sight.

Old Testament Scripture

There is something ironic in the uncontentious ease with which chapter 4 of *Dei Verbum,* a surprisingly short summary of the Christian outlook on the Jewish Scriptures, was accepted and integrated

---

40. The term *Schriftwerdung* comes from Hugo Rahner, "Das Menshenbild des Origenes," *Eranos Jahrbuch* 15 (1947): 197–248. The concept, however, is equivalently used by Karl Rahner repeatedly in his book *Inspiration in the Bible.*

into the document. The content of the chapter reflects, once again, a largely patristic point of view that modern biblical scholarship, both inside and outside Catholic circles, has not been able to integrate fully into contemporary exegesis. In fact, while the pre-conciliar patristic *ressourcement* proclaimed the "unity of the two Testaments" as central, Old Testament scholars were much less enthusiastic about joining ranks with a "Christian reading" of the Bible.

One must also say that chapter 4 is based, almost entirely, on the most ancient layers of Christian tradition about the Bible which, due to the rise of critical scholarship, lost much ground and were eventually ignored by modern exegetes. Its medieval reception was resurrected in Henri de Lubac's monumental *Exégèse Médiévale,* the first volume of which was published in 1959, at just about the beginning of the Council, but de Lubac's study never gained much attention in the post-conciliar Catholic renewal; in fact, the English translation of these volumes had to wait for more than thirty years![41]

Dei Verbum's approach to the Old Testament is best rendered in the first sentence of article 15:

> The salvation plan of the Old Testament has been ordered for the main purpose of preparing the coming of Christ, the Redeemer of all and of the messianic kingdom, to announce prophetically this coming (see Lk 24:44; Jn 5:39; 1 Pt 1:10) and to set up for it signs through various types (see 1 Cor 10:12).

Such an approach results in an almost exclusively Christian view of the Old Testament books, as the continuation of the text illustrates:

> The books of the Old Testament, in accordance with mankind's condition before the time of salvation inaugurated by Christ, make manifest to all the knowledge of God and of man, as well as the way in which God, being both just and merciful, deals with the human being.

It is remarkable how this document, when viewing the Old Testament as books, focuses exclusively on its universal and ongoing relevance. The text offers no word about the role of Jewish exegesis, or the

---

41. *Medieval Exegesis,* vols. 1–2, trans. Mark Sebanc (Grand Rapids, Mich.: Eerdmans, 1998–2000).

meaning of these texts for their original or contemporary addressees. Equally astonishing is the fact that the Pontifical Biblical Commission's document of 2002, entitled *About the Jewish People and Their Sacred Scriptures in the Christian Bible,* signified a full return of the pendulum to its opposite extreme by showing only minimal esteem for mainstream patristic exegesis, settling instead for a double track of meaning for the Old Testament, one Jewish and one Christian, the latter being set up side by side with a Jewish reading of Scripture which can still be carried out from a perspective of mere expectation. In the Christian reading, Jesus is "for us still the One to come." Nonetheless, when He comes, "He will have the traits of the Jesus who has already come and is already present and active among us."

This effort of combining a positive appreciation of present-day Jewish exegesis with a Christological fulfillment of the Old Testament is hardly present in *Dei Verbum.* After explaining the historical role of the Scriptures for the Jewish people of old, the conciliar text grounds the "permanent value" *(perennem valorem)* of the Old Testament texts in a Christological perspective. Originally they prophetically anticipated the economy of salvation, but then this history came to its end, exhibiting no resources for justifying "a Jewish reading of the Bible." Moving in the opposite direction, the Biblical Commission's document states that such a "Jewish reading of the Hebrew Bible is both possible and necessary." Such a reading stands "in continuity with the Jewish Sacred Scriptures from the Second Temple period, a reading analogous to the Christian reading which developed in a parallel fashion." While we cannot fully discuss the Biblical Commission's document here, the basic features of its divergence from *Dei Verbum* must be pointed out. These can be summarized in three paragraphs:

First, the Biblical Commission made no attempt to integrate into the Catholic, and especially patristic, exegetical tradition its new approach to the Jewish interpretation of Scripture. One remains perplexed how new paths for dealing with Jewish exegesis may be opened without first studying patristic and medieval tradition on the rather complex issue of the *"Judaica interpretatio."*

Second, the Biblical Commission's document seems to say that both Jewish and Christian exegetical traditions are equally legitimate or should be embraced on equal footing. Actually, by referring to two different "faiths" (and stating in the same paragraph that the rabbinical traditions exclude faith in Jesus), its puzzling statements about "two irreducible" readings of the Old Testament may lead us to think that by "readings" the document deals with nothing more than the literal sense, without engaging the reader's faith. The ancient sense of *littera,* however, cannot be identified with either the modern literal sense or "the historical and critical meaning" aimed at by modern exegesis.

Third, there remains the possibility that the Biblical Commission was pursuing here a goal more pragmatic than theological. If that was indeed the case, one must point out, also pragmatically, that Jewish-Christian cooperation in achieving a literal reading of the Bible is a tradition spanning two thousand years. Therefore, its future can neither be meaningfully discussed without an awareness of this long history, nor advanced without an exploration of the common elements of the Jewish and Christian faiths which, in the past and on both sides, transcended the positivistic historical-critical method of modern exegesis.

The last paragraph of chapter 4 (no. 16) of *Dei Verbum* is surprisingly and regrettably short. Using well-known and old formulas, *Dei Verbum* states the relationship of the two Testaments: the New Testament is hidden *(latet)* in the Old, the Old shows its meaning *(patet)* in the New. Accordingly, the text continues, the proclamation of the gospel recapitulates and resumes the texts of the Old Testament so that they both acquire a new meaning and obtain their own full meaning. In doing so, the two Testaments mutually enlighten and explain each other. In spite of its simple grammar, the meaning of this paragraph is complex and convoluted. It also leaves a number of questions unresolved. In particular, it lacks clarity about the sense in which the "fulfillment" of Old Testament texts is achieved by the New. How do texts obtain a full meaning *(completam significationem)* in *other* texts so that this full meaning is indeed their own, and is, therefore, neither added nor superimposed? In its document written forty years later, the Biblical Commission appeared rather perplexed about *Dei Verbum's* formulation of this "fulfillment," stating that it is "an extremely complex notion" (no. 21) and then, in a lengthy development, took issue with various failed schemes of this concept, all termed "fundamentalist," and thus unacceptable.

At this point, we realize why *Dei Verbum* is incomplete: it needed to provide more specific guidelines about the relationship of the two Testaments, probably by appealing both generally to Christology, and specifically to the theandrical nature of the acts of Christ. As acts performed by the Incarnate Son of God, they transcend the limitations of history and therefore equally impact past and future. Since their subject is the Divine Logos, they become retroactively and anticipatorily effective. This fact can validate their ongoing actuality and a continued reading about them within the framework of a universal salvation economy.

New Testament Scripture

The fifth chapter of *Dei Verbum* is again short and profoundly steeped in patristic thought. It begins by extolling the superiority of the New Testament as that part of the Bible which presents God's word and salvific power in a pre-eminent way *(praecellenti modo)*. The text does not hesitate to assert that Christ alone has "words of life eternal" (cf. Jn 6:68); he came at the "fullness of time" (Gal 4:4) and the mystery he revealed may not be approached in any other way (cf. Eph 4:4–6). Moreover, among the writings of the New Testament, the four canonical gospels are foremost, for they give firsthand witness to the life and teaching of the Word Incarnate.

The Scriptures are put on three different levels of dignity and importance, based on their closeness to Christ. On the highest level we find the four gospels, then the rest of the apostolic writings, and finally the books of the Old Testament in two subcategories of "law" and "prophets." This grouping of the Bible as a graduated collection of books is explicitly present in the patristic heritage. In his

Commentary on John, Origen asks in what sense all Scripture may be called "gospel" and ends up with a similar hierarchy of biblical books.[42] By this system, Origen subsumes all Scripture under the one term "gospel," meaning the proclamation of Christ in the humility of his Incarnation and in his glorious risen life.

The conciliar document also asserts the "apostolic origin of the four Gospels" (no. 18). The statement is non-ambiguous: "The Church always held and everywhere holds" *(semper tenuit et ubique tenet)* this conviction. This leaves little doubt that the Council meant to affirm the apostolic origin of the gospels as a tenet of faith taught by the consensus of all Church Fathers and the Magisterium. The rest of paragraph no. 18 further explains this statement. It uses the term *apostolici viri* as it was used by Tertullian to express that the apostolic authorship of the gospels does not necessarily imply literary authorship by one of the Twelve. The term, however, does mean that each gospel takes its origin from apostolic preaching and is correctly attributed either to a specific Apostle (Matthew or John) or one of the collaborators of the Apostles (Mark or Luke). This is also the sense in which St. Irenaeus understood the canonical gospels.[43]

In spite of *Dei Verbum*'s statement to the contrary, the majority of leading Catholic biblical scholars in the post-conciliar period began to call the canonical gospels anonymous works. It became customary, in fact, to regard the so-called "superscriptions" in the ancient manuscripts ("Gospel according to N.") as later additions without historical foundation. Martin Hengel's studies on the *Überschriften* of the Gospels (which prove the ancient origin and reli-

---

42. A concise summary of Origen's thought on this matter is found under the heading "The Old Testament Is Gospel" in George T. Montague, *Understanding the Bible* (New York: Paulist Press, 2006), 28–39.

43. The short paragraph in Irenaeus (*Adv. Haereses,* III, 1) expresses a clear logical sequence in three steps:

    1. Matthew preached the Gospel and put it in writing in Aramaic—during that time Peter and Paul preached in Rome;

    2a. after their death (= ἔξοδος) Mark gave written form to Peter's preaching, and

    2b. Luke, a companion of Paul, wrote another Gospel—

    3. finally John, the Lord's disciple who rested on His breast, wrote a Gospel in Ephesus of Asia Minor.

ability of these superscriptions) are still not known well enough in Catholic literature, while the popularity of Raymond Brown's writings discouraged contrary opinions.[44] All this happened on account of the post-conciliar shifts in Catholic scholarly positions on the authorship of the four gospels, which we may summarize in the following points.

First, the credibility of Papias's witness supporting the apostolic origins of the Gospels of Matthew and Mark has decreased because of a curious alliance between modern critical scholarship and the anti-millenarist bias that led Eusebius to make derogatory comments about Papias. Eusebius himself, however, never doubted Mark's ties to Peter's preaching or the fourth gospel's Johannine origin. He only criticized Papias with regard to the attribution of the Book of Revelation to the Apostle John, claiming that he was uninformed and of poor judgment. Similarly, by suggesting that perhaps all second-century sources on the gospels (Justin, Irenaeus, Clement of Alexandria, Tertullian, and others)[45] depended on Papias, modern critics questioned all patristic evidence about the apostolic origin of the gospels.[46]

Second, by adopting the two-source hypothesis and assuming that Matthew's gospel depended on Mark, scholars judged it improbable that Matthew, an eyewitness, could have written a gospel that relied on Mark, who was not an eyewitness. In addition, the early tradition (represented also by Papias) about an original Aramaic form of the Gospel of Matthew was ruled out by linguistic arguments showing that the Greek text was not a translation from a Semitic original.

Third, most post-conciliar publications further declared that the identification of Luke's gospel with "that of the Apostle Paul" was critically pointless, since Paul knew very little about the historical

44. Martin Hengel, *Studies in the Gospel of Mark* (London: SCM Press, 1985). Brown, *The Critical Meaning of the Bible*, 69–71.

45. The anti-Marcionite prologues and the Muratorian Canon could be included as well.

46. It is routinely overlooked that Papias *quotes another older tradition,* and thus the hypothesis of making Papias the "creative" source of all this tradition is absurd. Moreover, Hengel has shown that the superscriptions and Papias's source ("the presbyter") must have been contemporaries; hence we have multiple attestations of an older tradition.

Jesus. Furthermore, the Church Fathers' tendency to identify Luke's work with Paul's "τὸ εὐαγγέλιόν μου" was thought to be based on an anachronistic understanding of the word εὐαγγέλιον, for in the first century εὐαγγέλιον meant an oral message of salvation; only in the second century did it begin to connote a literary composition. The Pauline link in Luke's gospel was also discredited by showing that the image of Paul in Acts was historically inaccurate, and thus neither Acts nor Luke's gospel could be attributed to an author who knew Paul. As a result, there was no reason left for considering Luke's gospel "apostolic."

Fourth, the *Quaestio Johannaea*—the debate on the authorship of the Fourth Gospel—was solved, or rather dissolved, by identifying "the beloved disciple" with an anonymous figure of the early Church, and the "John" of the Johannine writings with one or several early Church figures, presbyters and/or prophets, but certainly not the son of Zebedee. On this point, in addition, a claim was introduced that John the Apostle suffered early martyrdom. Using old liturgical calendars and the assumption that Jesus' prediction of the martyrdom of the sons of Zebedee must have been based in the synoptic tradition as a *vaticinium ex eventu,* scholars began to assume that the early Church preferred to suppress the tradition about John's martyrdom, rather than accept a non-apostolic authorship for the fourth gospel.

These four points, which permeate the present state of research as a whole, summarize a definite tendency in Catholic biblical scholarship that runs contrary to *Dei Verbum.* The document abstained from discussing the shades of meaning for the concept of literary authorship in antiquity, and intended to keep an open mind about the role of further redactors and editors. Unfortunately, in the post-conciliar climate, the open-ended approach of the document was misinterpreted as a signal that the doctrinal guidelines of the past had lost their validity and *denial of the apostolic origin* of the canonical gospels was apparently *opinio communis* in Catholic publications.[47]

47. See for example, Daniel J. Harrington, *The Gospel of Matthew* (Collegeville, Minn.: Liturgical Press, 1991), 8. But the pendulum might have begun to move back in

An even more damaging conflict between *Dei Verbum* and its Catholic reception concerns the historicity of the canonical gospels, which the document addresses in no. 19, a text largely based on the introductory verses of the Lucan double work, Luke 1:1–4 and Acts 1:1–4. Without making explicit statements about the literary genre of a gospel, it focuses on the process by which the apostolic preaching about Jesus was shaped into stable forms of a mostly oral tradition, and was eventually channeled into four literary works that later became the canonical gospels. The document emphasizes that this tradition pays equal attention to "deeds and words" *(fecit et docuit, fecerat et docuerat)*. Such a view has been widely contradicted by scholars who use the Gospel of Thomas as a "fifth gospel," overlooking the fact that this writing does not contain narratives and lacks interest in Jesus' "deeds," including his passion and resurrection. Rejecting the Gnostic trend, *Dei Verbum* cannot recognize the apocryphal gospels as gospels, either in the form of "revelatory discourses" or "dialogues" between Jesus and his disciples; yet with a fairly tolerant attitude, it did not exclude the possibility that, at the composition of the canonical gospels, collections of sayings (the so-called *Testimonia*) had been preserved either in the oral or written form, and eventually influenced the composition of the canonical gospels.

Dei Verbum insists that if and when the authors of the canonical gospels participated in the process which led from oral to written forms of Tradition, they did so selecting only a portion of the available material which they then recorded in writing *(auctores conscripserunt quaedam. . .seligentes)*. While the document recognizes the possibility that the original gospel writers used a mixture of oral and written sources *(e multis aut ore aut iam scripto traditis)*, yet it clearly asserts that the composition of the gospels does not rely merely on the memories of eyewitnesses, but also on a fuller understanding *(pleniore intelligentia)* provided both by the disciples' post-resurrection encounters with Jesus and the enlightenment by the

---

support of the position of *Dei Verbum* as in, for example, a new German publication by Hans-Joachim Schulz, *Die apostolische Herkunft der Evangelien* [The Apostolic Provenance of the Gospels] (Freiburg in Br.: Herder, 1995).

"Spirit of truth" *(eventibus gloriosis Christi instructi et lumine Spiritus veritatis edocti).*

Indeed, *Dei Verbum* collects a number of insights formed by recent scholarship about the process of redactional activities accompanying the formation of the gospels. The model presented by *Dei Verbum* includes compositional changes of the material either for the sake of topical or doctrinal synthesis *(quaedam in synthesim redigentes),* or accommodation to the needs of the local communities *(vel statui ecclesiarum attendendo explanantes),* or even for retaining an exhortative focus of preaching and teaching *(formam denique praeconii retinentes).*

One can confidently state that the document provides a balanced methodology by which the transmission of the Jesus tradition appears as a possibly complex and protracted process, allowing a number of alternative hypothetical scenarios, yet not prescribing any particular source theory. It certainly does not impose any particular synoptic source theory; it does not even mention Matthean or Marcan priority. It avoids references to both ancient and recent theories about the chronological order of the gospels. But, equally important, *Dei Verbum* does not speak about the evangelists' "creative" expansion of tradition, the "retrojection" of post-resurrection prophetic utterances into the activities of the earthly Jesus, or the formation of Dominical sayings from Christologically rewritten Old Testament material and apocryphal texts. No mention is made of a possible accretion to the Jesus tradition from creative prophecy and exegesis for the sake of solving doctrinal or moral problems for the early Church. *Dei Verbum* does allow much room for the activities of the Paraclete teaching the apostolic communities the "fullness of truth" (see Jn 16:13), without allowing the insertion of fictional narratives, the invention or exaggeration of miraculous happenings, and gratuitous biographical details. While abstaining from drawing a concrete division between the authentic and the apocryphal (oral) tradition, the document consistently embraces the whole canonical Jesus tradition as historical and normative and refuses to allow the revision of the Church's understanding of Jesus through extra-canonical sources.

A Balance of the Council's Work

A present-day review of the theological content of *Dei Verbum* leads us back to a list of satisfactory gains and accomplishments, as well as to a set of desiderata, that is, goals to be reached by further study and renewed emphasis on introductory disciplines for the study of the Bible.

By its most significant impact on the theological thinking of the Church, *Dei Verbum* has restored the outlook of the patristic and medieval tradition by demanding that scriptural inspiration be handled in the context of revelation, and further that revelation be looked at in the context of a salvation economy. This approach opened up for modern times a wealth of traditional theological thinking: texts of patristic exegesis, preaching, catechesis, and liturgical texts and rites, as well as the whole world of ancient spirituality, including monastic theology.

The discrepancies that divide the modern historical consciousness from the biblical outline of history have become more apparent, requiring a new approach. We face more acutely than ever before the need to reconcile the present-day history of religions, the philosophy of religion, the theology of culture and history, or put more simply, the theology of "man" and of "time" embedded in those pre-critical assumptions characteristic of Christian theology throughout its development.

Recent decades have seen renewed efforts to return to the unity of the Bible as a framework of interpretation. Often called "canonical interpretation" or "canonical criticism," this new approach is connected most importantly with Brevard Childs and his vision of biblical interpretation. The theology of *Dei Verbum* has much to learn from and much to offer this trend. Although both the views expressed in *Dei Verbum* and the foundational ideal of canonical interpretation are honestly committed to the use of historical criticism and the reading of the Bible in the framework of Christian faith, they nevertheless also steer clear of the agnostic or skeptical presuppositions of the Enlightenment. At the same time, canonical interpretation has not yet discovered and embraced the fullness of the patristic heritage in terms of the Rule of Faith, the context of Sacred Tradition, and the Magisterium.

Even though *Dei Verbum* initiated a new synthesis of biblical inspiration, the post-conciliar years were unable to follow up on these initiatives in any significant way. Our understanding of the patristic tradition of inspiration is still fragmentary and obscure. We cannot tell with clarity what the Church's tradition really teaches about the divine authorship of the biblical books, how the divine and human sides of biblical authorship are related, and how the human intermediaries of revelation are to be seen in their multiple functions of initiating and furthering the written records of divine revelation. In order to bring greater clarity, the following specific tasks may be confronted:

First, we must discover how the formation of the Bible transmits the charism of the "prophets and Apostles" as intermediaries of the divine Word to "hagiographers," the biblical authors establishing written records of revelation for the ongoing spiritual nourishment of God's People.

Second, we must also see how the "subjective inspiration" that affected the hagiographers resulted in biblical texts (sacred or inspired books in the sense of an "objective inspiration") and in the Church's firm possession of the canon.

Third, we must revisit the issue of a "verbal inspiration," which transcends both pre-critical naïveté and critical arrogance with a post-critical theological sobriety recognizing the importance of the canonical text's accuracy and the Church's ongoing vigilance over the scriptural text.

Finally, we must explore the ecumenical relevance and potential of the New Testament canon, one of the few elements of the Christian heritage that, in the course of Church history, has survived most storms of disunity and disintegration.[48] It may be of importance

48. The canon of the New Testament is essentially a product of the second century's anti-Gnostic battle in which, among other things, the Apostle's Creed also took its shape. In spite of the controversies that later enveloped Revelation and Hebrews, all

to investigate the causes that made this collection of twenty-seven books so resistant to all forces of division that today all Christian schools of theology are able to use the same critical text of the New Testament. We should see if we can find paths leading to common avenues of interpretation and theological methodology beyond a common canon and canonical text.

Christian Bibles today have the same table of contents and no proposals for altering the New Testament canon have received significant support.

X. INSPIRATION, CANON, AND INTERPRETATION

A Systematic Presentation

The previous chapters of this book have anticipated the method to be used for a systematic presentation of a "theology of Scripture." I repeat here only that the lack of monographic studies on the doctrine of inspiration in ancient and medieval traditions presents today the greatest obstacle to the completion of this task.

The Point of Departure

Particularly important when determining the point of departure for a systematic theological understanding of inspiration is this question: Is the "divine authorship" of the Bible the correct fundamental assertion on which the theology of inspiration is to be based? Karl Rahner, even while raising concerns about the approach taken by *"Schultheologie"* (the theology of the "textbooks" used between the Second World War and the Second Vatican Council), seemed to agree with their approach on this point. He assumed, as most textbooks of his time did, the validity of the thesis evident in the title of Cardinal Bea's article *"Deus Auctor Scripturarum,"* and, further, he assumed that this principle of the divine authorship of Scripture was unanimously and unambiguously taught by the Church Fathers and the medieval theologians.

However, Alonso Schökel's *The Inspired Word* has shown that this assumption must be further investigated and, in any case, further qualified or refined. Ancient tradition applied the concept of a literary authorship infrequently, cautiously, and, at best, only analogously to the divine "authorship" of Holy Scripture. Furthermore, it is not clear that the fundamental question about Scripture centers on the issue of a double (human and divine) authorship.[1] In fact, it remains to be seen in just what sense Catholic theology should apply to God and man a common notion of literary authorship. A careful reading of *Dei Verbum* brought us to the conviction that the Council's greatest accomplishment was to show a path by which the theology of inspiration could be rescued from the impasse of the "double authorship" by recasting it in the framework of a newly developed theology of revelation, defined in Trinitarian and Christological terms and inserted into the context of salvation history.

Trinitarian and Christological Framework

The primary paradigm of the mystery that a theology of inspiration must treat is not that of the "God Who Writes" but of the "God Who Speaks." The opening phrase of a treatise on biblical inspiration is not about *Deus auctor Scripturae,* but much more aptly about God as described in the scriptural verse: "In many and various ways God spoke in the past to our ancestors by the prophets, but in these last days he has spoken to us through the Son, whom he appointed heir of all things, through whom he also created the worlds" (Heb 1:1–2).

In the background of the image of God addressing his rational creatures by words stands the Christian concept of God: God as communion, the internal and external mutual communion between Father and Son through their Spirit. In the mystery of a threefold Oneness, a triad of communication, understanding, and love, in fact

---

1. The concept of revelation as a sacred history of "facts and deeds" in which God acts through the mediation of human agents ("prophets and Apostles") preconditions in both Old and New Testaments the concept of "inspired authors" and the divine authority ruling over their literary activity. We have verified that this concept is foundational for a Christian appropriation of the books of an "Old Testament" (see chapter I) and for the formation of a "New Testament" as a collection of books, see chapters II and III.

a communion by love, defines both self-possession and mutuality, both absolute aseity and relational mutuality.

God's speaking *ad extra,* that is, to his creatures, must be understood as an extension and expression of the internal mystery of his Triune exchange, which constitutes his inner life. When he chooses to create his rational creatures and to invite them into his inner life, the speech by which he addresses them must be seen as part of his "salvation plan," a chain of actions by which he attracts those he created into personal communion with himself. God's "word" is not a mere metaphor by which God's self-expression is compared to a human use of sounds—phonemes linked through grammar and syntax, a system by which finite rational beings post signs for exchanging various states of human consciousness. On the contrary, God's Word is essential to his nature: his inner life consists of eternal and uninterrupted speech.[2] When he creates rational beings—angelic or human—the purpose of his action is to extend his "speech" of knowledge and love. Equivalently, we can say that his acts of creating rational beings endowed with free will are directed toward the inclusion of these creatures in his inner life. He does not engage in such activity—either the creation or the elevation of the creature to a level of supernatural existence—by any constraint. Such a claim would be incompatible with God's absolute freedom and autonomy. But, in fact, by sending his Logos, his Word, into the world to take up a life in the flesh, God has revealed this intention as "the mystery of his will" which he brought to fullness in Christ (see Eph 1:9), a mystery hidden for ages past but manifested "now," in the "now" of the Christian revelation to "the saints," the members of his holy people (see Col 1:16).

The main elements of such an opening paradigm are easily identified in the scriptural passage of Hebrews 1:1–2, quoted above.[3] God's

---

2. I would like to refer to a text by St. Bernard, commenting on Ps 62: *Semel locutus est Deus. Semel utique quia semper. Una enim et non interpolata sed continua et perpetua locutio est. Sermones de diversis* 5, 2, vol. VI–1 of *Sancti Bernardi Opera Omnia,* ed. J. Leclercq (Rome: Editiones Cistercienses, 1970), 99. I propose the following translation: "God spoke only once, once only because he keeps on speaking for ever. For He is one single, uninterrupted, and eternal speech act."

3. The original Greek text is heavily endowed with Hebraisms: God spoke "in" the

"speech" is not merely verbal; it consists of "words and deeds." All his "speaking" is focused on his speech through the Son but also involves "all things," meaning the whole of creation and of history. It is structured by time, beginning in a past that goes back to our ancestors, centers on "the last days" in which his Son enters history, and aims at the completion of history when the Son becomes fully the heir of "all things."

In this outline, Christ, the Incarnate Word, constitutes the peak of divine revelation. His actions and teaching must, therefore, be considered as those events and words by which God revealed himself most closely and clearly. While the terms "inspired speech," "divine self-disclosure," and "Word of God" are analogous concepts which can be applied in different degrees to the deeds and words of salvation history witnessed to in the Sacred Scriptures, the "words and deeds" of Jesus constitute the *"primum analogatum"*—the concrete realities to which these concepts refer first and foremost, properly and directly. All other realities can be called the "word of God" only insofar as they participate by some linkage or resemblance to the one and only revelatory Incarnation of the Son of God.

Revelation in and through History

The biblical outline of revelation clearly isolates creation as an initial and universal revelatory act apart from the particular history of salvation, which begins with the election of Abraham and leads on, through the forming of the People of Israel and the vicissitudes of its history, to the arrival of the Messiah who comes not only to save his people from their sins (Mt 1:21), but also to be "the Savior of the world" (Jn 4:42). This means that the mystery of the Incarnation is inserted into a particular milieu characterized by a particular

---

prophets, then "in" his Son. This preposition "in" ("*bᵉ*" in Hebrew) refers to the human agents not only as spokesmen, but, in their concrete and individual reality, as actors. In the Vulgate, which translates both occurrences as "in," this vision was effectively transmitted, for the Latin writers of the Middle Ages saw in *auctor* and *actor* the same concept differentiated only by spelling.

historical and cultural setting: with a mother divinely chosen at a given point in history, within the framework of the small ethnic and national community that God had started, watched over, and cultivated. As a poem by Isaiah describes it,

> My beloved had a vineyard on a very fertile hill. He dug it up and cleared it of stones, and planted it with choice vines; he built a watchtower in the midst of it, and hewed out a wine vat in it; and he looked for it to yield grapes, but it yielded wild grapes. (Is 5:1–2)[4]

In this more restricted and specific framework, not only does God linearly prepare and pedagogically develop his entrance into human history; he also anticipates and extends the mystery of his coming to man as one single and continuously penetrating divine action that cumulatively permeates the human being's existence as it is laid out in time. One may indeed say that only "when the time had fully come," at a particular moment or designated time, did "God send forth his Son, born of woman" (Gal 4:4). Yet all moments of this salvation history reflect the same light, each according to its age and context, like individual mirrors, reverberating from the one and only Sun shining over them all. Thus from Abraham through Moses and the whole history of Israel, one single "coming of the Lord" is anticipated. As the gospels testify to one central and full arrival of God in the flesh, so the apostolic Church was initiated by one universal sending, resulting in God's coming to all nations of the globe and all times of history "until the close of the ages" (Mt 28:20).

Prophets and Apostles

It is an essential aspect of this scheme of revelation that it centers on the Incarnation and expands on the same, namely on "God becoming man," so that in all its parts it operates through the media-

---

4. Resumed in Ps 88, this image is part of the most sweeping presentation of Israel's history by Jesus, the Parable of the Wicked Tenants (Mt 21:33–43; Mk 12:1–9; Lk 20:9–16), expanding on a frequent phrase of Jeremiah: "I have persistently sent all my servants the prophets to them, day after day" (Jer 7:25; 25:4; 29:19; 35:15; 44:4).

tion of human beings, chosen and sent by God to transmit his word to the rest of the world.[5] This reality of the Incarnation is strongly emphasized in Hebrews 1:1 quoted above, which compares God's speech "through the prophets" to his speech "through his own Son"; it is equally articulated in the Parable of the Wicked Tenants, a parable which, present in each synoptic gospel, describes first a chain of prophets sent by the owner to the tenants and finally the arrival of the Son whom they equally maltreat and even kill. Prophetic mediation of God's word is paired up with a further extension of the same paradigm in Luke's gospel: "I will send them prophets and apostles, some of whom they will kill and persecute" (11:49). In this Tradition has seen an allusion to the two Testaments, each transmitting the divine message by its appropriate human mediators and replicating by anticipation or extension the destiny of the crucified Son of God.[6]

From Spoken Message to Written Record

The study of biblical inspiration in its strict and proper sense begins at the point where we focus on a specific question: How, when, and why did God's revelatory word become stable and permanent as a text in written form, which was then ready to be redacted, edited, and transmitted from generation to generation under the auspices of a community of believers and its leadership?

First, one must realize that the transition from spoken to written word characterizes mankind's cultural history in general. In the history of God's chosen people, the introduction of written documents sought to obtain three main goals: anchoring historical remembrance, stabilizing and standardizing moral and legal rules, and creating a permanent framework for worship. This process per

---

5. This is the central vision of the second century, which was already in possession of a "canonical principle."

6. St. Paul sees the triple parallel of "Prophets—Jesus—Apostles" with regard to both the mediation of God's message and its violent rejection on the part of the intended recipients in a famous text that is still under some debate, yet cannot be proven to be an interpolation. The text refers to "the Jews who killed both *the Lord Jesus* and *the prophets*, and drove *us* (that is, Paul and his fellow missionaries) out" (1 Thes 2:15).

se can be observed in every culture and religion. In the culture of Israel two special features appear as the topical and theological center of Israel's sacred literature: the basic and constitutive event of the Exodus, followed by a journey through the desert and the conquest of a homeland. Israel's relating itself to a sacred tradition connected with the figure of Moses meant that God's word was transmitted as "Torah," or Way of Life—the remembrance of God's great deeds and commandments to which Israel responded by establishing its moral, legal, and cultic institutions. This proves that the roots of the Bible are buried in the experience of the Exodus, an experience through which God himself gave an education to his people, revealing himself as Creator and Savior, as the initiator of Israel's origins through the patriarchal ancestors who also gave them Moses as a lasting mediator between God and his people. This view of Moses as a mediator of the Torah already implies the institutional permanence of the Mosaic revelation, which thus had to lead through channels of oral traditions and written documents to a final crystallization of the Torah in the Pentateuch.

Another foundational event in Israel's development was the exile and restoration. Through a series of new historical upheavals and divine interventions, this event corrected and completed Israel's understanding of both God and itself, resulting not only in a repossession but also a re-interpretation of the significance of the Exodus and of the Torah. In this two-phased history of Israel's movements first from Egypt to the Land, then from the Land to Babylon and back, Israel became a paradigm of God's dealings with mankind. The road is marked by covenants broken and renewed, the experience of being chosen and rejected, forgiven and restored, and of possessing, in fact, the precarious yet permanent status of being God's own people.

On account of both human need and divine providence, the process outlined here began to generate its literary reflection; the people of Israel began to face the need not only of recalling and remembering the Torah and the interventions of its prophets, but also of systematically documenting and preserving the written records of its religious history.

Although scholarship still remains rather vague and undecided about the exact dating of most books of the Hebrew Bible, it is amply proven that the formation of Scripture reached new intensity right after the Exile and obtained growing momentum all the way until the reconstruction of the Temple. Although there is no reason to doubt either the literacy of the leaders of the Exodus or the flourishing of a rich and varied literary life during the monarchy, only in the post-exilic period did the sacred literature of the Israelites obtain the form in which we know it today and Jesus and his contemporaries knew it two thousand years ago. The post-exilic period witnessed another important event. Due to the appearance and the rapid expansion of Hellenistic culture, the Hebrew Bible was translated into Greek and eventually new books written in Greek were inserted into the literary heritage of the Old Testament. In this way, not long before Jesus' time, the biblical culture of Judaism went through a massive expansion, spreading in the Greco-Roman world in *koine* Greek, an international language that then prepared for a new *Schriftwerdung,* that is, the composition of the New Testament books, when, in the last years of the first century, the teaching of Jesus and of his first disciples obtained their crystallized form.

As we have stated from the very beginning of this book, the apostolic Church considered its mission to be joined essentially to the interpretation of the Scriptures. Moreover, while explaining Jesus' "words and deeds," it produced an additional set of sacred books. The first conscious reflections about this new *Schriftwerdung* surfaced shortly after the process came to its close. Then there appeared among Christians a growing awareness that the Church's faithful perseverance in the teaching of Jesus and his Apostles required guaranteed resources, a faithfully preserved and identified set of writings transmitted as documents containing authentic records of the first Christian communities. Concretely, however, this process took place within a cultic context centered on the Eucharist, which provided the flow of tradition both with consistency and permanence with an increasingly manifest need for the stability of the written word. In this sense we argued for a "Eucharistic cradle" or a "Eucharistic provenance" of the

New Testament, essentially ordered to the extension of Christ's presence in space and time and in the daily lives of the Christian churches.

Theology of Inspiration

The Definition of Inspiration

In a technical sense, "biblical inspiration" means the divine action stimulating the human authors of the biblical books to produce their work, and the divine charism bestowed upon the biblical authors, enabling them to produce those literary works which make up part of the Bible. Traditionally the theology of inspiration worked with a "single-author model," which is, in fact, a model easily applicable to cases like the authentic Pauline epistles, each of which we assume had one author responsible both for the work as a whole and all its parts as we have it today in its original form.[7] However, biblical scholars assume more often than not that most books of the Bible were produced over the course of a historical process which has run through different stages of composition and redaction involving several human authors. In these cases "biblical inspiration" is to be conceived as a divine grace guiding all individuals involved in the process and bringing about as its final product the canonical text of the book in question. For example, in the case of the gospels, an oral phase of the tradition starting with the apostolic Church's proclamation *(kerygma)* and catechesis was continued by the work of some individuals who stabilized and finalized the oral text and set themselves the task of composing the final written products, published in the canonical gospels under the names of Matthew or Mark or Luke or John.[8]

7. This "single-author model" is part of the Bible's conceptual framework of the human transmission of God's word: God *speaks* to his people by using individuals as human intermediaries. Thus, even for quoting the written text of the Bible, most often it is the *viva vox* that remains primary in the biblical imagery of inspiration. Not only Heb 1:1–2, quoted above, but also 2 Pt 1:21 regard the word of God transmitted in scripture as *speech*. Nonetheless the Bible presents itself as prophetic or apostolic "scripture" transmitting what God *said* through Moses or the prophets, and the apostolic teaching originating with Jesus. See above in chapter III.

8. It is here that we can see the relevance of what we said about the liturgical ambience in which the synoptic gospels were formed and shaped. See above, chapter IV.

A correct understanding of the concept of inspiration must also avoid the simplistic view that considers the process reduced either to the individualistic notion of one person's enlightened intellect and guided will, or to the romantic notion of a collective consciousness "emerging," without a definite and divinely chosen person's conscious and responsible activity. In most cases *in concreto,* inspiration cannot be adequately distinguished from revelation: God himself, in his self-disclosure to Moses or to Jeremiah or to Peter, accompanies "his word," the revealed message, in order that it may be expressed, transmitted, and eventually preserved in written form in the canonical books, and that the apostolic Church may recognize these as "God's word" addressing his Church. Formally, however, a distinction between revelation and inspiration can be readily made, for, technically speaking, inspiration concerns God's influence, which causes his word both to be communicated in written form and to be recognized as such by those to whom God has entrusted the care of his Church, while revelation as such implies only transmission of knowledge (conceptual and experiential) not necessarily accompanied by promptings that this knowledge be also expressed.

The Subdivision of Inspiration

We can distinguish between subjective and objective inspiration. The first is often regarded as inspiration in its primary and proper sense: the divine charism itself by which human beings are led and assisted to produce literary works conveying God's word. But in a secondary and derivative sense we can also speak about "objective inspiration" as a term used to describe the sacred text itself: that inspired quality or ultimately divine provenance characterizing the text as God's word. This distinction appears in the way Christian tradition attributed special dignity to the biblical texts by either referring to their prophetic and apostolic authors or speaking of them as vehicles for God's word, as texts containing divinely intended meaning, which are then to be used by human readers in the Church. Inspiration in its subjective sense would seem to be an extension of the charism of revelation, while inspiration in the objective sense would seem to reside in the consciousness of the Church as a set of presuppositions concerning biblical texts: certain writings must be regarded as sacred by all who read, preach, or interpret them in the Church.[9]

A theological treatment of biblical inspiration must aim at linking these two sides: we must show how the written transmission of revelation through chosen human spokesmen eventually constitutes "sacred texts," which the Church must hold in special esteem, venerate as receptacles of God's word, and interpret by searching with faith and humility for their divinely intended meaning.

Double Authorship Linked with Instrumental Causality

While the Magisterium has consistently retained the vocabulary of a "double authorship"—attributing the scriptural books both to God and to human "authors"—we have also seen that in both ancient tradition and in more recent times, as well as in *Dei Verbum,* this double authorship was affirmed only in an analogous and not in a univocal sense. It was important to see how the anti-Marcionite statements of the Church Fathers, which assigned God's *auctoritas* to the Old and to the New Testament *pari modo,* left open the question whether God was the "literary author" of the biblical books. The Councils of Florence and Trent, using the same language, replaced the anti-Marcionite concern with a canonical agenda and again spoke not exactly about authorship, but rather authority. This approach ultimately led both Councils to list, for the first time at an ecumenical council, all the books of the Bible: books written at various ages and by various authors but all with divine authority. Finally, the First Vatican Council and the papal encyclicals that followed *(Providentissimus Deus, Spiritus Paraclitus*, and *Divino Afflante Spiritu)* inserted the same expression into a new context: the biblical books of both Testaments have come about *Deo auctore.* No part of the ca-

---

9. There are further shades and subdivisions on both the subjective and the objective side of inspiration. It seems that, beginning with Origen, for many Church Fathers objective inspiration practically coincided with the presence of a "spiritual sense" in the text. As was noted in chapter VI, "For Origen the main consequence of inspiration is the presence of a spiritual meaning in the text."

nonical text can be attributed to merely human origin.[10] It is then in this specific context that pre-conciliar textbooks usually began to compare and to coordinate two literary authorships, one divine and the other human, the first conceived as that of a "principal author" or "principal cause," and the second as a subordinate or instrumental cause, with their relationship explained by the Thomistic doctrine of "instrumental causality."

If literary authorship is defined as literary self-expression, then it brings with it the limitations imposed by talent, education, culture, temporality, etc., and therefore cannot be applied to God in the proper sense of the word.[11] One might still ask, however, if at any point during the last four ecumenical councils (Florence, Trent, Vatican I and II) God was declared to be "author" of the Scriptures in a specific sense.

We have seen that *Dei Verbum* seemingly arrived at the concept of a "double authorship" by applying the term "author" with quite similar meaning to God and the human author. Yet a closer look revealed an important distinction. While it states emphatically that the human authors were "true authors" *(veri auctores),* fully using their faculties and abilities *(facultatibus ac viribus suis utentes),* such language was not used about God. He is not said to be *"verus auctor."* The emphasis is shifted in the opposite direction. The conciliar text points out that God exercises his authorship indirectly: *"Ipso in illis*

---

10. It is at this point that it becomes clear why we must contradict the attempts of "ending" the theology of inspiration by simply denying a "supernatural origin" to the books of the Bible.

11. One might object by saying that Jesus could have written books and his books would have had, in the proper sense of the word, the second divine Person for their author. True, but of course he wrote no book. One might attempt another question: Do Jesus' *ipsissima verba* have him as their literary author? The answer must be in the affirmative. This concept was known to the Church Fathers. St. Augustine began his commentary on the Sermon on the Mount by writing: *"Aperuit nunc [Jesus] os suum, qui prophetarum aperuerat ora." De sermone Domini in monte* I, 1, 2 (PL 34, 1231), quoted by St. Bernard, *Sermo in festivitate Omnium Sanctorum,* in *Sancti Bernardi Opera Omnia,* 331. In my translation: "Jesus opened now his mouth, he who had previously opened the mouth of the prophets." Something similar appears in Origen's thought as he arranges the meanings of the word *"euaggelion"* on an analogous scale, meaning most strictly the words of Jesus himself and on a gradual scale all manifestations of the Logos in creation or salvation history. See *Commentarium in Joannem,* vol. 1, 15–25, *Sources chrétiennes* 120bis, 35–39.

et per illos agente," meaning that he is "acting in and through them [the human authors]." Thus, Karl Rahner's distinction between *Verfasser* and *Urheber,* the first meaning a literary author, the second an "originator," might have left a mark on the wording of *Dei Verbum.* God cannot be called the *auctor,* in the full sense of the German word *Verfasser* only the "originator" *(Urheber)* of a biblical book.

We cannot assign to God the imperfections of human literary authorship; neither can God be considered a co-author in juxtaposition to the human author, nor can the application of "instrumental causality," invented for two finite created causes acting in subordination to each other (pen and hand, flute and artist), constitute much more than a metaphor. Especially as a principal author, God is not writing a personal letter to Philemon, and in Acts, God does not describe *his* (the author's) personal experiences due to a shipwreck. Such aspects of personal authorship do not apply to the divine "author." Can we say that God revealed himself in the works of Isaiah as a major Hebrew poet or can we fault him for his halting and monotonous style in the works of Ezekiel? Rahner was then right in showing the insufficiency of the scheme of "double authorship" when he stated that the same thing cannot have two causes simultaneously and under the same aspect.[12]

It was Luis Alonso Schökel who effectively moved beyond the paradigm of double authorship. He put the concept of inspiration, as proposed by Lagrange and refined by Benoit and Rahner, into a triple context which previous treatments of inspiration lacked: the

12. It is worth quoting it in German for the text is based on the German notion of the *Urheber* or "originator," as opposed to *Verfasser* or literary author: "Es kann also diese Schrift, das ist die Frage, nicht unter derselben Rücksicht, namlich der der literarischen Verfasserschaft zwei Autoren haben. Man beachte: Wir sagen nicht: dasselbe Werk kann nicht zwei Verfasser, einen göttlichen und einen menschlichen, haben; sondern wir sagen: es kann nicht sein, dass beide Urheberschaft von vornherein unter derselben Rücksicht in derselben Dimension auf eine literarische Verfasserschaft abziele. Denn sonst würde eine Wirkung unter derselben Rücksicht zwei Ursachen entstammen, was unmöglich ist." Karl Rahner, *Über die Schriftinspiration* (Freiburg in Br., 1961), 25. In his attached footnote (n. 7) Rahner points out the insufficiencies of "instrumental causality": both a writer and his pen, he says, are claimed to be the cause of the whole written text, with the writer being the *causa principalis* and the pen a *causa instrumentalis.* However, they do not cause the text from the same point of view: the pen cannot be said to be a writer or an author.

historical context of patristic exegesis, the context of theories on literature, and the theological context of Christology (unity of human and divine nature).[13]

In that same work, Alonso Schökel demonstrated the following five points:

First, the general statement that God is the author of the biblical text is, indeed, an article of faith.

Second, the long-standing patristic tradition does not allow us to narrow and reduce this concept of authorship to a pure function of being "the originator" (Rahner's *Urheber*): "[The patristic texts] all seem to favor the conception of God's activity in inspiration which is *better* described as 'literary author' than as 'origin.'"[14]

Third, when God is said to be the author of literary works, this does not mean that he manifested himself in the biblical books in the same sense in which human authors express themselves in their literary works. The statement "God is the author of Scripture" leads us to the realm of analogy, not to the application of a univocal term.

Fourth, Alonso Schökel finds in the sources of revelation four main analogies of inspiration: instrument, dictation, messenger, and literary character created by an author. All these serve to illustrate the linkage of two "authors," one human and one divine. By the charism of inspiration the human author is subordinated to the divine author

13. See *The Inspired Word,* trans. Francis Martin (London: Herder, 1967), 49–90. He attempted to investigate a fourth context, that of "the psychology of inspiration," but, as he states in a postscript, this aspect would need "a more detailed discussion" (213). In fact, the whole chapter 7, "The Psychology of Inspiration" (177–216), is a misnomer, mixing the speculative analysis of the charism of supernatural inspiration and the experimental study of "the human process of literary creation" (177). The author himself sees the hybrid character of this chapter and remarks: "We are but following in the footsteps of those who have written treatises on the subject of prophecy and inspiration." In other words, here Alonso Schökel goes little beyond summarizing Benoit's articles and suggests that the reader could skip the whole seventh chapter and "go on to chapter 8" (177, n. 1).

14. Ibid., 84. Emphasis added. The question still remains whether the problems of the modern concept of "authorship" should not prompt the theologian to abandon the terminology of "double authorship" and, before attributing it to God, to divest him of the misleading attributes of a human author or, perhaps more conveniently, to remove from the concept of authorship those of its aspects that cannot be applied to a divine authorship.

just as the individual, human nature of Jesus is linked to God's divine nature in the oneness of the Son of God, so that there arises also for the Bible a certain "communication of idioms," a notion frequently mentioned in Christology, in which the same Scripture is both "word of God" and "word of man." Furthermore, just as with the two natures in Christ, so the two authorships in Scripture, the human and the divine, co-exist "without commingling or confusion." Thus no imperfection is attributed to God, nor does the *human* author's activity become exempt from its finite nature and limitations.

Fifth, Alonso Schökel concludes his inquiry with the justification of the expression "inspired word" as the "verbal body in which revelation and grace have become incarnate." He also emphasizes that in Scripture we face "the mystery of the union of the divine and the human."[15]

Alonso Schökel's book certainly took an important step toward harmonizing the biblical and patristic notions of inspiration with the way literary criticism understands the origin of a literary work. However, it has left in suspense what has been a central concern of modern biblical research for a long time: the social aspect of inspiration.

The Social Aspect of Inspiration and the Role of Providence

In recent times, the concept of "authorship" in connection with biblical books has been largely relativized. We have become aware that, in many cases, the biblical texts were written not by one but by many authors, and this form of authorship usually involves a historical chain of consecutive human authors and redactors. Accepting the importance of the "social aspect of biblical inspiration" does not mean that one must subscribe to a nebulous concept of collective authorship whereby one attributes the origin of a book to a community's anonymous creative resources, positing, for example, that the Gospel of John was created by a "Johannine community," or assuming that the "early Church communities" had created sayings of Jesus anonymously in various ways at liturgical gatherings amidst some communal pro-

15. Ibid., 87.

phetic experiences. These theories reflect current trends in social sciences rather than the objective data of historical research. Especially because of the low level of literacy in ancient times, one must assume that the biblical texts had individual authors. Having said this, however, it is true that in many cases, before being canonized, the biblical texts underwent repeated reworkings at the hands of redactors and editors. Therefore, collective inspiration, in this sense of a succession of writers and redactors, must be seriously considered.

Rahner correctly emphasized that the divine author must be thought of as a transcendental cause. The Thomistic systems of inspiration tried to relate God's transcendental primary causality to divine predestination and even *praemotio physica* (a concept of Thomistic philosophy which requires that for every act by a finite cause there must be a logically prior act by the divine "First Mover"). Such an attempt, however, risked reducing the role of the divine author to something banal and common, treating it as identical to all other cases in which the ultimate divine causality interacts with finite human acts. There is, however, a tradition in patristic and medieval thought which assigns to biblical inspiration a role analogous to divine providence, yet special: the role of "watching over salvation history." For God's salvation plan is nothing else than the history of the Word, touching off a chain of incarnate self-disclosures in every event of that history, including among others the creation of the books of the Bible, a historical process culminating in Christ and continuing through the ongoing expansion of the Body of Christ, the Church.[16] Rahner's description of inspiration as a divine activity fundamental to the formation of the Church, has the potential of being further developed into the theological concept of God's special providential guidance,

16. A remarkably concise summary of this view is found in St. Bernard's *Homilies in Praise of the Virgin Mother* (better known as *Homiliae Super Missus Est*): "Do you think that any one of these [names] has been here superfluously placed? By no means. For if no leaf falls from a tree without a reason, nor does one sparrow fall to earth without the heavenly Father's notice, should I think that from the mouth of the Evangelist one single word flows superfluously, especially in *the* history of the Word? No, I do not think so. All these are full of heavenly mysteries and each of them flows with heavenly sweetness, but they should have a careful reader who knows how to extract honey from the rock and oil from the hardest crag." In *Sancti Bernardi Opera Omnia*, 14.

accompanying with fixed, privileged, and registered utterances the long process by which the Incarnate Word involved himself with mankind's history and revealed himself as the goal of this very same history of salvation.[17]

The Theandrical Character of the Biblical Word

The discovery of parallelism between the Incarnation and bibli-cal inspiration is an important feature that must pervade every kind of discussion of the matter. Several patristic scholars have pointed out the frequency with which this parallelism is mentioned by the Church Fathers. In his book on inspiration, Karl Rahner spoke of the Divine Word's *"Schriftwerdung"* ("becoming Scripture") as analogous to the German concept of *"Menschwerdung"* ("becoming man"). On this point Alonso Schökel supported Rahner's sugges-tions and offered the further thought that the two opposite Christo-logical heresies, Nestorianism and Monophysitism, were applicable also to opposite erroneous views of the Bible, the former character-izing mainline Protestantism, the latter more typical of conservative and fundamentalist theologies.[18]

The Catholic truth about the Bible lies in an equal affirmation of its divine and human components, "unconfused and inseparable," allowing no material distinction between the parts to be assigned either solely to God or solely to the human author. Both God and man are responsible for the entire text. Yet one must express caution against pushing this analogy too far. The inspired author and the Holy Spirit who inspires him are not linked by anything even resem-bling the hypostatic union. There is here no personal union between "two authors"; their union is not that of two different natures in the identity of one person. There is here not only a distinction of two natures but also a distinction in the manner of causality, that is, the way in which the respective distinct persons exercise their authorial

17. See a summary of Rahner's description of inspiration in Alonso Schökel, *The Inspired Word*, 220–22.

18. See ibid., 84–87. Three years earlier Louis Bouyer expressed similar thoughts in a remarkable short article: "Où en est le mouvement biblique?" [At what point is the biblical movement?], *Bible et Vie chrétienne* 18 (1956): 7–21.

role. On the level of personal self-expression (an essential feature of literary authorship), they remain distinct: one infinite and the other finite, one omniscient and the other limited in knowledge, one omnipotent and the other limited in power.

The analogy between inspiration and incarnation has been only initially explored in theological literature, partly because the two sides of inspiration, its subjective and objective aspects (inspired authors and inspired texts), are rarely treated under separate headings. While in more recent times inspiration has been primarily explored from a subjective and psychological point of view (as a charism given to the biblical author), ancient texts paid more attention to the human and divine characteristics of the inspired text and spoke of a double structure of the inspired word. The latter approach often looks at the "letter" as comparable to the flesh or the humanity of the divine Word, and at the "spirit" or "spiritual sense," as a transcendental reality "behind" or "under" the letter. For the Church Fathers not inerrancy but this divine/human structure of the text seemed to be the most important consequence of inspiration. Even after decades—in fact, almost a century—of patristic renewal, present-day Christian exegesis is still confronted with a major gap between its own approach to the Bible and that of the early Church. While it is often said that the Church Fathers were not sufficiently aware of a "fully human" authorship on the part of the biblical writers, it also seems to be true that, in contrast to ancient exegesis, today's interpreters are unable to give account of a divinely intended meaning of the text which transcends the human author's conscious intentions. Consequently, the modern exegete is typically unwilling to admit that such inspired (that is, divinely intended) meaning could be in the text unless it is demonstrably present in the finite and limited state of consciousness of the human author. Thus it is quite important to realize that the same paragraph of *Dei Verbum* (no. 12) which insists on how important it is "to search out the intention of the sacred writers" also requires that "no less serious attention must be given to the content and unity of the whole of Scripture if the meaning of the sacred texts is to be correctly worked out."

Here we cross an important threshold: canonical interpretation—
the unity of the two Testaments as a presupposition for biblical exegesis, and understood from a theological perspective transcending
historical and critical preoccupation—cannot be affirmed unless we
realize that in the act of inspiration, God uses the human writer as
God's instrument without the possibility that his sovereignty would be
handicapped, reduced, or limited by the deficiencies of the human instrument.[19] What the theology of inspiration has not yet fully worked
out is, therefore, not only a clearer differentiation between incarnation
and inspiration, but also the discovery of the quasi-sacramental character of the biblical text and a better use of the categories of modern
sacramental theology for enlightening the composite (divine/human)
nature of the inspired text.[20]

Inerrancy and the Truth of the Bible

The Present-Day Status of the Question

Much of the recent discussion about biblical inspiration has tak-
en place in the shadow of modern biblical criticism. In the wake of
the Enlightenment, the central issue of biblical criticism became the
question of inerrancy, which began to be treated as the most important consequence of inspiration.[21]

19. Cardinal Avery Dulles states among the basic rules of the theological use of the
Bible: "No efforts will be made to limit the meaning to the conscious intentions of the
human author who may have composed the particular passage under consideration."
"Criteria of Catholic Theology," *Communio* 22, 2 (1995): 310. About the "authorial inten-
tion" as a criterion in the theological interpretation of Scripture see also: A. Dulles, *The
Craft of Theology* (New York: Crossroad, 1992), 78–79.

20. For a recent evangelical perspective on the analogy of inspiration/incarnation,
see Peter Enns, *Inspiration and Incarnation* (Grand Rapids, Mich.: Baker Academic,
2007), 17–22 and 167–70.

21. "The final effect of inspiration for our consideration is inerrancy, the quality
by which the Bible is protected from error." R. F. Smith, "Inspiration and Inerrancy,"
in *The Jerome Biblical Commentary*, ed. R. Brown, J. Fitzmyer, and R. Murphy (Englewood Cliffs, N.J.: Prentice Hall, 1968), 312. *The New Jerome Biblical Commentary* published by the same editors in 1990 presents a rather different picture of inerrancy. In the
corresponding revised part of the volume Raymond F. Collins writes: "The concentra-
tion on inerrancy tends to reduce theological discussion about inspiration to a concept
that was first introduced into the theological discussion in the nineteenth century. The

If the biblical text is, indeed, inspired, it must not have any attributes incompatible with divine authorship. Obviously, a literary work whose main author is God cannot contain error. Yet, when the Church and its theologians began dealing with biblical inerrancy in response to rationalist attacks on the Bible, they could not help taking from their opponents a number of their suppositions. Rather than defining inerrancy from the point of view of Christian doctrine, they found themselves defending a concept of inerrancy in terms which the rationalists assumed, as a divine guarantee of truth, covering each and every sentence of the Bible. It was typical for a rationalistic reading of the Bible to regard the sacred text as nothing but propositional statements, for each of which the believer had to defend truthfulness in the sense of *adaequatio rei ad intellectum,* a faultless correspondence of "reality" to its "understanding by the mind." Such an outlook also tends to presuppose that with every sentence the biblical author's goal was to convey precise and distinct ideas of truth revealed about God and man, as well as the world and its history in its relationship with God. Cardinal Newman's mistaken notion about the *obiter dicta* came from his effort to identify the way in which the Bible mirrors the cultural environment of the human authors without also claiming the presence of revealed doctrine. Instead, rather than include these elements in the tapestry of a composite whole in which ordinary perceptions and insights are tools for expressing a general view of the world, Newman tried first to separate and then to exclude these elements from the inspired text.

Without the benefit of a functioning Magisterium, in recent times Protestantism has dealt with the question of "biblical inerrancy" in two opposite ways. In liberal Protestantism, and perhaps even in mainline Protestantism in general, inerrancy lost its relevance

---

term 'inerrancy' has never appeared in a conciliar text, although found in papal encyclicals and the original rejected schema of Vatican II on revelation. . . . Indeed the Scriptures themselves never claim to be inerrant. Finally, a serious philosophical reflection on the nature of biblical 'truth' and 'error' must take into full consideration the literary form and the level and function of language." Raymond F. Collins, "Inspiration," in *The Jerome Biblical Commentary,* edited by R. Brown, J. Fitzmyer, and R. Murphy (Englewood Cliffs: Prentice Hall, 1990), 1033.

and ceased to be discussed or defended. At the same time, for more fundamentalist Protestantism it became heavily defended territory, even a touchstone or litmus test. This produced various clashes both within and outside evangelical groups against the claims of science, history, and at times even archeology and textual criticism. In Catholic theology, on the other hand, the question of biblical inerrancy moved more slowly and more cautiously through what were nonetheless significant phases.

Confrontation with Scientific Truth

Issues related to creation and evolution were either settled or defused before the first decades of the twentieth century. Consequently, there is in Catholic theology no significant tradition of "creationism" and no acute awareness of irreconcilable conflicts between Christian faith and the theory of evolution.[22] Both theologians and the rest of believers slowly became aware that the biblical sources reflect the naïveté of ancient cultures not yet in possession of scientific thinking. On the whole, the statements made in Pius XII's encyclical *Divino Afflante Spiritu* about "literary genres" and God's condescension to the cultural limitation of those he addresses provided satisfactory tools for deciding these issues.

Confrontation with Historical Truth

While in the course of the last fifty years the natural sciences have launched fewer attacks on the Bible, and in some cases have

---

22. The recent flare-up of a discussion about mitigating the theory of evolution with a claim of "intelligent design" is often based more on misinformation or lack of philosophical reflection on both sides, by biblical theologians and scientists. Catholic journalists arguing for a "fully random" version of the evolutionary theory usually cannot distinguish between transcendental and categorical causality and thus regard any inclusion of a "divine purpose" in the process of evolution as incompatible with randomness. Unfortunately the participants in the debate usually do not possess enough background in mathematics to understand the modern concept of "randomness," nor in biology to understand the substantial differences between the evolution of life from organic matter and the evolution of a new species, or the process of "hominization," that is, the evolution of the human species as again a further case, different from the origin of non-human animals. Catholic involvement in the "intelligent design" controversy was at times regrettably lacking in clarity about the concepts involved.

become more neutral or respectful toward the limitations of ancient cultures, the historical sciences have dug up new reasons for questioning the veracity of the Bible. Belief in the historical accuracy of biblical accounts has swung back and forth like a pendulum with every major discovery. The advances in archeology, the finding of papyrus manuscripts, the reconstruction of ancient Egyptian, Mesopotamian, Persian, and Greco-Roman (and other) civilizations brought about publication of reports conveying opposite messages. Beginning in the 1950s, there appeared, on the one hand, popular publications claiming to prove the historical liability of biblical accounts, while, on the other hand, time and again journalistic assessments of archeological finds or historical discoveries attempted to settle the score on biblical "errors" about issues as diverse as the star of Bethlehem and the exodus of the Jewish ancestors from Egypt.

Quite frequently Christian apologetics and secular historiography ended their debate in an impasse. Biblical historians reminded their secular counterparts that applying the demands of modern historical sciences to the biblical account was in itself completely anachronistic and set "unfair expectations" for the biblical authors. In addition, later stages of research often validated or rehabilitated what was earlier quoted as a surely fictitious feature in a biblical narrative.[23] Cardinal König's memorable intervention at the Second Vatican Council represented in some ways the whole atmosphere surrounding the question of biblical inerrancy in the 1960s: "The scientific study of oriental history has demonstrated that the notions of the Bible about history and the natural sciences may sometimes deviate from the truth." The three examples of historical inaccuracies that he quoted (Mk 2:26, Mt 27:9,

23. A celebrated example is the description of the pool of Bethesda (or Bethzatha, with a number of other variant transcriptions of this name) with five arcades in Jn 5:2. First believed to be a classical example of Johannine "creativity"—a symbolic feature incorporated into the story—by a number of early modern critics, like Loisy, later it was vindicated by the archeologists who unearthed the pool in a shape of a trapezoid with a portico on each side, and partitioned in the middle by a bridge holding the fifth portico. The Copper Scroll found in Qumran has confirmed the name and the location as well. But the dating of the pool and the porticos or its exact way of functioning as a cultic place is still under discussion. See James H. Charlesworth, *Jesus and Archeology* (Grand Rapids, Mich.: Eerdmans, 2006), 592–93.

and Dan 1:1) should not have impressed anyone at the Council, for they had been known for a long time. Indeed, the first example, concerning the reference to Abiathar, and the second one, concerning a quotation of Zechariah cited by Matthew under the name of Jeremiah, had already challenged the ingenuity of the Church Fathers.[24] Only the third was the result of modern scientific history. Interestingly, all three errors quoted by König are due to a confusion of names. In such cases the transmission of the biblical text usually favors the better known over the less well known: Abiathar over Ahimelech in Mark 2:26, Jeremiah over Zechariah in Matthew 27:9 and Jehoiakim over Jehoiachin in Daniel 1:1.[25] Most modern commentaries pass over these "errors" as inaccuracies, which are "close enough" approximations for those times in which quotations and references were made by memory. At the Council the journalists who orchestrated a worldwide uproar were not knowledgeable enough to realize that the examples cited dealt with no "modern advancements" in biblical history, but age-old problems of small details, which arose from the difficulty of remembering Hebrew names and transcribing them with Greek letters.

One could say that this incident ultimately helped the Council and was instrumental in creating *Dei Verbum*. But in spite of all the merits of the new document in replacing "inerrancy" with the holistic and positive concept of "the truth of the Bible," its new and final version did not live up to all expectations. It seems that, in the euphoria of the last session of the Council, at which the final draft of

24. The quotation from Zechariah under the name of Jeremiah is probably the oldest objection to Matthew's "formula quotation" for which the Old Testament prophet is mentioned. The commentary of W. C. Davies and Dale Alison in Matthew, *The International Critical Commentary*, vol. 3 (Edinburgh: T & T Clark, 1997), 568, enumerates ten solutions, of which six come from Church Fathers (two from Eusebius, one each from Justin Martyr, Origen, Jerome, and Augustine), one from Luther, and only two from modern authors. This is not a difficulty with inerrancy in view of "modern advancements" in biblical studies.

25. A recent commentary on Mark by J. Marcus quotes D. N. Freedman in connection with Mk 2:26 stating that, in transmission of texts, "a better-known name often supplants a lesser-known one." See J. Marcus, *Mark 1–8*, The Anchor Bible 27 (New York: Doubleday, 1999), 241. This is really an old textual difficulty, but it was somewhat veiled by the presence of several textual variants. Those who read "*in the days* of Abiathar" think that the author is aware that he just randomly refers to a biblical story about David. See Vincent Taylor, *The Gospel According to Saint Mark* (New York: Macmillan, 1966), 217.

Dei Verbum was created, there was little awareness that at the core of the controversies, which had existed for about two hundred years, a long-lasting cultural struggle was being played out in all the academic communities of both historians and philosophers, and further that this cultural crisis could not be resolved in a single document, even a well-written one. Beyond the dispute about the Bible's truthfulness (regardless of what term was used, "veracity" or "inerrancy") there lay the agenda of a secular culture, trying to reconstruct and explain Christian origins on a purely rationalistic basis, eliminating the supernatural from mankind's religious history, and, in particular, from the documents of biblical revelation and salvation history.

The Truth of the Bible in Dei Verbum

Although *Dei Verbum* contains only one sentence about the truth of the Bible, its convoluted grammar and the history of its repeated redactions reveal a number of problems, not all of which were resolved in the end. This one paragraph must be quoted in its original Latin and in a somewhat annotated translation:

1) Cum ergo omne id quod auctores inspirati seu hagiographi asserunt,

2) retineri debeat assertum a Spiritu Sancto,

3) inde Scripturae libri veritatem

4) quam Deus nostrae salutis causa Litteris sacris consignari voluit, firmiter, fideliter et sine errore docere profitendi sunt.

In its official English translation:

1) Since all that the sacred authors, or hagiographers assert

2) must be held as asserted by the Holy Spirit,

3) therefore one must proclaim that the books of Scripture firmly, faithfully, and without error

4) teach that truth which God, for the sake of our salvation, wanted to put into the Sacred Writings.[26]

26. This is the translation that became most widely known, as it is contained in the introduction to all recent editions of the New American Bible. "That truth" in no. 4 is

In the first two lines the verb *asserere* is repeated: it was consciously chosen in order to indicate that a statement, by becoming part of the Bible in any accidental way, that is, by just being mentioned or reproduced, would not be endorsed automatically by the authority of the Holy Spirit; a text may merely quote or report a view without assenting to it. In such a case the statement is not asserted by the author, and thus is not asserted by the Holy Spirit either. An old-fashioned example is the passage by the Psalmist quoting the impious "There is no God" (Ps 14:1). A more serious, yet still rather obvious example, is a proverb quoted in the letter to Titus: "Cretans are always liars, vicious brutes, lazy gluttons" (Ti 1:12), which must not be thought of as an assertion by the Holy Spirit. Thus the "truthfulness of the Bible" is legitimately evoked only for those statements in which the scriptural author indeed intends to teach,[27] and not for those in which he merely reflects an accepted opinion of contemporary knowledge or culture.

It seems to be of importance that the conciliar text uses active voice for the human author's "assertion" and passive voice for describing a concomitant assertion of the Holy Spirit: *"hagiographi asserunt, . . . assertum a Spiritu Sancto."* This formulation, with its asymmetric parallelism, was chosen on purpose: what the author as-

---

the most problematic phrase of the English text. The original text has only *veritatem,* not *illam veritatem.* The problem with translating it as "that truth" is partly linguistic: in Latin there is no definite article. In any European language, other than English, one would correctly translate it with the definite article: *la vérité* or *die Wahrheit* or *la verità,* etc. But in English to speak about "the truth" modified by a relative clause, "the truth which God. . .wanted to put" might appear strained. So the translators might have followed stylistic considerations when inserting the demonstrative pronoun: "that truth, which. . . ." However, the resulting text is now rather misleading: one gets the impression that the Council, by inserting the expression *sine errore,* returns to the concept of inerrancy, but in the next phrase limits inerrancy to "that kind of truth" (not including any other kind of truth) which serves the cause of salvation. It helps little to point out that the Council explicitly rejected this latter interpretation when stating that it allows no "material limitation" to the Bible's truthfulness, not even a limitation by subject matter (like "pertaining only to faith and morals").

27. At the Council an amendment was proposed to replace *asserere* by *docere.* The Theological Commission did not accept it, for fear that it would make it seem that the "truth of the Bible" were restricted to doctrinal passages. Yet the Commission noted that *asserere* means a formal statement, and that mere casual mentioning would not satisfy this criterion.

serts becomes asserted by the Spirit. The formulation suggests that the human author and the Holy Spirit do not make their assertions in the same way. The human author makes his statement on the basis of a human mind which involves subjective limitations of knowledge and certainty, while the divine Spirit transcends all such limitations. Of course, God's use of a human being to mediate his speech necessarily involves deficiencies and imperfections, but God can still use such instruments to express infallibly what he intends to be deposited in the biblical text.

The triple modifier "firmly, faithfully, and without error" expresses traditional doctrine. The last of them, "without error," was not originally included in the draft, but was inserted at the insistence of a sizable group of Council Fathers who wanted to be sure that the doctrine of "inerrancy," used by magisterial documents for centuries, be preserved and stated explicitly in the document.[28] This was first inserted in a somewhat complicated way and the last phrase (no. 4) obtained its final form only after all other changes. This detail is important for a correct interpretation of the text. In the first proposal for emending the text, the proposed formulation was *"Inde Scripturae libri veritatem salutarem firmiter et fideliter et sine errore docere profitendi sunt,"* meaning, "The books of the Bible teach salvific truth firmly, faithfully, and without error." However, the expression *veritas salutaris* gave the impression that the document was restricting the Bible's inerrancy to those texts which spoke of a certain kind of issue, that is, to texts

28. The contention that the language of "inerrancy" is a novelty in Catholic theology and was not used before the nineteenth century is a typical half-truth of a certain rhetoric which became fashionable after the Council (see above the passage by Raymond F. Collins quoted in n. 21). Following Collins, dismissal of this allegedly nontraditional concept of inerrancy is the best proof for the importance of the insertion of *"sine errore"* into the document. For he writes: "The truth of Scriptures lies not so much in that its passages are without error, but that through them God manifests his fidelity to his people, bringing them into loving union with himself." One must also keep in mind that the doctrine of inerrancy—the exclusion of error from the Bible—was stated equivalently by the earliest Church Fathers such as Clement of Rome, Irenaeus, Tertullian, Hyppolitus, and others. It is true, of course, that in ancient patristic sources the lack of error regards a whole range of concepts: falsehood, deception, lies, and the like, but also logical inconsistency and factual error, which are claimed to be incompatible with the Bible.

speaking about our salvation.[29] Therefore, a significant number of the Council Fathers were dissatisfied.

After various proposals, the spokesman of the subcommittee explained that their draft (with the expression *veritas salutaris*) was in agreement with the papal encyclicals: it does not restrict inerrancy materially to certain parts of Scripture but only formally, namely, according to the point of view from which the Bible teaches the truth, since truth is revealed not for the sake of information but for the sake of our salvation. The subcommittee obviously thought that its statement about the Bible's truth as *veritas salutaris,* untarnished by error, would provide a well-balanced position that should satisfy all, including those who, in agreement with Cardinal König, wanted to admit that the Bible contained errors about non-religious issues, the so-called *veritates profanae.* Hence the subcommittee retained the expression *veritas salutaris.* At this point a crisis seemed inevitable. A number of Council Fathers appealed to Pope Paul VI. The pope, in a letter written to the subcommittee, expressed his own concerns and "perplexity" *(perplessità)* about the matter, and asked that the issue be sent over to the Theological Commission of the Council. After stormy exchanges in the Council and in the press, the Theological Commission removed the phrase "salvific truth" and replaced it with "the truth which, for the sake of our salvation, God wanted to be expressed in the Holy Scriptures."[30] Considered now as unambiguous, the final text passed with virtual unanimity and, as it seemed, the Council survived its last major crisis by reaffirming inerrancy in a way both new and yet also in agreement with traditional teaching.

29. The expression *veritas salutaris* seems to come from the decree of the Council of Trent on Scripture and Tradition. It was quoted in (the old edition of) Denzinger's *Enchiridion Symbolorum* under no. 783 (31st edition, under the care of Karl Rahner, Herder, 1957) and thus was well known to all the experts of the Council. Besides, Karl Rahner was one of the key members of the subcommission preparing the draft.

30. I think this is the correct translation. One must criticize the official English translations, which added the demonstrative adjective *that.* However such a translation would assume a Latin text saying *illam veritatem* and imply the restriction of the truthfulness of the Bible to a certain *kind* of content. The English translation has in fact misled a number of readers who thought that such interpretation is within the confines of Church teaching. We face here a problem concerning the correct reception and dissemination of the Council's teaching.

However, in the aftermath of the Council, even this apparently clear formulation of inerrancy kept causing further debates and disagreements. A notorious example is found in recent post-conciliar discussions about the virginal conception. As is generally admitted, the authors of the infancy narratives of both Matthew and Luke believed and stated that Jesus was conceived by his mother without sexual intercourse. However, some biblicists invoked *Dei Verbum* when questioning if, in Catholic doctrine, one must, indeed, retain the notion of virginal conception, since—they maintained—it is not clear that this truth is being asserted by the Bible as a salvific truth, that is, as a doctrine necessary for our salvation. After all, the truth of the Incarnation (which is certainly salvific truth) does not necessarily imply Mary's virginity *ante partum,* and thus one may not be obliged to follow what the evangelists only personally believed about it and expressed not as a truth necessary for our salvation.[31] Of course, such an interpretation goes a long way beyond the intentions of the Council by its speculation about the evangelists' "authorial intent." It would turn the concept of "the truth of the Bible" into an elastic and customized notion, open to manipulation and incapable of any normative role.

How True Is the Bible? A Summary

"If God is the author of the Bible, it must not contain anything unworthy of him." This type of statement is probably the oldest formulation of the principle of "inerrancy" and can be found with frequency in the writings of the anti-Gnostic Church Fathers of the second and third centuries. Falsehood is incompatible with divine authorship: God's word does not communicate lies or errors. This leads us to the following statements.

---

31. Raymond E. Brown in his *The Birth of the Messiah,* 2nd ed. (New York: Doubleday, 1993), 528, n. 28, quotes no. 12 of *Dei Verbum* in the sense which the Council wanted to exclude. For he writes: "A faithful Catholic would have to ask: Should one rank the biological manner of Jesus' conception as a truth God wanted to put into Sacred writings for the sake of our salvation?" Ranking or not ranking certain biblical statements among the truths covered by inerrancy was explicitly rejected in the conciliar debates about "salvific truth."

First, Scripture's truthfulness implies absence of error, but the concept of "inerrancy" must be handled with care so that it may avoid two dangerous flaws. On the one hand, Holy Scripture is not a set of propositional statements; its truthfulness must not be measured simplistically by mere comparisons to objective (historical) facts or correct abstract (logical) reasoning. Much of Scripture's content is poetry; another large portion expresses commands, wishes, and prayers—subjective states of mind of all sorts. On the other hand, where Scripture states facts or conveys reasoning, the truth it expresses is cast in human thought forms and verbal expressions, so that truth cannot be fully assessed without reference to the human history and culture in which the Word became flesh. God not only accommodates himself to the mind and culture of the hearers and of the readers of his word, but in Christ God became man and also the subject of knowledge acquired and expressed in a human way.

Second, we must conceive of the truth of Scripture by analogy to Christ's human knowledge. Just as his thoughts and words were embedded in the particular limitations of his own age and culture, so does Scripture reflect the particularities and limitations of the cultures in which God's people made their journey of salvation history from Abraham through the last apostolic witness contributing to the composition or redaction of the New Testament.

Third, in the way Paul speaks in Philippians 2:8–10 of the Incarnation of the Son of God and John speaks in John 1:14 of the Logos becoming flesh, we can speak of the word of God becoming Scripture. In the scriptural word the Son manifests his intention to "empty himself" and "take upon himself the form of a servant," becoming human in a physically bounded world, in which the perception and transmission of truth is conditioned by space, time, point of view, discourse, context, historical circumstance, and, ultimately, the human being's exposure to constant change.[32] This analogy implies important cautions.

The truth of a scriptural word is contextual with both the work of

---

32. This is the main thesis of Enns's *Inspiration and Incarnation,* 167–73.

the human author (and his literary work as a whole) and that of the divine author (the whole of the canon and the whole of salvation history with its Christological peak and goal). The "divine pedagogy" and "condescension" of which the anti-Marcionite Church Fathers (beginning with Irenaeus) spoke, mostly in defense of the imperfections of the Old Testament, must be extended to all of Scripture.

Furthermore, just as Jesus "grew in age and wisdom" from infancy to maturity as a human being, each book of the Bible had a true process of formative development which divine inspiration both moved and guided so that the "final product" of the canonical text would be properly obtained.

Therefore, divine inspiration does not imply that each passage and sentence of the biblical text must be found free of error from every conceivable point of view. The grammarian, the scientist, the psychologist, the philosopher, the historian, and others may point out a particular passage which, when examined from some limited point of view by some specialized endeavor of human learning, can be found faulty. But such a realization does not prove that God's word asserts error. Rather, it only means that God's message is expressed, at one or another point of salvation history, with the imperfections characteristic of human existence. Nevertheless, in the way it serves both the human author's concretely defined purpose and its divine author's salvific purpose, every passage expresses the truth which it is supposed to express according to God's salvific will.

However, one must be careful to avoid the mistranslation and/or misinterpretation of *Dei Verbum* that formally attributes inerrancy only to all that the biblical author intends to assert for the purpose of man's salvation and thus restricts inerrancy materially to those statements of the Bible that teach doctrine necessary for man's salvation. A correct interpretation would emphasize that all parts of the Bible are relevant to and teach about salvation history, and would add that different biblical texts carry out this objective in different ways but each does so without asserting error. It would be incorrect to attribute inerrancy selectively to some parts of the Bible and to deny it to some others according to what is or is not, in the subjective judgment of the reader, religiously relevant and written for the sake of salvation. Here, we must remember again the Pauline text we found so important at the beginning of this book: "Whatever was written in former days was written for our instruction" (Rom 15:3). Paul made this statement in reference to his Christological exegesis of Psalm 69:10 and then extended it to "all scriptures" as written in service of the Church. When reading in the gospels of Matthew and Luke that Mary conceived Jesus virginally, we cannot take the liberty of excluding this from the compass of the Bible's truthfulness by declaring it irrelevant for our salvation. Quite to the contrary, the exegete's task is to find the salvific importance of the gospel narratives and receive the evangelists' message with the consent of faith to both fact and meaning.

The Analogy of the Incarnation and the Truth of the Bible

This ancient model, which compares biblical inspiration to the Incarnate Word, has great potential and promise for the future, but it currently remains in the shadows, waiting to be rediscovered and further developed. Its presence in the writings of Origen and the Origenian tradition has been noticed, yet its influence on patristic thought in general is not clear.[33] According to this model, the peak of biblical inspiration is found in the gospels, and not just in the texts, but in the words and deeds they report. Since they were to transmit the acts and teaching of Christ, the gospels originated with the Word Incarnate, and give literal expression to the closest union between God and man. All other parts of the Bible can be called "gospel"— God's Good News for man—because they participate in this foundational mystery of the Bible. The Old Testament was to be the antici-

---

33. The first book of Origen's *Commentary on John* is an extended, step-by-step demonstration that every part of the Old and New Testament may be properly called "gospel," for each belongs to the same economy of salvation. De Lubac sees in this concept the key to Origen's system of exegesis in which "the Gospel is the first-fruits of all scriptures." Henri de Lubac, *History and Spirit: The Understanding of Scripture according to Origen*, trans. A. E. Nash (San Francisco: Ignatius Press, 2008), 223–35. A more recent and surprising rediscovery of this "incarnational analogy" appears in Enns, *Inspiration and Incarnation*, a book dealing with Old Testament exegesis.

pation of God's self-disclosure in Christ, and thus it is prophetically inspired. It was fulfilled, became intelligible, and reached its goal in Christ. This fulfillment was not simply passive—mere completion and interpretation. Rather, Jesus, the God-Man, read it, quoted and prayed it, and fulfilled it by his sacred manhood, body and soul, mind and heart, intellect and will and affections. The New Testament extends the gospel apostolically through those whom Jesus, the "one sent," has himself sent into all the world and all the ages: those upon whom the Spirit was poured from his risen body.

This model of inspiration has the great advantage of manifesting the analogous character of inspiration. It also expresses quite explicitly that, in their inspired character, the Old and New Testaments are directly and indivisibly linked. This model might hold the key, or at least one important key, to the controversial issue of the Bible's truth and inerrancy: it frames an obvious corollary by showing that the Truth of the Bible is Christ himself, pure and absolute. At the same time, the gospels indisputably manifest the full humanity of Christ, his growth from the womb to infancy, childhood, and adulthood. Moreover, there is no doubt about his full immersion into the culture of his time, the human limitations which determined his individual life on the level of perception, thought, and feeling. The much debated concept of "salvific truth" obtains a new clarity in Christ, since his whole life, death, and resurrection were *"propter nos et propter nostram salutem."* It is beyond doubt that his human life of thirty-some years took place within the context and limitations of the contemporary culture, in the way he thought, argued, quoted Scriptures, and functioned amid human experiences of anxiety, questioning, reasoning, anguish, and pain. In this perspective, one may more easily find the correct way of understanding the biblical truth as analogous to and consonant with the truth of God's Incarnate Word. This truth is not mathematical, not logical, not scientific, not historiographic: it is the truth of God's authentic self-disclosure.[34]

34. Contrary to what most non-professionals think, mathematical truth is neither absolute nor complete. Modern mathematics lacks no awareness that the truth of any

This "incarnational model" still needs thorough probing and research from at least two points of view. We should strive to discover exactly how it sufficiently reflects the Church's traditional faith and understanding of biblical inspiration, if it does so at all. Furthermore, we should evaluate its relation to the Christological dogmas, and should attempt to understand it by a fuller application of Christology.

---

theorem depends on the system of axioms on which it is built. After Goedel's proof, it is generally admitted that also in mathematics the truth of consistency cannot be obtained within the system, that is, by a mathematical proof. By logical proof I mean here implications demonstrated by logical rules. By scientific truth I mean a truthful statement resulting from independently repeatable experiments leading to identical conclusions. Historical truth is demonstrated in reference to credible witnesses and their testimony, evaluated by the rules of historical criticism. Such instruments are valuable in setting limits of credibility; they do not dictate what may or may not elicit faith in the Incarnation.

EPILOGUE

We cannot demonstrate better the importance and actuality of the topics treated in this book than by showing their manifold connection to the proposals *(Propositiones)* formulated by the twelfth Synod of the Catholic Church, "The Word of God in the Life and Mission of the Church," held October 5–26, 2008. After Vatican II, such Synods of the Church have been held in order to exercise in pastoral practice the doctrine of collegiality among the bishops by means of regular meetings in which representatives of the worldwide assembly of the Catholic hierarchy discuss, at the discretion of the pope, the most important theological and pastoral topics of the time. The theme of the Synod of 2008 highlights a first-ranking concern of Pope Benedict XVI, who has always shown special interest not only in furthering biblical research and promoting cooperation between biblical scholarship and other theological disciplines, but also in renewing Catholic exegesis by linking it more intimately with tradition, especially the biblical interpretation of Church Fathers, and by more deeply rooting it in faith and attention to the Magisterium.

At its end the Synod, working under the leadership of Canadian Cardinal Marc Ouellet, formulated its conclusions in fifty-five proposals, which were published and submitted to the Holy Father for further reflection and action. It is in the opening paragraphs (an introduction followed by the first two propositions) and part 1 (nos. 4–13) that we find many references to issues treated in this book.

These first thirteen proposals reveal that, in terms of theological reflection, the Synod's work can be seen as nothing other than an extension and continuation of the Apostolic Constitution *Dei Verbum*.

The theological content particularly of the first eleven propositions resembles a commentary on the Council's teaching about divine revelation, itself clearly and somewhat more succinctly formulated in the first two chapters of *Dei Verbum*. However, in proposition 12, in a rather abrupt and surprisingly curt style, the tone changes and, rather than continuing with its commentary on *Dei Verbum,* the text states:

> The Synod proposes that the Congregation for the Doctrine of the Faith clarify the concepts of "inspiration" and "truth" in the Bible, along with their reciprocal relationship, in order to better understand the teaching of *Dei Verbum* 11. In particular, it is necessary to emphasize the specific character of Catholic Biblical hermeneutics in this area.

At first reading, one is be tempted to be alarmed: How can the Synod expect the Congregation for the Doctrine of the Faith, an administrative organ of the Holy See, to produce a document to make up for what *Dei Verbum,* a document of the Second Vatican Council, failed to achieve? However, this perspective is incorrect. One should rather say that the Synod transmits to the Congregation, and through it to the Holy See, two sets of problems regarding *Dei Verbum*—problems which the Synod itself, because of its composition and juridical status, was not able or competent to remedy. On the one hand, the text of *Dei Verbum* on inspiration and on "the truth of the Bible" (as a holistic formulation of the question of inerrancy) is much too short for conveying a "doctrine." On the other hand, what we today call the "reception" of a teaching or doctrine, that is, the way in which these brief and insufficiently detailed statements of the document have been used after the Council (mostly for authenticating various and diverse tendencies in exegesis), appears disturbing or at least unsatisfactory for the episcopate represented by the Synod. Now the Synod has turned to the Congregation for the Doctrine of the Faith not so much as an organization endowed with theological expertise but as an organ of the Magisterium capable of providing *authentic interpretation of a text* that, by itself and without further interpretation, cannot give enough clarity and certainty for posting both limits and guidance for Catholic exegesis.

This need is expressed by the text of the proposition under three aspects. First, it asks for more clarity about what biblical inspiration means. As we have seen above, this request can hardly be fulfilled without resorting to concepts clearer than those which the text of *Dei Verbum* employs. In traditional Church doctrine "inspiration" connotes both inspired authors and inspired texts, the subjective and the objective aspects of one and the same issue. *Dei Verbum* does not consider these two concepts distinctly and consequently cannot delineate their relationships. Furthermore, the scheme of "double authorship," one divine and the other human, is insufficiently explained by *Dei Verbum*, mainly because this issue was obscured by the controversies immediately preceding the Council (like those about Rahner's essay on inspiration), and also on account of insufficient research on its history and lack of critical reflection on its philosophical implications.

Secondly, the proposition asks for more clarity about "the truth of the Bible." Obviously this request shows dissatisfaction with the famous sentence in no. 12 of *Dei Verbum*. What was greeted with enthusiasm in 1965 as "the solution" for Pope Paul's *perplessità* appears forty-three years later as not much more than a cosmetic solution to a problem regarded as unsolvable by many modern exegetes. The post-conciliar abuse of this sentence of *Dei Verbum* has grown into a major problem: it has ended up reducing the Bible's freedom from error, or inerrancy, to teaching in truth the *"veritates salutares,"* an erroneous interpretation of the text not accepted by Pope Paul VI and not to be re-introduced through the back door. But then the text does need authentic interpretation, guided by careful study of the concept of truth and error as it pertains to a divinely inspired text and by further clarification of the issue.

Thirdly, the Synod asks for more doctrinal clarity concerning the "reciprocal relationship" of inspiration and truthfulness in the Bible. The word "reciprocal" is a very fortunate expression in the proposition. The scholastic textbooks defined inerrancy as the main "consequence" of inspiration. The Synod instead speaks of a reciprocal relationship, that is, a relationship of mutual implication (in mathematical logic: "if and only if") between the two. This is, it seems, a helpful step toward bringing forward the discourse about inspiration. For it is the "inspired text" that teaches the truth without error, while the mind of the "inspired author" must not be considered necessarily immune from all error, except insofar as it contributes, in a way that is both fully authorial and intended by God, to the composition of the book. We see here, at the end of the paragraph, a shining light indicating the end of the tunnel. The mutual relationship of inspiration and inerrancy may well be what lies at the bottom of an authentic doctrine of the Church Fathers about the linkage of inspiration and inerrancy.

The rest of the Synod's propositions make it quite clear how much is at stake for the Church when she demands unambiguous clarity for the teaching about inspiration and the truth of the Bible and about their mutual interdependence. Not only do catechesis (no. 23), daily preaching (no. 15), daily liturgy (nos. 14, 18, 19), and an authentic renewal of consecrated life (no. 24) depend on it, but in an even more intimate way, Catholic theology as taught in seminaries and schools and preached from pulpits cannot fulfill its role of animating the life of the Church without a broadened concept of exegesis, a new, more constructive and intimate relationship between historical-critical studies and theological interpretation of the Bible, and a more cooperative connection of biblical and theological studies on the one side and theologians and pastors on the other.

The Synod openly laments the disappearance of the perspective of faith from exegesis, which alone can turn the ancient scripture into documents addressing the present. It demands, instead of a "positivistic and secular hermeneutics, denying the presence or the accessibility of the divine in the history of humanity," a "hermeneutics of faith" as promulgated in *Dei Verbum* (no. 26). Furthermore, the Synod calls attention to the fact that

> an unproductive separation exists between exegesis and theology, even at the highest academic levels. A worrying consequence is uncertainty, and a lack of solidity, in the formative intellectual journey of some future candidates to ecclesial ministry. Biblical theology and

systematic theology are two dimensions of that lone reality we call "theology." (no. 27)

Proposition 29 points out that reducing the study of the Bible to "historiography" has peculiarly disastrous consequences for the use and understanding of the Old Testament, an area in which lack of an adequate theology of inspiration leads to thoroughly inadequate exegetical practices. Beginning with proposition 5 the Synod repeatedly makes the demand that, as was stated by *Dei Verbum,* Holy Scripture be read "in the same Spirit in which it was written,"[1] because "the same Spirit, who is the author of the Holy Scriptures, is also the guide to their correct interpretation."

However, the ultimate outlook of the Synod is not negative. Its vision is permeated by the hope that the objectives of *Dei Verbum* and of the Second Vatican Council in general will be obtained through arduous and generous listening to the Word of God, audible and even tangible and sacramentally efficient in the celebration of the Eucharist: "Therefore, we vividly hope that a new season of great love for the Sacred Scriptures on the part of all the members of the People of God will flow from this assembly, so that a relationship with the person of Jesus will come from their prayerful and faithful reading over time" (no. 10). With practical wisdom, the text continues: "In this sense, it is hoped, to the extent that it is possible, that every member of the faithful should have a personal copy of the Bible." This is a clear sign that the Synod proclaims the active presence of the Spirit not only in the Church in general but in every Bible-reading believer.

---

1. This is in no. 12 of *Dei Verbum,* quoting the Encyclical *Spiritus Paraclitus* of Benedict XV and referring to St. Jerome's *In Galatians* 5:19–20 (PL 26, 417A).

Bibliography

Allert, Craig D. *A High View of Scripture?* Grand Rapids, Mich.: Baker Academic, 2005.

Alonso Schökel, Luis. *The Inspired Word.* Translated by Francis Martin. London: Herder, 1967.

Balás, David L. "Marcion Revisited: A 'Post-Harnack' Perspective." In *Texts and Testaments,* edited by E. W. March, 95–108. San Antonio, Tex.: Trinity University Press, 1980.

Balás, David, and Jeffrey Bingham. "The Patristic Exegesis of the Bible." In *The International Bible Commentary,* edited by William R. Farmer, 64–115. Collegeville, Minn.: Liturgical Press, 1998.

Balthasar, Hans Urs von. *Thomas von Aquin: Besondere Gnadengaben und die zwei Wege des menschlichen Lebens: Kommentar zur Summa Theologica II–II, 171–82* [Thomas Aquinas: Special Charisms and the Two Ways of Human Life: Commentary on the Summa Theologica II–II, 171–82]. Vol. 23 of *Die Deutsche Thomas-Ausgabe,* edited by H. M. Christmann. Vienna: Pustet, 1958.

Bauckham, Richard. *The Theology of the Book of Revelation.* Cambridge: Cambridge University Press, 1993.

———. *Jesus and the Eyewitnesses.* Grand Rapids, Mich.: Eerdmans, 2006.

Bea, Augustinus. "'Deus auctor S. Scripturae.' Herkunft und Bedeutung der Formel" [God the Author of Sacred Scripture: Provenance and Significance of the Formula]. *Angelicum* 20 (1943): 16–31.

Benoit, Pierre. *Inspiration and the Bible.* Translated by J. Murphy-O'Connor and M. Keverne. New York: Sheed and Ward, 1965.

Bernard of Clairvaux. *Sancti Bernardi Opera Omnia* [The Complete Works of Saint Bernard]. Edited by J. Leclercq, C. H. Talbot, and H. M. Rochais, 8 vols. Rome: Editiones Cistercienses, 1958–1977.

Bingham, D. Jeffrey. *Irenaeus' Use of Matthew's Gospel in Adversus Haereses.* Louvain: Peeters, 1998.

Bouyer, Louis. "Où en est le mouvement biblique?" [At what point is the biblical movement?]. *Bible et Vie chrétienne* 18 (1956): 7–21.

Brown, Raymond E. *The Critical Meaning of the Bible.* New York: Paulist Press, 1981.

———. *The Birth of the Messiah.* 2nd edition. New York: Doubleday, 1993.

———. *An Introduction to the New Testament.* New York: Doubleday, 1997.

Bultmann, Rudolph. "The Study of the Synoptic Gospels." Translated by Karl Kundsinn. In *Form Criticism, Two Essays on New Testament Research,* edited by C. F. Grant. New York: Harper, 1962.

Campenhausen, Hans von. *The Formation of the Christian Bible.* Philadelphia: Fortress Press, 1972.

Chapman, Stephen. "Reclaiming Inspiration for the Bible." In *Canon and Biblical Interpretation, Scripture and Hermeneutics,* edited by C. Bartholomew, vol. 7, 167–206. Grand Rapids, Mich.: Zondervan, 2006.

Charlesworth, James H. *Jesus and Archeology.* Grand Rapids, Mich.: Eerdmans, 2006.

Chatillon, J. "L'influence de saint Bernard sur la scolastique" [The Influence of Saint Bernard on Scholasticism]. In *Saint Bernard théologien, Analecta S. Ordinis Cisterciensis* 9, no. 3–4 (1953): 268–88.

Collins, Raymond F. *Introduction to the New Testament.* New York: Doubleday, 1982.

———. "Inspiration and Inerrancy." In *The New Jerome Biblical Commentary,* edited by R. Brown, J. Fitzmyer, and R. Murphy. Englewood Cliffs, N.J.: Prentice Hall, 1990.

Crehan, J. H. "The Analogy between *Dei Verbum Incarnatum* and *Dei Verbum Scriptum.*" *Journal of Theological Studies* 6 (1955): 87–90.

Cullmann, Oscar. *Early Christian Worship.* London: SCM Press, 1953.

———. *Die Christologie des Neuen Testamentes* [The Christology of the New Testament]. Tübingen: Mohr, 1957.

Daniélou, Jean. "Christos Kyrios." *Recherches de sciences religieuses* 39 (1952): 338–52.

———. "Saint Bernard et les Pères Grecs" [Saint Bernard and the Greek Fathers]. In *Saint Bernard théologien, Analecta S. Ordinis Cisterciensis* 9, no. 3–4 (1953): 46–55.

Davies, W. D., and Dale Allison. *The Gospel According to Saint Matthew.* 3 vols. Edinburgh: T & T Clark, 1991.

De Lubac, Henri. *Exégèse medievale* [Medieval Exegesis]. 4 vols. Paris: Aubier, 1960–1964.

———. *Medieval Exegesis.* Translated by Mark Sebanc. Grand Rapids, Mich.: Eerdmans, 2000.

———. *Scripture in the Tradition*. New York: Crossroad, 2000.

———. *History and Spirit: The Understanding of Scripture according to Origen*. Translated by A. E. Nash. San Francisco: Ignatius Press, 2008.

Dulles, Avery. *The Craft of Theology*. New York: Crossroad, 1992.

———. "Criteria of Catholic Theology." *Communio* 22, no. 2 (1995): 303–15.

Ellis, Earl. "Pseudonymity and Canonicity of New Testament Documents." In *Worship, Theology and Ministry in the Early Church*, edited by M. Wilkins and T. Paige, 213–24. Sheffield: Sheffield Academic Press, 1993.

Enns, Peter. *Inspiration and Incarnation*. Grand Rapids, Mich.: Baker Academic, 2007.

Farkasfalvy, Denis. *L'inspiration biblique dans la théologie de saint Bernard* [Biblical inspiration in the theology of Saint Bernard]. Rome: Herder, 1964.

———. "Theology of Scripture in St. Irenaeus." *Revue bénédictine* 78 (1968): 319–33.

———. "Prophets and Apostles, the Conjunction of the Two Terms before Irenaeus." In *Texts and Testaments*, edited by E. W. March, 109–34. San Antonio, Tex.: Trinity University Press, 1980.

———. "Bernard the Theologian: Forty Years of Research." *Communio* 17, no. 4 (1990): 580–94.

———. "The Presbyters' Witness on the Order of the Gospels as Reported by Clement of Alexandria." *Catholic Biblical Quarterly* 54 (1992): 260–70.

———. "The Papias Fragment on Mark and Matthew and their Relationship to Luke's Prologue: An Essay on the Pre-History of the Synoptic Problem." In *The Early Church in Its Context, Essays in Honor of Everett Ferguson*, edited by Abraham J. Malherbe, Frederick W. Norris, and James W. Thompson, 92–106. Leiden: Brill, 1998.

———. "The Eucharistic Provenance of the New Testament Texts." In *Rediscovering the Eucharist: Ecumenical Conversations*, edited by Roch A. Kereszty, 27–51. New York: Paulist Press, 2004.

Farmer, William R., and Denis Farkasfalvy. *The Formation of the New Testament Canon*. New York: Paulist Press, 1983.

Ferguson, Everett. "Canon Muratori: Date and Provenance." *Studia Patristica* 17, no. 2 (1982): 677–83.

Feuillet, André. *Études johanniques* [Johannine Studies]. Paris: Desclée de Brower, 1962.

———. *The Apocalypse*. New York: Alba House, 1965.

Fitzmyer, Joseph. *To Advance the Gospel*. Grand Rapids, Mich.: Eerdmans, 1981.

Forest, Aimé. "Saint Bernard et notre temps" [Saint Bernard and our times]. In *Saint Bernard théologien, Analecta S. Ordinis Cisterciensis* 9, no. 3–4 (1953): 290–96.

Fuller, Reginald C. "The Deuterocanonical Writings." In *The International Bible Commentary*, edited by William R. Farmer, 179–80. Collegeville, Minn.: Liturgical Press, 1998.

Gamble, Harry. *The New Testament Canon, Its Making and Meaning*. Philadelphia: Fortress Press, 1985.

———. *Books and Readers in the Early Church: A History of Early Christian Texts*. New Haven, Conn.: Yale University Press, 1995.

Gnuse, Robert. *The Authority of the Bible, Theories of Inspiration, Revelation and the Canon of Scripture*. New York: Paulist Press, 1985.

Gundry, Robert H. *Mark: A Commentary on His Apology for the Cross*. Grand Rapids, Mich.: Eerdmans, 1993.

Harnack, Adolph von. *Marcion: Das Evangelium von fremden Gott, Eine Monographie zur Grundlegung der katholischen Kirche* [The Gospel of the Unknown God: A Monograph on the Foundation of the Catholic Church]. 2nd ed. Leipzig: J. C. Hinrichs, 1924.

Hengel, Martin. *Studies in the Gospel of Mark*. Translated by John Bowden. London: SCM Press, 1985.

———. *The Johannine Question*. Translated by J. Bowden. London: SCM Press, 1989.

———. *The Four Gospels and the One Gospel of Jesus Christ*. London: SCM Press, 2000.

Hoffmann, R. Joseph. *Marcion: On the Restitution of Christianity*. Chico, Calif.: Scholars Press, 1986.

Irenaeus of Lyon. *Adversus Haereses* [Against Heresies]. Edited by A. Rousseau, L. Dutreleau, C. Mercier, and B. Hemmerdinger, 10 vols. Sources Chrétiennes. Paris: Cerf, 1965–1982.

Iverson, Kelly R. "A Further Word on Final *Gar*." *Catholic Biblical Quarterly* 68 (2006): 79–94.

Kaestli, D., and O. Wermelinger, eds. *Le Canon de l' Ancien Testament* [The Canon of the Old Testament]. Geneva: Labor et Fides, 1984.

Karrer, Otto. *Die geheime Offenbarung* [The Secret Revelation]. Einsiedeln: Benziger, 1948.

Kürzinger, Josef. *Papias von Hierapolis und die Evangelien des Neuen Testaments* [Papias of Hierapolis and the Gospels of the New Testament]. Regensburg: Pustet, 1983.

Lang, A. "Die Bibel Stephan Hardings" [The Bible of Stephen Harding]. *Cistercienser-Chronik* 51 (1939): 250–56.

Marcus, J. *Mark 1–8*. The Anchor Bible 27. New York: Doubleday, 1999.

Martin, Francis. *Sacred Scripture: The Disclosure of the Word*. Naples, Fla.: Sapientia, 2006.

Meade, David G. *Pseudonymity and Canon*. Tübingen: Mohr, 1987.

Metzger, Bruce M. *The Bible in Translation*. Grand Rapids, Mich.: Baker Academic, 2001.

Montague, Georges T. *Understanding the Bible*. Mahwah, N.J.: Paulist Press, 2007.

Origen. *Commentarium in Joannem* [Commentary on John]. Edited by Celine Blanc, 5 vols. Sources Chrétiennes. Paris: Cerf, 1966–1992.

Rahner, Karl. *Über die Schriftinspiration* [Inspiration in the Bible]. Quaestiones Disputatae 1. Freiburg in Br.: Herder, 1961.

———. *Inspiration in the Bible*. Translated by C. H. Henkey. New York: Herder, 1961.

Reicke, Bo. *The Epistles of James, Peter and Jude*. The Anchor Bible 37. New York: Doubleday, 1964.

Riché, P., and G. Lobichon, eds. *Le Moyen Age et la Bible* [The Middle Ages and the Bible]. Paris: Beauchesne, 1984.

Roberts, Colin H., and T. C. Skeat. *The Birth of the Codex*. London: Oxford University Press, 1983.

Schmidt, Karl Ludwig. *Der Rahmen der Geschichte Jesu* [The Framework of the Life of Jesus]. Berlin: Trowitch und Sohn, 1919.

Schulz, Hans-Joachim. *Die apostolische Herkunft der Evangelien* [The Apostolic Provenance of the Gospels]. Freiburg in Br.: Herder, 1995.

Smalley, Beryl. *The Study of the Bible in the Middle Ages*. Oxford: Blackwell, 1952.

Smith, Raymond F. "Inspiration and Inerrancy." In *The Jerome Biblical Commentary*, edited by R. Brown, J. Fitzmyer, R. Murphy. Englewood Cliffs, N.J.: Prentice Hall, 1968.

Stuhlmacher, Peter, ed. *The Gospel and the Gospels*. Grand Rapids, Mich.: Eerdmans, 1991.

Sundberg, Albert C. "Canon Muratori: A Fourth-Century List." *Harvard Theological Review* 66 (1973): 1–41.

Taylor, Vincent. *The Gospel According to Saint Mark*. New York: Macmillan, 1966.

Tertullian. *Adversus Marcionem*. Introduction, translation, and commentary by René Braun. 5 vols. Sources Chrétiennes. Paris: Cerf, 1990–2004.

Theron, D. J. *Evidence of Tradition*. Grand Rapids, Mich.: Baker Book-house, 1958.

Trummer, Peter. "Corpus Paulinum—Corpus Pastorale." In *Paulus in den neutestamentlichen Spatschrifte,* edited by Karl Kertelge, 122–45. Freiburg in Br.: Herder, 1981.

Vanni, Ugo. *Lectura del Apocalipsis* [Reading the Apocalypse]. Pamplona: Verbo Divino, 2005.

Vögtle, Anton. *Das Buch mit sieben Siegeln* [The Book with Seven Seals]. Freiburg in Br.: Herder, 1981.

Wilder, Terry L. *Pseudonymity, the New Testament and Deception.* Lanham, Md.: University Press of America, 2004.

Index

Inspiration and Interpretation: A Theological Introduction to Sacred Scripture
was designed and typeset in Minion by Kachergis Book Design of Pittsboro,
North Carolina. It was printed on 60-pound Natures Book Natural and bound
by Thomson-Shore of Dexter, Michigan.